Culture as Catalyst

CULTURE AS CATALYST

Edited by
Isolde Brielmaier

**The Frances Young Tang
Teaching Museum and Art Gallery**
Skidmore College

Table of Contents

Welcome
Ian Berry
6

Culture as Catalyst: An Introduction
Isolde Brielmaier
8

CHAPTER 1

Whiteness and "Default Culture"
24

Fuck the Grammys: The Conundrum of "Transcending" Race and the Politics of Excellence
Treva B. Lindsey

Panel Discussion
Matthew Cooke, Treva B. Lindsey, Dara Silverman

CHAPTER 2

Migration and Borders: Visible and Invisible Walls
54

Books, Borders, and Democracy
Tanya Selvaratnam

Panel Discussion
Hassan Hajjaj, Richard Mosse, Tanya Selvaratnam

CHAPTER 3

Mass Incarceration and the Prison Industrial Complex
80

What I Would Change about Incarceration after Thirteen Years in Prison
Johnny Perez

Panel Discussion
Elizabeth Hinton, Duron Jackson, Johnny Perez

CHAPTER 4

Technology, Visual Culture, and the Politics of Representation
108

Decolonizing "Artificial" Art Making: The Impact of AI on the Art Ecosystem
Amir Baradaran

Panel Discussion
Amir Baradaran, Farai Chideya, Michael Joo

CHAPTER 5

#feminism?: Activism and Agitation in the Digital Age
132

Considering a New Feminism
Kimberly Drew

Panel Discussion
Kimberly Drew, Natalie Frank, Amy Richards

CHAPTER 6

Memory and Monuments: (Re)Claiming Public Space

156

The Questions That Answers Hide

Karyn Olivier

Panel Discussion

Dan Borelli, Titus Kaphar, Karyn Olivier

CHAPTER 7

Get Up, Stand Up: Rights and Responsibilities of Citizenship

180

Immigration, Discrimination, and the Journey to Citizenship

Minita Sanghvi

Panel Discussion

Sam Durant, Eric Gottesman, Minita Sanghvi

CHAPTER 8

Culture Now: Appreciate / Appropriate

200

Exploring the Limits of Cultural Appropriation in Popular Music

Matthew D. Morrison

Panel Discussion

Jessica Andrews, Renee Cox, Matthew D. Morrison

CHAPTER 9

On Navigating Forgiveness, Redemption, and Rejection

224

Is Forgiveness Enough?

Lyle Ashton Harris

Panel Discussion

Alexandra Bell, Lyle Ashton Harris, David Karp

CHAPTER 10

Food Futures: Food Justice, Sustainability, and Well-Being

242

Fighting Metabolic Dominance

Anthony Ryan Hatch

Panel Discussion

Kate Daughdrill, Anthony Ryan Hatch, Leah Penniman

Contributors

270

Acknowledgments

275

WELCOME

Three years ago, we welcomed Isolde Brielmaier as our first Curator at Large at the Tang Teaching Museum. Isolde's signature program at the Tang was the Accelerator Series of panel discussions, and we are pleased to document her impressive achievement in this volume. Isolde convened ten panels of leading artists, scholars, and activists from 2016 to 2019. The evenings included conversations on critical topics including race, responsible citizenship, and navigating forgiveness, culminating with a packed house in the Tang's Payne Room for an electric night on the future of food justice and sustainability.

The innovative thinkers that gathered for these community conversations remind us of the power of civil discourse and how the skills of genuine listening, critical thinking, and honest speaking are key to building empathy and knowledge. *Culture as Catalyst* is a compilation of their provocations—a compendium of diverse ways to make new connections, craft pathways to understanding, and think radically about the urgent issues facing our world today. Amazing things happened. Conversations were fueled by anger, reflection, curiosity, and vulnerability and marked by a consistent challenge to remain open, look closely, listen carefully, and speak confidently. And in the end, we were inspired to move.

In 2016, we also welcomed Rebecca McNamara as Mellon Collections Curator at the Tang (now Associate Curator) to lead important parts of the Accelerator Series and corresponding publications. Rebecca was a key partner on all aspects of these projects and managed the editing and production of this volume with great savvy. Along with Isolde and Rebecca, I add my sincere appreciation to the thirty panelists that came to the Tang over three years to create these dialogues with the Skidmore community. To Jessica Andrews, Amir Baradaran, Alexandra Bell, Dan Borelli, Farai Chideya, Matthew Cooke, Renee Cox, Kate Daughdrill, Kimberly Drew, Sam Durant, Natalie Frank, Eric Gottesman, Hassan Hajjaj, Lyle Ashton Harris, Anthony Ryan Hatch, Elizabeth Hinton, Duron Jackson, Michael Joo, Titus Kaphar, David Karp, Treva B. Lindsey, Matthew D. Morrison, Richard Mosse, Karyn Olivier, Leah Penniman, Johnny Perez, Amy Richards, Minita Sanghvi, Tanya Selvaratnam, and Dara Silverman: thank you!

To the dedicated Tang staff and to our faculty and staff colleagues that work alongside us each day at Skidmore College—thank you for the encouragement, participation, and work that helped shape the content of these timely conversations and provided a stage for our students to share their stories. I particularly thank Jennifer Barthelmas, Jean Tschanz-Egger, Michael Janairo, Annelise Kelly, Barry Pritzker, Rachel Seligman, Patti Sopp, Tom Yoshikami, and kelly ward. Very special thanks to designer Beverly Joel and editor Andrea Monfried who joined with us to make the formative document in your hands.

Special thanks to The Andrew W. Mellon Foundation for supporting *Accelerate: Access and Inclusion at The Tang Teaching Museum*, a three-year project at The Frances Young Tang Teaching Museum and Art Gallery at Skidmore College from which the Accelerator Series was born. In particular, thanks to Gene Tobin and Alison Gilchrest for championing our work and guiding our proposals. We look forward to more work with Mellon as we look to sustain the community relationships we've built over these past three years. Thanks also to the Alfred Z. Solomon Residency Fund that allowed us to bring some of our speakers to campus. Thank you to our academic leaders at Skidmore for their critical support of our ideas that became this transformative series, especially to our former Dean of the Faculty and Vice President for Academic Affairs Beau Breslin, and our current Dean of the Faculty and Vice President for Academic Affairs Michael Orr.

At the culmination of these important and reflective three years at the Tang, we focus on questions: What did we learn? How do we move that learning beyond our museum staff, Skidmore faculty and students, and Saratoga Springs neighbors that attended these ten evenings into the larger world? How do we best continue working toward realizing the values of access, justice, and empathy that were articulated?

Culture as Catalyst is one response and an example of how teaching museums can offer distinctive and unique experiences that break down barriers, build audiences, and nurture uncommon ways of navigating our complex world.

Ian Berry
Dayton Director

CULTURE AS CATALYST
An Introduction

Isolde Brielmaier

As a concept, "representation" is multilayered, particularly with regard to notions of social difference, and extends far beyond what we see, hear, read, and experience. In the context of the essays and conversations that compose this book, "representation" also encompasses the tremendous impact of popular visual culture—art, media, entertainment, fashion, technology—on the construction of ideas, meanings, and value. And representation is shaped by those who do the "representing"—individuals, communities, and issues; by those who are being represented; and, perhaps more important, by the sometimes-problematic nature of these representations in relation to truth, equity, and power. Thus, the dynamics around representation inform our engagement with and positioning within the sociopolitical and economic systems that structure our lives. And these systems involve and affect individuals, communities, and nations in ways that change who we are, what we think and feel, and how we live.

In this moment, our world's culture workers are taking up salient social issues, which often leads to the representation of those issues in artistic, creative, and physical forms. Many of these urgent topics are discussed in this book and intersect directly with the power and politics of representation—or of *mis*representation, which itself has deep historical roots. As criminal justice reform advocate Johnny Perez has noted in many discussions, to continually incriminate and incarcerate Black and brown people, which we in the United States have been doing since the founding of this nation and even earlier, we must first criminalize them in the eyes of our society. Problematic imagery contributes to criminalization—and there are problematic images everywhere.

Yet if our popular visual culture has the ability to paint people and ideas in a negative light, it also has the power to transform these perceptions. Through the simple act of a visual or other embodiment of something people don't know or understand, individuals can bring about change by working critically and inventively across cultures and industries. In 2016, I, along with Ian Berry, Dayton Director of The Frances Young Tang Teaching Museum and Art Gallery at Skidmore College, and the museum's team, took this thinking as our starting point for a public forum to explore and debate these points. We wanted people to get "comfortable with being uncomfortable" as we collectively pushed through difficult ideas, histories, and experiences about representation in its myriad forms. We considered the key political, social, and economic issues that culture workers are contending with, many quite fervently, on local, national, and global scales. We wanted to examine these topics from numerous angles, each with an eye to the ways in which visual culture has intervened in shaping and engaging these themes. For example, why not talk about race by examining whiteness and white privilege as well as by examining what "whiteness" really looks like? Or debate the immigration crisis by looking at both the literal and figurative borders that human beings construct in order to block movements by other human beings? The result was the Accelerator Series: ten conversations aimed at envisioning and bringing about real change.

Culture as Catalyst combines transcripts from the Accelerator Series conversations with meditations by a selection of the panelists along with contemporary artworks. At the book's core is the belief that popular visual culture is powerful and can not only denigrate but also elevate. The words and images of pop culture are grounded in the present-day social, economic, and political landscape; at the same time, they draw inspiration from the visual realm. The juxtapositions between words and images—in this book and in the world—explore and highlight the ways in which art and visual culture contend with and intervene in critical social issues.

Ten key topics that dominate our economic, political, and, above all, social psyche—beginning with whiteness and "default culture" and ending with food justice—structure both the conversations and the book. Our goal for the interdisciplinary focus has been to forge a way forward, often through complex historical and contemporary terrain. And especially to urge each of us, honestly and openly, to do the difficult work of interrogating how we see and interact with those around us.

White privilege is an absence of the negative consequences of racism. An absence of structural discrimination, an absence of your race being viewed as a problem first and foremost.

—Reni Eddo-Lodge, *Why I'm No Longer Talking to White People About Race*, 2017

Historic power structures in the United States, which developed along lines of race and class, are still active in the present moment. Whiteness stands at the pinnacle of these structures and as a standard against which much is measured within the social and cultural context of the United States. Matthew Cooke, Treva B. Lindsey, and Dara Silverman explore what happens when whiteness and white people are charged with examining themselves, their privilege, and the ways in which they consciously and unconsciously uphold and benefit from institutions built upon white supremacy. Rather than taking these institutions as assumed or "fixed," the panelists maintain that they can and must be dismantled and reconfigured.

In her frank analysis of whiteness, Lindsey speaks of the ambivalence a marginalized group has in regard to the assumed "default, or dominant, white mainstream culture." Foremost for her, however, is the larger project of dismantling white supremacy; it is an effort, she asserts, that all must prioritize and undertake. Lindsey notes the psychological labor required: "This is about a humanity project of questioning and learning the spots of inhumanity that we have had, and what it means to care for somebody and understand that their nonliving or dying impacts all of us…if I died right now…that should impact you, right? But there are millions of me dying right now that we don't give a damn about." Many scholars and activists working today seek to shift the burden of representation and regular engagement (or "labor") around race and racial issues onto those who occupy spaces of power and privilege because of their whiteness. And in so doing, both physical and psychological space can be cleared for the centering of other bodies and voices.

> **I was and still am that same ship which carried me to the new shore, the same vessel containing all the memories and dreams of the child in the brick house with the toy tea set. I am the shore I left behind as well as the home I return to every evening. The voyage cannot proceed without me.**
>
> —Luisa A. Igloria, *Juan Luna's Revolver*, 2009

The current global discussion about the international movements of people—both voluntary and forced—extends far beyond political boundaries. It calls into question how we think about issues of identity and citizenship; how we define home and a sense of belonging and/or displacement; and perhaps, above all, how and what we define as the legal and political rights of human beings. Of utmost importance is delving more deeply into concepts of mobility and migration from both local and global perspectives.

In their conversation, Hassan Hajjaj, Richard Mosse, and Tanya Selvaratnam examine the multilayered aspects of borders both visible and invisible. Selvaratnam, in her essay, writes, "When those in positions of political power seek to divide us with physical borders and walls, our imaginations are the most effective tools we have to keep cultural borders open." She explains that reading was and is a means for her, and by extension all of us, to traverse boundaries and engage in the free exchange of ideas. She extends this everyday act to the making of art and other forms of culture that both tie people to a particular place but also extend their connections to others in distant locations. Through cultural production, we can bridge divides as well as recognize and overcome differences.

An attempt to create a new conceptual terrain for imagining alternatives to imprisonment involves the ideological work of questioning why "criminals" have been constituted as a class and, indeed, a class of human beings undeserving of the civil and human rights accorded to others.

—Angela Y. Davis, *Are Prisons Obsolete?*, 2003

Those who have been incarcerated become muted—visually, figuratively, literally. It is, as Elizabeth Hinton, Duron Jackson, and Johnny Perez assert, a tortured existence that no current system can redeem. Along with the roots of mass incarceration, they examine the present-day criminal justice system, especially as it impacts communities of color. And they question the economic and political interests served by the United States with the world's highest rate of incarceration.

Perez, a human rights and criminal justice reform advocate, opens his essay with an assessment of American hypocrisy concerning mass incarceration: "As a nation, we pride ourselves on holding onto the principles of decency, compassion, and the preservation of humanity [yet] criminal justice policies in the United States do not reflect [those values]." His text chronicles his thirteen-year incarceration, much of which was spent in solitary confinement. Perez uses his experience to rethink how the United States seeks to punish and reform. How can we find a way forward? He touches on the critical impact of perception and representation—particularly in film, television, and print media—on how we see crime and people who allegedly commit those crimes and on how we believe it is best to penalize them. The panelists discuss the possibility of dismantling what many call the criminal "injustice" system and work as a society to reconceive punishment and reform or rehabilitation.

> **The technology you use impresses no one.
> The experience you create with it is everything.**
> —Sean Gerety, ThinkAdvisor.com, 2019

At the current moment, technology in all of its varied forms is changing at light speed, touching every aspect of our lives. "Immersive technology" (often encapsulated within the broad term "artificial intelligence") has given rise to a new era in virtual experiences, particularly since about 2015. In visual fields, including art and media, there are tangible implications around the ways in which technology, and specifically AI, intersect and intervene in our world. Artists, activists, and creatives have drawn on immersive technologies to generate projects that are intent on challenging the social, political, and economic ramifications and complexities of the technology itself.
In particular, journalists and scholars have called on this new medium to shift the linear style of visual storytelling to allow for multiple paths and entry points. At the same time, AI has the potential to reinforce stereotypes, contributing to massive economic and social disruptions and alienation, and to implement new systems of invasive monitoring and control.

What do these new developments in technology mean for education, entertainment, social policy, and systems of codified knowledge?

Who regulates immersive technologies? Who will be part of these new cultures, and who will be left out? Amir Baradaran, Farai Chideya, and Michael Joo observe that the disconnect between the invention and the consumption of technologies such as VR and AR has made evident a tendency to homogenize people or "users"—a tendency predicated on who is devising the technology and on a specific idea of who the user is. We are not mere bystanders to evolving technologies, however: how we interact with, support, or reject certain technologies can have lasting effects on our daily lives and the lives of the generations that follow— and we can make those decisions to elevate diverse voices and fight for greater justice.

It's no surprise that a generation of women who were brought up being told that they were equal to men, that sexism, and therefore feminism, was dead, are starting to see through this. And while they're pissed off, they're also positive, bubbling with hope. One obvious outcome of being brought up to believe you're equal is that you're both very angry when you encounter misogyny, but also confident in your ability to tackle it.
—Kira Cochrane, *All the Rebel Women*, 2013

Maintaining ownership over our own history and narrative is critical. This has not always been the case for women, but over the last several decades, in part due to the rise and, more important, evolution of women's movements, the situation has shifted. The digital realm and its new and ever-changing technologies have paved the way for a fourth-wave feminism. Advanced platforms allow women to come together, organize hashtag campaigns, and build grassroots movements. Social media has created a permanent arena within which women can share their stories, engage with current issues, and secure a means to enact social and cultural change. In addition to social media, some of the issues foregrounded in fourth-wave feminism are intersectionality, inclusivity, racial equality, gender neutrality, gender expression, sexual harassment, workplace equality, image authorship, sex positivity, and call-out culture.

The differences in scope, impact, and reach between digital space and "real time" are notable. Social media has, without question, provided the greatest vehicle yet for current feminist thinking and for the transnational spread of a powerful and inclusive feminist ideology. Yet there are still questions around whether this fourth wave is truly intersectional. Women of color have brought attention to the idea that many white women call out issues relating to gender but not to race, for example. Many young people have raised concerns around the term *feminism*, which is rooted in gender binaries that may not consider members of LGBTQIA+ communities. Clearly, each feminist movement faces new challenges and must evolve new tactics.

Kimberly Drew, Natalie Frank, and Amy Richards discuss these changing ideas and ideals of feminism and how different types of cultural production can respond to, reinforce, or reshape them. Frank, for instance, uses her painting to assert agency and dignity over how women and their bodies, sexuality, and power are represented. Her paintings and drawings of primarily white women—sometimes featuring her own renditions of well-known stories, such as Pauline Réage's 1954 erotic novel *Story of O*—seek to challenge visual perceptions of these women, who vary in class, status, and profession, and also to challenge her viewers, asking them to consider varied platforms of representation. Again, representation for marginalized or disenfranchised people in particular is vital: Drew, a writer and curator, wonders "what the fruits of this next era will be… I have… watched as women have excluded trans women from notions of feminism time and time again. I wonder how we will take charge of this triumphant moment, how we will document ourselves, and most important, how we will all hold ourselves accountable."

**People are trapped in history
and history is trapped in them.**
—James Baldwin, *Notes of a Native Son*, 1955

The debate over whether to remove public monuments that celebrate complicated individuals or events is connected to our sense of history and memory and also to our understanding of what is, and should exist within, "public space." Power, agency, and voice affect how we construct, contend with, and come to terms with contentious aspects of our histories and how these histories, events, and communities are visualized, concretized, and memorialized. When these statues, plaques, flags, and other markers are removed, debate arises over erasing certain histories. At the same time, we are opening new ground for rewriting and expanding our historical narratives.

Dan Borelli, Titus Kaphar, and Karyn Olivier discuss these questions of memorialization, commemoration, and the ways in which "history" is constructed visually and physically. They further explore who are the decision makers for monuments in public spaces and play with the idea of permanence: can monuments be temporary? Olivier's project statement for her 2017 public interventionist installation *The Battle Is Joined* declares, "Monuments are established with the assumption that we as a nation have collectively decided that something should be remembered, honored, and celebrated. In reality, we don't have equal voices in this mandate, but in my insertion, the intention will be for each of us to see and imagine our critical role in the ever-evolving American story." Working toward that equality and that inclusion—not just in moments and celebrations but in ordinary day-to-day life—is where the transformation can begin.

Citizenship is more than an individual exchange of freedoms for rights; it is also membership in a body politic, a nation, and a community. To be deemed fair, a system must offer its citizens equal opportunities for public recognition, and groups cannot systematically suffer from misrecognition in the form of stereotype and stigma.
—Melissa V. Harris-Perry, *Sister Citizen: Shame, Stereotypes, and Black Women in America*, 2011

Citizenship is a multifaceted idea. It connotes a sense of legitimate belonging as well as of social right; it is a form of agency, an active practice, and a dynamic relationship of accountability between public service providers and their users. It also implies home, purpose, and responsibility. However, the ways in which we conceive citizenship, especially in the United States, as well as the rights and responsibilities that we believe citizenship may or may not encompass, vary widely.

Citizenship, we often presume, is a monolithic ideal that each person has a "right" to claim after having undergone a vetting process, but it is actually far more complex and fluid. Sam Durant, Eric Gottesman, and Minita Sanghvi sift through the sometimes-fluid elements that make up "citizenship," acknowledging that these global yet varied ideas are imbued with each government's interests and inevitably bring with them a range of issues often tied to identity. Citizenship can mean different things depending on an individual's race, class, ethnicity, and sexual orientation as well as political and economic background. Contrary to mainstream thinking, it does not necessarily mean that each person—each citizen—has access and ability to participate in the act or right of belonging in the same way. We have to work to maintain what it means to be a citizen by voting, speaking out, and showing up to actively create change.

We can have no significant understanding of any culture unless we also know the silences that were institutionally created and guaranteed along with it.

—Gerald Sider, "Against Experience: The Struggles for History, Tradition and Hope among a Native American People," 1997

In an age in which images, ideas, and even sounds are widely accessible, the topic of cultural appropriation, particularly within popular culture, has become an increasingly charged issue. Questions of appropriation have long been a part of art, music, fashion, and street culture: artwork by Dana Schutz, Hank Willis Thomas, and Richard Prince; music by Elvis, Madonna, Miley Cyrus, and Bruno Mars; in fashion, Gucci's engagement with Harlem's Dapper Dan; pro sports mascots; Halloween costumes; the Kardashians. The line between appropriation and appreciation seems to grow ever narrower: *cultural appropriation* and *cultural appreciation* are slippery and often overlapping. This multidisciplinary and multi-industry topic necessitates an examination of power, history, capitalism, imperialism, and assimilation, along with an interrogation of who exactly "owns" culture.

Discussions about appropriation have long come up in conversations around art, music, fashion, and popular culture, but currently there is an increased focus on the topic. What might this suggest about the larger world we live in? Ethnomusicologist Matthew Morrison asserts that, since the 1980s, the term *cultural appropriation* "has emerged in popular discourse as a critique of the misuse of the cultural attributes or performances of one community by those who do not belong or cannot claim an immediate connection to that group." Today's debates, as demonstrated in the conversation between Morrison, Jessica Andrews, and Renee Cox, involve expected inquiries—those around authenticity, agency, authorship, and voice—and also complex, consuming examinations of the idea of cultural borrowing. When a person or group "borrows" or draws inspiration from another person or group, is this key to their expressive process?

The creator's intent is of great consequence in answering the question. The panelists suggest that a formal and respectful acknowledgment of source materials is essential, but more may be needed to resolve the longstanding and growing complexities of appreciation and appropriation.

> **You can't forgive without loving. And I don't mean sentimentality. I don't mean mush. I mean having enough courage to stand up and say, "I forgive. I'm finished with it."**
> —Maya Angelou, in an interview with Oprah Winfrey, 2013

Rejection, redemption, and forgiveness resonate across all communities, cultures, and perceived boundaries. What does it mean to "live in the gray," to allow ourselves to take a more fluid approach to how we

see others and how we choose forgiveness? Would a candid and frank exchange—one in which we share and listen with sincerity—be able to bring people together, to draw out our understanding, compassion, and empathy? "Forgiveness" can be many things: an idea, an action, a passive acknowledgment, a reactive response, or the process or act of letting go. For some people, forgiveness means redemption. For many, it feels like an ongoing generational process that dates back hundreds if not thousands of years. For artist Lyle Ashton Harris, forgiveness starts from within. For sociologist David Karp, restorative justice can be vital to forgiveness. Meanwhile, artist Alexandra Bell is more concerned with accountability, particularly in relation to large and thorny issues of racism. Bell, who is trained as a journalist and has worked in community advocacy, explains that she struggles with the amount of effort required to realize forgiveness, especially because those seeking forgiveness move on and remain in positions of privilege. How, who, and why we forgive can be divisive and personal, but we each must find our own ways to the goals of cooperation, growth, and harmony.

The nation's fiscal health is dependent upon the health of the next generation. When we consider the cost of inaction in a matter of national security, lives are at stake; so it is the case with the Child Nutrition Act.
—Debra Eschmeyer, *Huffington Post*, 2010

Healthy food nourishes the mind, body, and spirit. But not everyone has access to it or to the important information that it can deliver well-being to both individuals and communities. Equity and access lie at the core of food justice or food sovereignty—ideas rooted in the time-honored ethos of Indigenous peoples around the world. In this conversation, Kate Daughdrill, Anthony Ryan Hatch, and Leah Penniman underscore that these ideas are far from new. Access to food is not only a necessity for human existence, it can also be considered a right that must remain open to all. These factors are essential as we rethink the future of food with an eye to social justice, sustainability, and the well-being of all people.

Hatch says that it is critical to consider how we think about food and the history of its related terminology: "The term *food security* established by the US government meant to give the US government a way to describe patterns of access to food…It strikes me that the term *food security* places food in the context of a discourse of war." We must interrogate language around issues of food justice just as we interrogate the issues themselves—and especially who regulates access to food and who benefits from those decisions.

Individually and collectively, the conversations, essays, and artworks in this volume underscore the significant ways in which those on the front lines of culture, advocacy, and activism consider, confront, and engage social, economic, and political issues of the day. The thirty contributors to *Culture as Catalyst* examine the ways in which we see and think about the world around us and those who live in it. They lay out today's critical issues around race, class, sexuality, and more from their own points of view and posit an overarching challenge: that each of us look at ourselves and our actions in order to become allies, speak up, take action, and affect change. They assert that we must ask ourselves whether we are ready to take on this all-important task and then offer multiple catalysts for us to see differently, to think differently, and, above all, to act. ▲

WHITENESS AND "DEFAULT CULTURE"

Willie Cole
To get to the other side
2001
32 cast-concrete lawn jockeys,
mixed media, galvanized steel, wood
32½ × 198 × 198 inches
Tang Teaching Museum collection,
gift of Peter Norton, 2015.26.35

"The symbol of the lawn jockey is perceived as negative. But in this piece, I've turned [the lawn jockey] into a symbol of power by placing it in the position of power as a member of a chess team, but also giving it the embellishments of spiritual icons from African traditions… The lawn jockey is a stand-in for Elegba, the god at the crossroads, the presenter of choices. His symbolism might be the doorway, the cross, the colors red and black; the so-called traditionally painted lawn jockey has those same symbols." —Willie Cole

FUCK THE GRAMMYS

The Conundrum of "Transcending" Race and the Politics of Excellence

Treva B. Lindsey

"I'm the first Black woman to headline Coachella—ain't that a bitch!" uttered Beyoncé playfully from the stage of her stellar performance at the annual desert music festival. The two-hour-plus set was electrifying. Fans and critics alike sang the praises of the performance and its unapologetic celebration of Black cultural institutions, traditions, and expressive practices, especially those of historically Black colleges and universities. The fact that the performance was history making, however, is unsettling. Despite branding itself as an event including both well-known and relatively unknown artists, Coachella waited more than a decade to feature a Black woman as its headliner. Beyoncé's own remarks about being "first" reveal an ambivalence about marginalized people disrupting the default, or dominant, white mainstream culture.

The act of pioneering carries the weight of exceptionalism as well as of a reification of a white, masculine, heterosexual, cisgender, financially secure, and able-bodied status quo, that is, the default space for cultural significance. Beyoncé's callout of Coachella is often overlooked in favor of a narrative in which she emerges as a transcendent figure. In reality, however, her decision to center historically Black colleges and universities in her show challenged the festival's attempt to render her a symbol of its progress toward greater inclusivity. The show also derided the celebratory impulse that accompanies first-time access to white cultural spaces. "Beychella" illuminated a complicated relationship between African American women and dominant culture. When marginalized folks become the first in formerly—and formally and informally—exclusionary spaces, the excitement often overshadows a larger issue: that the default culture is used as a point of reference with which to assess or validate cultural and expressive practices. What is at stake in relying on a dominant culture for this kind of marker of achievement?

In cultural production, the desire among both white people and people of color for non-white artists to cross over or attain mass appeal stems from present-day assumptions as well as from underscrutinized ways of evaluating excellence and achievement. Prestige and accolades emerge from spaces deemed elite or discerning. White men, historically and contemporarily, act as "objective" arbiters of excellence; in fact, they reproduce a meritocracy centered around white maleness. For example, the paltry number of Black women Oscar winners reflects not a lack of talent in front of or behind the camera, but rather the insufficiency of standards established by a group of people who view culture through a lens that explicitly and unconsciously privileges a white status quo. Black women, and women of color more broadly, do not register as cultural producers to the organizations that are charged with recognizing artistic merit. Declarative statements about standards, universality, and quality inscribe a cultural context in which the opinions, ideas, and perspectives of white men shape what and who is lauded. Consequently, the concept of excellence is and has been determined by the precepts of a privileged and exclusionary group of people.

Acceptance in white spaces is often viewed as a sign of both progress and deracialized appeal. A favorable reception is posited as "transcending race," as opposed to countering racism and white supremacy. Beyoncé publicly rebuked Coachella; even so, the festival benefited from the tremendous success of her show. The almost instant sell-out of festival passes and tickets and the live-streamed performance (filmed for the 2019 Netflix documentary *Homecoming*) ensured that the festival nabbed countless headlines. Although the event was labeled Beychella, Coachella won because Beyoncé headlined. Coachella's organizers have an important stake in being more inclusive: profit. Beyoncé, too, had a vested interest: using a platform within default culture to foreground Blackness.

She also highlighted her disbelief at being "first." Disrupting the status quo isn't solely about entering predominantly white spaces; as marginalized cultures enter these restricted spaces, their overvaluation becomes clear. Crossing over, transcending are almost exclusively the provinces of non-white, non-male artists who appeal to white audiences. By problematic default, those artists identified as crossover or even transcendent are people of color who have been embraced by mainstream and "highbrow" white culture(s). A white artist awarded a BET Award and a Black artist awarded a Grammy do not resonate in the same way because default culture assigns more value to the Grammy.

The descriptions "Grammy-winning" and "Oscar-nominated" carry a distinct cachet. The hypervaluation of these honors reproduces a situation in which white male arbiters of cultural significance can claim their assessments are colorblind. While the myth of an objective meritocracy may be under attack by efforts such as April Reign's #OscarsSoWhite campaign, the power of white male cultural supremacy continues to shape default culture. Consequently, a racialized hierarchy remains intact. The illusions of meritocracy and colorblindness help to naturalize a system in which the ability to garner acclaim and accolades from these organizations signals excellence.

The superior value placed on white, male-dominated spaces also pervades the culture of electoral politics. In 2018, US voters elected an unprecedented number of women of color to Congress. Trumpeted as a watershed moment in democratic governance, it also led to pointed conversations about the predominance of white men in Congress and what that predominance means for legislation and policy. Almost immediately after they were sworn in, the first-term congresswomen of color made their presence known and felt. Their efforts to transform the default culture of Washington led to acutely polarized responses. Whether with harsh attacks or high praise, the media, fans, and critics alike fixated on Representatives Rashida Tlaib, Alexandria Ocasio-Cortez, Ilhan Omar, Lauren Underwood, and Ayanna Pressley. Viewed by some as the future of the Democratic Party and by others as its demise, these women challenge the status quo of Congress by both their presence and their comparatively progressive politics. Their voices, bodies, perspectives, adornment practices, and identities deviate from the norms exhibited by their male counterparts, who are mostly white, heterosexual, financially secure, able-bodied, and Christian. Although the congresswomen made history, their literal and figurative disruption of a space occupied historically and primarily by white men reveals that deeply entrenched ideas about who can and should govern rely on prejudicial and exclusionary cultural conventions and assumptions.

The first-term representatives brought to the legislative table their experiences as Black, Latina, Muslim, immigrant, and refugee women. These women of color refused to conform to the default culture of Congress or even of their own party. They cosponsor progressive legislation, speak out on hot-button political issues, and use social media as a means of connection. Unlike many of their white male counterparts, they spend little to no time with lobbyists or with the large corporate donors who wield considerable power in Congress. Tlaib, Ocasio-Cortez, Omar, Underwood, and Pressley alongside some of the veteran women of color, such as Representative Barbara Lee, form a defiant subculture within the default culture of Congress. Admirers, detractors, and the media, mainstream and otherwise, pay close attention to their words and actions, whether mundane or substantive. For some, these representatives are reshaping the political landscape and helping to normalize the presence of women of color in seats of power. For others, their refusal to adhere to the status quo is infuriating.

The adornment practices of these congresswomen—Ocasio-Cortez's bold red lipstick, Omar's hijab—unsettle the cultural landscape of electoral politics. Omar in particular is seen to deviate from mythical norms of US identity—especially those of white males—enraging her critics as much as her progressive and sometimes unpopular opinions do. Omar is a Black Somali Muslim refugee woman. Any of those identities counters the norm, but her embodiment of several "othered" identities renders her particularly vulnerable to resistance from the default culture of electoral politics. In the face of virulent Islamophobia in Congress and in US society more broadly, Omar dons her hijab and defies the Christian cultural hegemony that has existed throughout the history of US government. Death threats and other menaces do not deter her from embracing her identity, nor do they result in an assimilation into or a reproduction of Congress's default culture.

It is without question difficult to avoid the seeming ubiquity of default culture. Whether in pop music or electoral politics, the prominence of ideas about who belongs and who excels creates a context in which transcending can become aspirational for non-white people. Speaking out against hierarchized value might require an artist or politician to stop seeking the approval or adulation of entities created and led by white men. Substantive risk accompanies this approach, just as tangible value accrues to winning Oscar and Grammy awards or appealing to white, male, Christian voters. Pushing back against the demand to transcend or the racialized and gendered politics of excellence necessitates a divestment from default culture. Rarely if ever does divestment not come at a high cost. But the inability to imagine a world in which the default becomes the defunct, in which the status quo is radically transformed, reveals a cultural cowardice. Ain't that a bitch? ▲

34–35

MARCH 23, 2017

WHITENESS AND "DEFAULT CULTURE"

Matthew Cooke
filmmaker

Treva B. Lindsey
scholar

Dara Silverman
organizer

Isolde Brielmaier · **Junot Díaz, the Pulitzer Prize–winning writer, made an interesting statement in a 2015 interview: "We live in a society where default whiteness goes unremarked—no one ever asks it for *its* passport." What exactly is this whiteness that Díaz is speaking of? And what or how might that relate or not relate to "default culture"?**

Matthew Cooke · When I was fifteen years old, I remember smoking a cigarette across the street from my high school, Evanston Township High School, just north of Chicago. A couple of police officers came up and said, "You can't smoke across the street from the high school." And I said, "What the fuck is this? Is that what's up?" My friends said, "Dude, they're going to cart you off to jail." And I said, "No, they're not. You can't do that. You can't arrest somebody for smoking." And I kept walking.

But other friends of mine have told me stories of much lesser things that got them taken into custody. It was at that point that I recognized that there was some sort of…But that word *default* just bugs me for some reason. I think it's because I want to challenge it. Despite my perception of myself as being other—even though I elected into that position—I recognized at that moment that there was something I had in common with these particular police officers that afforded me a certain freedom to say, "Fuck you, this is the land of the free. You can't tell me what to do."

Dara Silverman · One part that's important for me about naming whiteness and being explicit about it is that as a white person, I'm never really asked to name it, I'm never asked to contextualize myself, and everyone's expected to understand where I come from.

Over the past few years, as the Movement for Black Lives has grown and as the Immigrant Rights Movement has grown, what we've seen is more and more communities of color fighting more publicly and saying, "White isn't the norm in our lives and in our experience." And so, for those of us who are white, it's really a question of how we start to see that the world we see isn't what everyone else is experiencing. It isn't what the majority of people in the United States are experiencing—we are in a privileged position. What does that mean every day when we're walking around with this privileged lens hiding all the things that we can't see?

Treva B. Lindsey · When I hear the word *whiteness*, I think power, and the invisible and yet hyperfelt and hypervisible ways in which it's able to function. I grew up in low-income housing in Northeast DC, and then I went to an elite private school. The very different ways that I saw my body engaged made a huge impact.

Similarly, I heard things like, "She talks like a white girl, that means she's educated." Being educated was read as white, and all of the things loaded into that are extraordinarily problematic. It at once normalizes and valorizes whiteness or some kind of vernacular speech but also demonizes African American vernacular speech by saying that it is less valuable. In one fell swoop, you're demonizing the spaces of Blackness, valorizing whiteness, and reinstating power.

The idea of whiteness being something of power—being a default when we don't name it and when we don't identify it within a system of power, within a system of privilege, within systems of marginalization—means that everyone else is at fault. So thinking about fault and how we think about "Who can be wrong? Who can be held accountable? Who can be seen as disposable?" within that context leads to the question, "Who becomes invisibilized by the invisibilizing of whiteness?"

IB   **I should point out that we're having a very US-centric conversation. We know people say race is a social construct; it's also very much a lived experience for many of us, including white people, right? And it looks very different when you move over to Europe; perhaps there are some similarities when you move to the global South. I want to be conscious that we're speaking specifically in this context.**

     When you talk about race, in most people's minds, it connotes Black and brown people—African American, Latinx, Asian, Chicanx. So how do we make that shift of putting more of the spotlight on the idea of whiteness as a race?

     Matthew, I know you're not fond of the notion of default culture or this idea that whiteness becomes an unspoken and presumed standard against which everything is measured.

MC   I just want to change *default* to *dominant*. We have a responsibility as human beings in this mysterious experience of life to figure out what it is that we're doing. What's the point? Why are we sitting in a room talking about a topic? Who cares? We could be doing other things. What's the point of being alive, of living, of making any of the little to large choices we're going to make?

     To me, there's a simple direction, which is the alleviation of unnecessary suffering. What is peace? Peace is the alleviation of not just violence but any type of suffering: the suffering that comes from being in a world without understanding, being in a world with communication that's broken down, the violence that comes from living a life that's unfulfilled, from doing work that gives you no feeling of satisfaction or no feeling of self-worth, from being spoken to, talked to, looked at, and in every way, shape, and form marginalized or disenfranchised. That's violence as well. So when I think about a purpose to life, of living in a purpose that brings about peace, that's the kind of peace I think we would all want, not only for ourselves but something we would want for all of our brothers and sisters in our immediate family and on the whole planet.

     When we sit here and talk about whiteness and the default culture, what I think about is a dominant culture. And a culture that, I've come to learn and understand, committed a genocide against Native peoples here, which is a travesty for all of us because what do we not get as a result of embracing that culture? We don't get all that wisdom, and all that understanding, and all that depth of how it is to live in harmony with the world, and with the earth, and with the gods as they represented them, and what about all those other elements that we just miss out on because of an ancestry that many of us today feel very, very challenged in facing?

     I'm talking about white people like myself. It can be very challenging to look at something. We might say, "Are you talking about me? I cut the tusks off the elephant? No. I didn't do that." I think that's why we're here, to talk about that and to challenge some of those ideas. I'd be uncomfortable myself as well, of course, because there's so much obviously that I can't see and haven't seen. But we need to face that reality of the history of a genocide against a culture, the history of having a slave trade and a slave labor force that created the most powerful economic structure on earth.

We have never, ever come to terms with what we did. From my perspective, there should be a memorial on every corner. There should be reparations. There should be an acknowledgment of everything that was done, not just to say, "I'm sorry," but so that we don't all have such a fragile identity that crumbles at the idea that by not giving proper homage to MMA or football, we're all going to fall apart. That is a weakness that we in ourselves deserve to heal. I don't want to be that type of person, so fragile.

TBL What's so interesting in this moment is that I often hear that the Movement for Black Lives is about claiming Black humanity. The idea that this is a humanizing project is a failure of recognizing the inhumanity that you're talking about. We have to look at the dehumanization of whiteness and white people to think about what allows people to do such harm to a community. What allows someone to participate in the genocide of Indigenous people? What makes it possible for someone to participate in the transatlantic slave trade and chattel slavery, to establish Jim Crow, to not afford women rights, to not guarantee food security for people, and to have all of these systems of marginalization that stem from notions of anti-Blackness, antifeminist, anti-queerness, anti-poorness that are circulated in these spaces?

We often talk about dehumanization as this reclamatory project for people of color or dehumanized people—people who have been actively dehumanized through these processes of violence. But I think the real question is a humanity question that is specifically targeting whiteness, that's targeting maleness, that's targeting positions of power in saying, "What kind of human do you have to be to cause this kind of harm?" And that is a really difficult conversation to launch, because, as you said, it's easy to feel attacked and to go into the space of fragility. In feminist spaces, we joke that masculinity is so fragile, but these little things make you feel like your masculinity is pulled apart.

There's something that is afforded a fragility in this kind of default or dominant position that we have to get past. And when we say "It's uncomfortable," it should actually be painful because what you may have to do, as we examine and self-reflect in these conversations around whiteness, is look at the history of dehumanity and inhumanity that is very much part of the history of whiteness.

IB **The notion of white fragility is something that needs to be looked at head-on, and that's part of the pushing through, right?**

DS A big piece of it for me, as a white person, is asking what it means to lose my humanity. As a Jew, what did my people give up for me to get white privilege? Not all Jews are white, but for Jews who are white, what did we have to give up? What made my grandmother, when she saw me running through the airport when I was six years old, turn to my mother and say, "She's really cute, but she's going to have to get a nose job."

I think about that and about the constraining of what it means to be female, of what it means to be white, of what it means to be presentable in mainstream culture. For me, as a woman growing up and coming out as a queer person, part of what that meant as well was asking, What are these norms that are put on me of what attractiveness is and what's acceptable?

And then I started to unpack my whiteness and to see the ways in which my family over generations gave up parts of our identity to gain what we saw as the privileges of whiteness. And what came with that was mental illness, was distance from our culture and from our identity, and was this separation, both from other Jews and from other white people. We had to figure out how to succeed. What is it that we gain from this capitalist system that benefits us if we buy into it?

When I think about white fragility, and this idea that Robin DiAngelo has put forward of white people being so scared of being critiqued, part of it for me is around asking, How do we love each other?

But for a lot of us who are white, it's also asking about the roots that we come from. What are the small towns that we come from? And how do we connect? How many people in the room have a relative who supported Trump or voted for Trump and now you're trying to figure out how to talk to them or how to relate to them? It's not just for white people; there are a bunch of us.

This is a gap that all of us are struggling with. How do we reach across that divide? What does it mean to say, "I'm going to value my whiteness above the lives of people who will be killed by the policies that this government is going to put into place"? And what do we benefit from when that happens?

IB   **We're making people uncomfortable.**

DS   But that's part of the goal, right? To really dig in on how we talk to our relatives who supported Trump. A friend called me this morning and said, "I called my mom and I tried to get her to call her legislator to speak out against the health-care bill," and the mom said, "People don't deserve handouts. I didn't get any handouts, so why should other people get that?" There's a disconnect between "People will die when they lose their health care" and "People don't deserve handouts." Where do we get the sense that government isn't actually about supporting all of us, particularly people who are struggling?

IB   **Where do we get that sense? I hear people saying, "Oh, my gosh. I can't believe how divided things are." But things have always been divided. There have always been these different camps, specifically along lines of race, gender, and sexuality. Let's focus on this idea of whiteness, which Matthew calls a dominant culture. It's interesting that you call it that because I don't see it as dominant. I don't want to give it power. It doesn't dominate my life. I feel fully dominant and in control. The reason I use *default* is that there is this implicit, unspoken standard that we are always** acknowledging in the art world and the academy. When we talk about race, the assumption is that we're going to be talking about Black people.

In the Whitney Biennial right now, there is a painting that many are finding problematic by the established, highly regarded painter Dana Schutz, who is white. This painting, *Open Casket,* is based on a photograph of Emmett Till, the fourteen-year-old who faced a severe beating and lynching in 1955, when he was laid to rest in an open casket. It is a large-scale painting where Emmett Till's face is abstracted and the body is somewhat clearer. It has set off protests; people have found it offensive—so much so that there have been calls for the museum to remove it and destroy it. The thinking here is that, A, it's displaying and using Black people's pain, specifically Emmett Till and his family's pain, as raw material; and B, it will eventually leave the Whitney exhibition and enter into the market.

Then there's a painting by Henry Taylor. He is now in his late fifties, and he has always painted Black life. He painted a portrait of Philando Castile bleeding to death in the back of his car. There's not as much pushback with Taylor's painting. For me, it brings up the idea of cultural authority: who has the right or who has the privilege of telling whose story? Where does this leave us?

TBL I'm of many minds about it. I consume Black death on a daily basis. But in the moment in which Emmett Till is killed, the media looked completely different, and the point of Mamie Till displaying the body of her brutalized, beaten son in that photograph was to galvanize something.

Now I can go on my phone, go to Facebook, Twitter, Instagram, Snapchat, whatever platform, and watch it on a loop in private. Black death has become a consumptive practice—and it always has been, right? But now we can say we're doing it in the guise of raising awareness, and I'm very careful about Black death as spectacle because this again speaks to the inhumanity of whiteness, not the dehumanization of Black people.

I don't have to reclaim Emmett Till's humanity in this moment, but I want to ask, Why would you make this piece? We need some real talk about what it means for a white woman to do a rendering of Emmett Till in the form that she did, in part given how a white woman's lie is what propelled the event in 1955. Quite recently, the woman who was at the center of this case confessed that she was lying about what happened, which is something pretty much every Black person already knew. But now she's on record, and it was actually in a fairly sympathetic article in *Vanity Fair,* where she said things like, "I wonder now. I think about his mother." Now you think about Mamie Till?

This analysis is an interesting instance of race and gender and class intersecting in what it means for a privileged white woman to render Black death and to make it visible to an audience that's largely not Black and brown and not in the neighborhoods that feel the afterlife of Emmett Till. The afterlife of Emmett Till is Philando Castile, is Trayvon Martin, is Sandra Bland, is Rekia Boyd. That afterlife resonates very differently. Then, Dana Schutz gave a completely tone-deaf response to the pushback that she received.

DS   In her response, she talked a lot about how she created the piece as a mother. And that in approaching it as a mother, she decoupled her race and her whiteness from this idea. I think for a lot of white people, the notion of a threat to their children is a new realization. There are studies that show that white parents start talking to their kids about race when they're twelve or thirteen and parents of color start talking to their kids about race—well, in the studies, they say five or six, but in my experience, it's…

IB   **Three or four. That's when it started in our household.**

TBL   Three or four.

DS   Because of social media, many white people are being faced with Black deaths so much more explicitly. There's been pushback in the communities that I'm a part of with people saying, "Don't share videos of Black people being killed. We are surrounded by this all day. It is in our lives. It is in everything around us. Don't share those videos." But for many white people, they haven't seen those videos or those experiences before, and somehow the history of lynchings and the history of attacks on communities of color and on Black and brown bodies hasn't gotten through until the past couple of years.

    The way that whiteness works has been to protect white people. It's part of the project of protecting whiteness to say, "We're not going to look at the hard parts. We're not going to see those parts that are so difficult. We're not going to see what it means to protect our communities so that we don't have to see the death and destruction that happens." For example, in the southeast part of the United States, people have events on plantations—white people have events on plantations—and don't think about what it means. They don't ask, "What does it mean to have a celebration on a place that was literally seeped in the blood of enslaved Africans?"

MC   We're certainly experiencing the reality of being very, very far down a slippery slope of idiocy. Part of it is just a commodification problem in general, and the commodification of human beings. But this idea that it's the same thing to talk about an issue and raise awareness of it as it is to do something about it is part of the huge problem.

    Also, law enforcement, as an apparatus, has continuously, since the birth of the nation, been used as an oppressive device to stamp out Native Americans, to keep African Americans on the plantation, to go hunt them down if they escaped, or what have you, and that still exists in every form today in the prison industrial complex.

IB   **Absolutely.**

MC   When we talk about stuff historically, it's not just historically. It is the precursor to how we live today. We have the largest prison system in the history of humankind, and it is disproportionately targeted against not-white people, and most white people don't know it.

    Even though numerically more white people are killed by police officers than not-white people, it's disproportionate by population. The thing is that white people are the collateral damage in a war against not-white people that's been going on for hundreds of years. Another casualty of this ongoing war is this cultural acceptance of commodification of basic human values, which we see right now in this horrific portrait of somebody.

TBL But there's no point in US history where the Black body isn't a commodity, right? It's not shocking that we continue to consume the Black body. The productive and reproductive labor of Black bodies produces wealth in this country. But we were brought here as chattel, as property. The continuation of that is convict leasing, what we now know is the prison industrial complex—which is still about containment, of course, but also about this establishing of property.

You talk about this hyper-commodification and this reality, but there's no time in history where Black bodies weren't tied to commodification. And that's why the response is so visceral and painful for a lot of folks witnessing this. You can write that idea into a narrative of awareness and motherhood, but then it is such a troubling thing to think about Black motherhood in particular.

IB **Especially over the summer.**

TBL Over last summer. There are mothers who are actively in this legacy. It's a terrible thing to think the legacy of Mamie Till—Sybrina Fulton, Trayvon Martin's mom; Lucy McBath, Jordan Davis's mom—is somehow similar to white privileged motherhood. There's this idea of motherhood as a universalizing experience or womanhood as a universalizing experience. Well, Black motherhood was used to create antiwelfare rhetoric.

Right now in the prison industrial complex, we have the opioid crisis and we have opioid patients. We were crack whores and crack moms and had crack babies. We were criminalized and fed into the prison industrial complex in unprecedented ways, both in terms of the actual institutions of prisons but also in the decimation of our neighborhoods, communities, and families as a result of that. Black motherhood has been demonized, seen as invalid, seen as not valuable, and yet Black mothers have nursed this nation, figuratively and literally.

She could have done a portrait of Emmett Till. Why is it his death that was chosen? What would it mean if she had painted the picture that was next to the casket of him in his suit and smiling versus the picture of his body brutalized and assailed? What is the value of that? It is saying to us collectively that the only value Black bodies have in forwarding this conversation is to be dead bodies. That our violated bodies are what propels conversations. How many violated bodies do we need to see, to witness, to bear witness to, before we bear *with*-ness to what's happening?

DS That is such a huge question that we have to grapple with in this moment because the other epidemic that we're seeing in the United States is of white male shooters. Most of the shootings that happen in the United States are done by white men. Most of them are done with guns that were purchased legally.

Also, the narrative has shifted around opioids and the heroin epidemic—living in upstate New York, it's something that's talked about in very sympathetic tones, which is not the way that it was talked about in the 1980s or 1990s. There's a question of how white people are humanized around suffering, whether it be around heroin or around white murderers who are killing across the country every day, and there is no legislative will to limit the purchase of guns.

One of these situations happened just recently. A white man came up from Maryland to New York City...

TBL   To kill Black men. But the news framed it as "Army Vet Shoots Homeless Black Man Who Had Eleven Prior Cases." I know the victim's criminal record. I don't know the shooter's criminal record. I have no idea about the shooter. I know he's an Army vet.

I remember Renisha McBride, a sister who was killed in Detroit. The headline said something like, "Homeowner Shoots Drunk Woman on Porch." I didn't have to know the race of the person to know what *homeowner* meant, to know what that was signaling. And I knew who the drunk woman was, regardless of the fact that there was no race mentioned anywhere in that headline. The media apparatus has a way of letting us know this. So as soon as I saw "Army Vet"...

DS   You knew.

TBL   I knew who was being referred to. And then "Homeless Man Who Had"—it's just all of these signals: Who's disposable? Who's not? Who gets to be heard about? Who gets to be written about? Who's valuable? The politics of disposability in our nation suggests all of these things in very real ways. Crack whores, crack babies are disposable; opioid patients aren't. That doesn't mean I agree—we should have always approached drugs as a public health issue—but it's not like white people just started doing drugs yesterday. White people have always done drugs, but the arrests for Black and brown people are at disproportionately higher rates. Even now we see the legalization of marijuana. Who's going to profit off of that? And who's still incarcerated because they were doing that?

DS   In some places, corners that used to be the heaviest corners for Black drug dealing have now become gentrified by white marijuana shops. But if you have a previous conviction for selling marijuana...

TBL   You can't have a marijuana shop!

DS   You can't do it. And so again, when something becomes commodified and legalized, then it becomes a purview of white people, and it's preserved in that way: with laws to preserve the wealth for white communities. It's this question of, How do we reach white people to get more and more white people to recognize this as well? Which I'm not at all saying to people of color in the room, but actually to the other white people in the room.

IB   **I'm so glad you're saying this because I want to get to the doing, too. What are the takeaways? What can we do?**

MC The war on drugs was completely invented as a means for social control. It was racist from its inception. Opium laws were targeted at the Chinese; marijuana laws were targeted at Mexicans. There were news articles that said, "Marijuana gives Mexicans superhuman strength." That was a real story that existed. The goal was to galvanize the constituency so that certain politicians would get the votes and be able to get jobs or whatever benefits they were looking to get for their particular community. And the same thing for cocaine with African Americans. There were stories about "cocaine-crazed Negroes" attacking white women in the streets. This was used as evidence that we needed to have cocaine laws levied particularly against Black people.

The reality, though, was different. There were studies done at the time that showed the highest rates of cocaine use were from white women in the suburbs. As many people know, it was mixed with all kinds of things: Coca-Cola was the alcohol-free alternative to a cocaine beverage.

So what are we going to do about it? And that can be incredibly confusing, especially in a day when, if our phone gets turned off, we don't know how to get anywhere. I don't know anything without technology. And major media corporations control 90 percent of our media. Boom, they control everything. We have to be inventive in each one of our talents, whatever that unique thing is that we're bringing into the world. For myself, as a filmmaker, what I can do is learn about the history of things outside of my upbringing and incorporate it and have heroes that are outside the dominant culture.

IB **I love what Matthew is saying in terms of everyone having a talent, having a focus, and paying attention. Not being afraid to be uncomfortable, to feel small, and to take all of that and channel it into whatever it is that you focus on or hope to focus on.**

DS There are two parts that I think about. One is interpersonal, right? Sometimes people say to Millennials, "You're snowflakes, and you're going to melt under the pressure." And I think the reality is that Millennials are incredibly resilient and don't want to put up with the shit that a lot of us have put up with for a really long time.

Turn to the people around you and be in conversation with them. There can be a real desire to be only with the people who agree with you, and I would encourage all of us, particularly the white people among us, to be in conversation and engage others. Not just in your class, and in the school, and in the town, and in the town that you come from, but to have conversations with people elsewhere. Even if they mess up and they don't have the "right" language, to not focus on the words but to ask, What is it that they're trying to get across? And how can I be in this with these white people who are around me?

The other piece is structural. As much as Donald Trump is our president and there is something horrific and disease-ridden in our government, we're also in what can be called the "moment of the whirlwind," where thousands of people are emerging and wanting to take action. We need to do really boring things, like go to a town meeting, which is mostly filled with older white people, and actually engage with them and make the conversation be about affordable care and defunding the military and putting money into our communities.

There is an anarchist idea of dual power: How do you take down the systems that are oppressive and build up alternative structures? How do we build food co-ops, and how do we build workers' cooperatives and health-care collectives? At the same time, how do we destroy the government and the systems that are controlling us in so many ways? We need to do both of those things at once. And to do that we all need to be organizers.

TBL What I say is, "Stay in your lane." And everybody's got lanes to do things for which they are uniquely gifted.

From the first time I went to Ferguson, after the Ferguson uprising and the killing of Michael Brown, one of the people I remember most is this woman in the community who cooked us food. Everybody knew who this woman was because, well, she could just cook, and that was her contribution to the movement. She could sustain us.

Not all of us are going to be out in the street, and not all of us are going to be crowding jails, not all of us are going to be writing books or making films or being an organizer that's doing that kind of work, but there are so many ways for you to be impassioned about something and to act. For me, it is about using our unique gifts and talents and skills, and learning and unlearning a lot of stuff, too.

And listen to marginalized folks—really listen, don't just hear. Because so many of the things that we're talking about institutionally, that we're saying we need to build, are what marginalized folks have had to build when things have fallen. Black Panthers, for instance, created free breakfast programs. They had medical centers and clinics—these are things you don't often hear about the Black Panther Party. You see the image of the guns, which is also part of the movement. But let's be very clear: these programs were actually coopted and initiated by the government and now they're on the chopping block.

And in the wake of that, organizers in over thirty cities around the country have created "books and breakfast" to refeed communities. People on the margins have always created things to sustain ourselves when we knew that dominant powers, default culture, would not provide those things. So look at models that already exist from people who've always had to create freedom dreams when the nightmare is right at their door.

Too many of us waited until the nightmare was at our door before we got concerned and motivated. So as much as I'm inspired by the hundreds of people at town halls, I'm wondering, when I was in Ferguson, at every Black Lives Matter march I went to, at rallies I've gone to for transwomen being murdered, or the ten girls who went missing in DC in one week, where is everybody at? Where have we been? Did it need to be you for you to have to feel the thing? And I know for a lot of people that's the reality that we're dealing with—that it has to affect you.

But again, this is about a humanity project of questioning and learning the spots of inhumanity that we have had, and what it means to care for somebody and understand that their nonliving or dying impacts all of us. And I don't mean financially or in this capitalistic way, but more like, if I died right now on this stage, that should impact you, right? But there are millions of me dying right now that we don't give a damn about.

So I ask us to think about that in the work that we do and imagine that the work that we're doing is literally saving a life because all of our lives are in jeopardy. And marginalized folks have already lived in that precarity, but now we fill it more grandly. Welcome to the struggle, for those who weren't here before. We welcome you. Understand that we may be a little skeptical, a little cynical, a little "where were you?" You have to sit with that, but still do the work while sitting with that.

Audience You all talked about history several times. Lately I've been thinking about history because I was watching this documentary on Netflix about hip-hop, about how people who created hip-hop are still alive and what has happened to hip-hop and why. I think that once someone doesn't know the history of things, there is no connection. My question is: What do you all think about or can speak to about the importance of history? Even between generations, between people?

TBL This is one of the reasons I did my PhD in history. I think it comes from how we defund public schools. Civics education used to be a part of education. I'm thinking about that work now. I'm thinking about what it means to create spaces of political education, because as we stand now, and with who we have leading the charge on education, and seeing the way states and municipalities are defunding public education in particular, we're going to have to use models that we've seen before to provide that space to offer these histories. The arts have a large part to do with how we're doing this.

There's a show, *Underground*, about the Underground Railroad and fugitive and enslaved resistors, agitators. It's historical fiction, but there's a way that people are learning about enslavement in a fundamentally different way from what and how they've been taught in schools. We see textbooks now that say "unpaid laborers" as opposed to "slaves." I say "enslaved persons" as a framing tool. That political and civics education is part of this work as well.

I hope that when people know better, they do better. That's not always true, because they can know better and still be invested in power and still make terrible decisions as they pertain to marginalized people. But I do believe that there's a core, critical mass of people who, if they knew how deeply entrenched the act of slavery is in how we function today, would have a different conversation around reparations—if we actually knew and had a large consensus about what enslavement meant.

The Dakota Access Pipeline protests look very different if we have a larger history about being on occupied land. I usually start by acknowledging the occupied land on which we sit. I think about what it means to say, "Water is life," and connecting that to Flint and to other places throughout the world that are struggling through water crises right now. There isn't a longer history about how people have talked about natural resources and land and ownership. People just don't know.

If we invest in and create spaces for political and civics education and advocate for the systems that formally educate to include these histories in the curriculum, it's important to do that advocacy but also know that it may not work and some people are not interested. We all are teachers and learners at different moments in our lives. And so we all can bring something to that conversation. But I think it's important that we create those spaces in the absence of our government creating them.

I am unapologetically about getting free, and so all of my work is unapologetically oriented in that way. More of us who have the privilege of writing in the academy have to put that on the line in doing the work that we do. As students, think about the projects that you choose. Ask yourself a question you never thought to ask yourself: Why do most of the workers on our campus look like this? Why do most of the students look like this? What's the history there? You can research that right here. You don't have to go anywhere. Research that and ask yourselves those questions.

DS   And build political education into any event that you do. For white folks in the room, we don't always have a lot of models of white people doing racial justice work. We don't hear about John Brown or about the Grimké sisters. There is a history of white people who have been doing racial justice work and who have been showing up again and again and again and who have been in accountable relationships with people of color. Not relationships where they made themselves smaller and said, "I'm just going to do whatever you say, and I'm just going to do childcare and fundraising." But were actually asking, "How can I organize my people and what does that mean for me to be organizing my people in this moment?"

Part of the work for white people is how we take action and take accountability through taking action. And know that we're going to make mistakes, but keep showing up because we can't see all the things that are there. That consistency and continuing to show up is a part of the work.

MC   Context is everything, and if we don't have history, we have nothing. The act of providing context that challenges institutionalized authority is resistance, and it's that step that makes us feel empowered and motivated.

At one point I was having an argument with people on Facebook about the term *race-baiting*. I went back to Howard Zinn for history. A hundred-year span of time seems to be completely missing from the mainstream US educational system. We're taught that slavery ended, and then there was Martin Luther King and then Obama. So I thought, What are the five points that I can make that can connect this time and this time?

I had a list of points, and it got longer and longer and longer until I realized, nobody's ever going to read that Facebook response. But I'm a filmmaker, so I made a piece, and it was nine minutes long. It's called *Race-Baiting 101*. I felt super awkward making it because I'm a white guy doing African American history in nine minutes. But I put it up and forty million views later, it's used in prisons around the country. And it's just a little bit of research and a lot of Facebook arguments. And it had some impact. Besides the hate mail and the death threats, there were significant numbers of white people who said, "Oh, I didn't know that, and I didn't get it, and now I get it, and I totally see that differently."

So if you found out something about the history of hip-hop, share it. It takes all of us or nothing's going to happen.

IB **Please share it. Write it. Investigate it. Research it.**

MC Rap it.

TBL Paint it, dance it, code it.

Audience When we talk about white people showing up, how do we challenge white supremacy without centering whiteness or re-centering whiteness?

DS This comes up all the time. One of the big pieces is naming race and also naming our own complicity in it, the benefits that we get individually from the system. It's not something that we created, but we're pulling some of the veils back to make it more apparent.

There is a stage that a lot of white people go through where they think, "Oh my God. I need to talk about being white, and I feel really bad about taking up space by talking about being white." And we spend ten minutes talking about how bad we feel in that moment. But it's also really important. You live in a racialized space. And so, as white people, how do we name that and then also not turn to the person next to us to say, "Was that okay? Did I do that right?" But instead turn to other white people and say, "How can we support each other in doing this?" And also be in accountable relationships with people of color and ask, "What could be most helpful in this situation?" People will tell you if you ask them.

I went to Bard College, not so far from here. Most of the people who worked on campus there were white. Not that they were just hiring white people, it's that that's who was doing service jobs there at that time. I was on work study, and I would ask, "Hey, what is it like working here?" And they'd say, "Well, it really sucks...I'm barely getting paid minimum wage and I've worked here for ten years." And there ended up being a union drive that a bunch of students ran in partnership with longtime cafeteria workers. They ended up unionizing, and they're still a union. I went back for my reunion, and people there said, "That union has meant that I've been here for twenty years." There's real power in building those relationships. Building those relationships across class with people who are working on campus and building them within the community of people who are here and not assuming that we have all the answers but also not assuming that we don't have any answers.

Audience The email invitation for this event had this image that I found to be quite striking. When I came in and saw the sculptures, I was taken aback because it reminded me of what my family used to call these figures when they didn't have the embellishments to be so assertive and aggressive looking. I apologize if this is hard for other people to hear, but they were called "yard nards." And it was the most humorous thing we could say at the time when we would see these horrible things in people's yards. I wondered what it was like for you all to come into this room, having these figures over here next to you this whole time?

IB I'm really glad you brought that up. These sculptures are three pieces from a much larger chess set created by Willie Cole in 2001 called *To get to the other side*. I'll read a brief description: "*To get to the other side* [is] a large floor-mounted chess board with game pieces comprised of embellished and transformed lawn jockeys. A powerful work, *To get to the other side* comments on the historical origins of the Jockey Boy statue as a Revolutionary War memorial figure while simultaneously referring to Cole's belief that it is a contemporary stand-in for the Yoruba god Elegba."

Cole has embellished each of these figures with blades and nails, jars, and other items. For him, there's this notion of getting to the other side within a Congolese belief system. Congolese people believe that you can live in multiple realms and that your life is essentially a journey from one realm to the other.

There's also a reference to what we refer to as Nkisi N'Kondi, or power figures, derogatorily referred to as fetishes. These figures are important staples within Congolese communities; they are cared for by a caretaker referred to as a Nganga, and they serve as ways to resolve disputes among individuals in the communities. So each of the nails and the blades stands for a particular issue that was discussed. And sometimes a tiny piece of hair was used to bind that person and their agreement. So the more nails and blades and inserts, the more powerful the figure.

Cole's sculpture is a reference and an homage to Congolese culture, but also an appropriation of an incredibly multilayered lawn jockey statue that has racist connotations—there are layers of class, layers of servitude. In chess, the figures are imbued with certain powers. There are pawns, who are all identical, who are guarding the king, the queen, the castle, and they all have to physically be moved in an effort to challenge your opponent. Here, taken out of the chess context, the figures are posed as one big question/problem: What is this? What do I do with it? How come this is here?

DS We were talking earlier about the exhibition at the Whitney, and I think there's something about the creation of art by people of color not meant for the white gaze.

I also think about what the art that was created for my culture is. Not to just reinforce the mainstream, but for me, as a Jew, what is the art that reflects a Judaism that isn't about colonization and isn't about maintaining or supporting state power? And that can represent something different? And how does that build a larger movement for decolonization and against colonization both here in the United States and in Israel? That's something that I have to grapple with as a white Jew.

TBL Dara, I'm glad you mentioned the white gaze. When I see these sculptures, I have a visceral response, particularly seeing the singular figure versus the whole installed sculpture, putting it in context, thinking about the very diasporic way that these pieces come into being. There are certain things you just got to know to know. And that happens in Black cultural production across the diaspora.

There are certain things that aren't for everyone to know. There are different literacies that we have with reading particular pieces. One of those literacies, for me, is America's racist history. So when I see these works, I don't see them outside of that. I see it in conjunction with all of these other things. In race- and representation-oriented classes, you hear "white gaze" as this thing that's deployed. We often don't get at the nuts and bolts of it, and the ways in which white bodies have needed Black bodies to be seen. What was so fascinating to me about seeing the sculptures in a panel to talk about whiteness is that it does signal the ways in which whiteness has engaged Black bodies in very significant ways—which impacts even how I see Black bodies.

How whiteness imagines Blackness is not my shame or my discomfort. But to think about this in the larger piece of the strategy, the routing: what is it to be menacing? "Menacing" has been used against Black folks, but what is menacing as a re-appropriated tool of resistance and armed resistance to these things? So I see this, and I also see Korryn Gaines in Baltimore, who was shot by the police, who was an armed Black mother trying to protect her child but is seen in this very complicated way. And notably Black folks really teetered as to whether they should support her or not. Because we, too, saw her as a menacing or bad mother, and we know the history bad Black mothering has in a US imaginary.

I can't escape the Americanness of the ways in which I process images, either. I have to unlearn that, too, so that I rail against individual and collective fears of Black men walking down the street. I get so many messages that tell me that I should be afraid. The white gaze is not specific to white people—I want to be clear about that. That's where dominance and default and power and privilege go, so I have to actually construct an oppositional gaze. It's like bell hooks's resistive practices—practices in order to see things differently and to not let those histories dictate the way I process and engage and move through the world.

Audience   A lot of white people are beginning to accept and come to terms with their privileged role as being oppressive, especially in communities that are largely upper or middle class and white, like this college. I'm wondering how white people can be part of this destabilizing conversation that's meant to unseat white power without taking over that conversation and making it a way in which to retain white power.

IB   **Dara, you touched earlier on that idea of decentering without becoming the center, or this idea of intervening within a space without taking it over.**

DS   There's something around taking risks. Sometimes we can get so caught up in "Is it the right thing to say? And am I going to be taking up too much space?" Part of it is also the roles that we're conscripted to.

In terms of your question about how we raise questions about race, how we do race work as white people without taking it over: sometimes you'll be given a little bit of space and will make mistakes. How do we take risks and know that we're going to make mistakes and keep trying? And build genuine relationships with the people of color who are around us? I was a white person in the Movement for Black Lives, and for so long it was so rare to see other white people who were in it. There would be these waves after Philando Castile was killed, after Sandra Bland was killed, after the burning of the Black churches... There would be this wave of white people who would come in and say, "Oh my God, I just realized we live in a racist country..."

TBL   [Throws hands up] What?

DS   Exactly. And they'd be around for a couple weeks and then a lot of people would fade away. Whether you stay in it for the long haul is part of what makes a difference. It's that consistency of showing up and showing up again and showing up again and not always being the person on stage. I've been doing this work for a long time. I am on stage right now, but in my town, I'm cleaning the floors and I'm cooking the food, and we're figuring it out together because we're in it together.

TBL   I also think you create spaces to do a certain kind of work that holds you accountable. I can be in my classrooms as a professor. I can be a race whisperer and a gender whisperer. But when I'm organizing and moving in other spaces, my work isn't actually talking to white people about race. That's something I've self-selected out of because there's the work of me being Black and getting to my car and not dying. That can be a real thing and real labor, unfortunately. Adding another thing to the labor of oppressed people is always a sticky thing for me.

    Let's first unlearn and get all the guilt and shame out and get all that bullshit out in the beginning to start this. Let's start from the place of stating that white supremacy exists, so what are we going to do? How uncomfortable are we willing to be? How willing are we to diminish our own proximity to power? When I think about movements right now, the tactic of going and getting arrested is not to put it on your Instagram. It's to actually flood the jails and make it impossible for them to hold everybody who's in there. That's not work you can ask undocumented people to do and yet they do it anyway because their lives are at risk. Sometimes we show up for ourselves because no one else is showing up.

    For those who are building spaces that are antiracist, anti-ableist, anticlassist, antisexist, antitransphobic, the question becomes: What are you willing to risk? "If freedom is in your vocabulary, then death is also in your vocabulary" is my riff-off of Malcolm X's powerful quote, "If you're not ready to die for it, put the word 'freedom' out of your vocabulary." We're fighting against a system that has literally killed to maintain itself.

    When you say, "Are you ready to die for this?" it seems very grand and up there, so I also ask, What are you willing to give up? Are you ready to be present? To show up?—which means you will be wrong at times. I'm wrong in spaces all the time, particularly around how I moved and thought about and learned as a nontrans person thinking about activism and asking my trans sibs to be in spaces when I know they're policed in a very different way than I am as a nontrans Black woman.

    Those questions of taking up space I appreciate deeply, but I also want to encourage you to create space and have that space to be accountable to the communities that you're fighting alongside. You're not speaking for them but speaking with them and in conjunction with the work that's going on. Within the Movement for Black Lives, we have times when we say, "This is a Black space," and we claim that very clearly. Or: "This is an all-women-identified space."

In the interim, that doesn't mean you get a day off when we're doing that work. That means, on that day, you get you and your cousins—cousins in the playful Black vernacular sense, your peoples—and you get them together and you have conversations about what we need to do and what work we need to do in this moment that would be most supportive to the agenda that's been given to us by these communities of color who are seeing the world in this way, and feeling and experiencing the world in this way.

MC Right now you might be in a space where if you started talking about a certain issue, there might be a couple other people here who you seem to be taking up space for, but there are so many other situations in which you will be alone out there and you will find yourself not amid the people who can speak up for themselves at all. You'll be at an immigration checkpoint or you'll be somewhere where someone's getting arrested right in front of your face.

Do you all remember the Milgram experiment? I'll jump to the conclusion: 65 percent of human beings will electrocute somebody to death if instructed to do so by an authority figure—65 percent. So whether we believe that that's by nature or nurture, we're genetically predisposed to obey and we have that working against us. We need to train and practice those modalities of resistance, that psychology of resistance, that psychology of saying, "No. No. I'm actually going to go, and I'm going to disagree with you." And maybe at first, it's with shaking hands and it's not with the right words. So what? And then you try it again, and the next time you're more comfortable with it—you might get checked here and there but it's so worth it. So many people's lives are just brutalized.

I've spent time in our prison system. And I encourage you, if you haven't, to take a tour. Just take a look at what's going on in prisons or the local jail or a courthouse. And watch how it functions, and observe that in a nation where everyone should have the right to a free trial, 95 percent of all cases are resolved by plea bargaining, which means that a prosecutor laid on the charges and told you, "You're going to need $50,000 to $100,000 to fight the case, so you might as well just plead guilty and you'll spend x amount of time and then you'll be out of there."

And the next thing you know you're spending a couple years in the most horrific, barbaric environment that one could not possibly imagine without taking a look at it. And I mean that. I've seen some horrible, horrible stuff in my life. And what I saw in LA County Jail and what I heard about, I couldn't have come up with it in the sickest corner of my mind. You'll never make a decision again to just vote for the corporate Democrat.

There are all kinds of reasons why we might not want to speak up or might not want to challenge something or feel self-doubt. Just give it a shot. The old way has brought us to where we are now, and it's not working; let's try anything else.

TBL Use the privilege of being able to take up space. Use your privilege right now. This is actually when a white person speaking of seeing someone stopped and unfairly treated at the airport matters differently. What can you do to be an interrupter of the kinds of violence that are impacting marginalized communities? Because even if it doesn't work in that exact moment, that person needs to know that somebody cares and that they weren't rendered both violated and invisible in that moment. So it is the day-to-day as well as these more concentrated moments. I'm not saying at every moment that you see something that you act, because you'd just be exhausted. But really take a look at those moments and ask, What can I do in this exact moment that stands between this person and the system that was designed to kill them?

And if you think of these systems as systems that were designed to kill people slowly and commodify people and commodify the worth of people, then I think it emboldens us more to contest that at every level. We think about the everydayness of this. And it reminds you that every day, marginalized people wake up marginalized people. So every day when you wake up with whiteness or the privilege of class or heterosexuality or whatever it is, use that to challenge so that we get closer to a world in which that privilege doesn't have that kind of power. ▲

MIGRATION AND BORDERS

Visible and Invisible Walls

Hassan Hajjaj
Mr. J. C.-Hayford
2012
Metallic lambda print on Dibond, Papillon matchboxes in white frame
35 × 24⅜ inches
Tang Teaching Museum collection, purchased with generous funding from Nancy Herman Frehling '65 and Leslie Cyphen Diamond '96, 2017.9

"When you say, 'rock star,' in my eyes and my friends' [eyes], it's normally a leather jacket, long hair, a guitar, and dark glasses. That's kind of a brand. I wanted to take this brand and turn it into my brand, my rock stars: it's my friends, it's people who have a similar journey from different parts…I've chosen these friends, which I call the underdogs, in that they're not mainstream. But they have this passion and they're born with something and they follow it. Even when they fall, they get up and keep fighting. When I started this project, I was very lucky because of my background…I've been very lucky to have these kinds of people around me. When you hear the title My Rock Stars, you expect musicians. And so I try to have the Henna girl, male belly dancer, the snake charmer, the bad boy done well. The underdogs are more attractive to me."
—Hassan Hajjaj

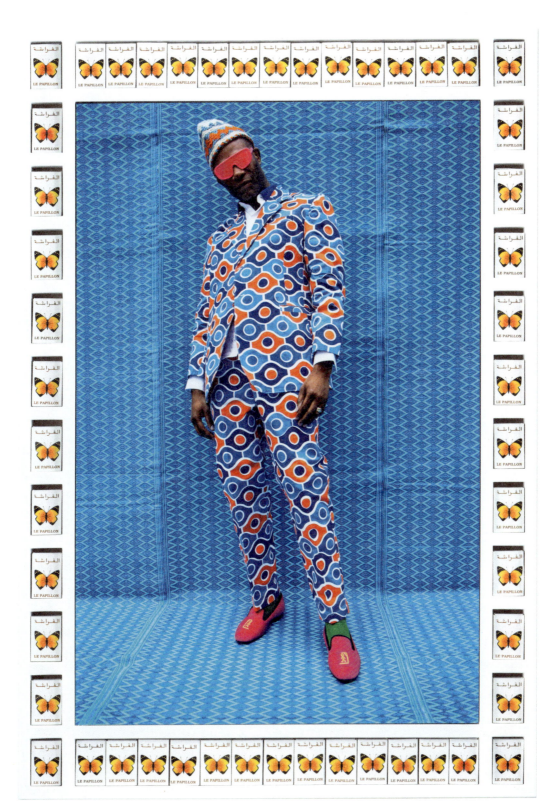

Books, Borders, and Democracy

Tanya Selvaratnam

[1] Azar Nafisi, *The Republic of Imagination: A Life in Books* (New York: Viking Press, 2014), 4.

[2] Ibid., 294.

When those in positions of political power seek to divide us with physical borders and walls, our imaginations are the most effective tools we have to keep cultural borders open.

From the time I could read, I haven't felt complete without a book in my hand or my bag or by my bed. Even in the car as my parents drove, I would read in the back seat until the natural light dimmed and I couldn't squint my eyes any smaller to discern the words on the page. When I was reading, I was someone else, somewhere else. I could escape my surroundings in Long Beach, California, and the unhappiness in my family home. I made friends with the characters in the books, getting to know their worlds and communities.

In my New York apartment, I have books on my shelves that date back to elementary school. Seeing them triggers memories of the times during which I read them. The older I get, the more my bookshelves overflow.

Soon after 2019 began, Marie Kondo, the Japanese home-organization expert, was all the rage. After watching her television show, people took piles and piles of clothes, records, and books to donation centers and secondhand stores. I decided it was time to clean up my own shelves. I said "thank you" to the books I knew I wouldn't peruse again and put them in bags to give away. But when I came across *The Republic of Imagination* by Azar Nafisi, I started reading it again.

Nafisi wrote, "Long before I made America my home, I inhabited its fiction, its poetry, its music and films."[1] She wrote about her admiration for James Baldwin: "Baldwin genuinely believed that literature had a vital role to play as a sort of social glue. He felt there was, as he put it, 'a thread...which unites every one of us' and saw a deep-rooted and necessary affinity between our everyday lives, anxieties, joys and sorrows and the act of writing."[2]

Baldwin was my father's favorite writer, and he eventually became mine, too. A copy of *Tell Me How Long the Train's Been Gone* had been on my father's office bookshelf. As my father lay dying from lung cancer in his hospital bed, I read to him from *The Fire Next Time*. When I was starting the Federation, a coalition of artists, organizations, and allies committed to the concept that art is essential to democracy, I turned to Baldwin's words again and again, and in particular, to this quote: "The

3 James Baldwin, "The Creative Process," in *Creative America* (New York: Ridge Press, 1962), 1.

4 Nafisi, *The Republic of Imagination*, 294.

5 Ibid., 16.

precise role of the artist [is] to make the world a more human dwelling place."[3]

But can art save democracy? The question is a provocation in its implication that there's a democracy to be saved: the United States has never truly been one. The question then becomes: How can art be used to build the democracy we are striving toward?

Nafisi wrote, "In a democracy, the arts tend not to threaten the state." She also asserted, "Writers are truth tellers, and that can sometimes put them in conflict with the state."[4] In her 2003 bestseller, *Reading Lolita in Tehran*, she recounted how every Thursday for two years, she gathered seven female students in her living room to read forbidden Western classics. Reading was rebellion; reading was an act of defiance against totalitarianism. In both democracies and totalitarian regimes, there's an element of people having to succumb to a system of governance. Nafisi has stated that "fiction is an antidote" to conformity, "a reminder about the power of individual choice."[5]

We know we are sliding toward authoritarianism when artists become perceived as enemies of the state, when cultural exchange becomes a threat. We know that this is happening in the United States in 2020. The measures taken to build physical walls and ban entry from specific countries have been explained in terms of national security. But in truth, they have been much more about suppressing freedom and eroding our shared humanity; they have been intended to instill fear. When children are separated from their families at the border, they are imprinted with trauma that will track them for the rest of their lives.

Making borders more rigid is an attempt to block the free exchange of ideas. Take, for example, the saga of bringing *The Jungle*, a play set in a refugee camp in Calais, France, from London to St. Ann's Warehouse in Brooklyn, New York. Many of the cast members had lived in the refugee camp, and three were from countries on the ban list. It took intense legal maneuvering as well as letters from luminaries such as Sting and the mayors of New York and London to persuade the US government to let the actors cross the border. Matthew Covey, the lawyer who worked on the case, said to the *New York Times*, "The issue of refugees is on everyone's mind right now, so a powerful artistic piece coming out of that context is very compelling, and when this first came in, we said, 'We have to do this, and we have to make it work.'"[6]

Senator Kirsten Gillibrand, in her plea to the State Department about the case, said, "Welcoming refugees is what the Statue of Liberty stands for and what our nation stands for, and this play is so important because it gives refugees a chance to bring their powerful experiences to the United States."[7]

Near the building that houses St. Ann's, droves of tourists take photos against the backdrop of the Manhattan and Brooklyn Bridges: bridges not walls. They also take photos of the Statue of Liberty in the distance. This gift from France has at its base the Emma Lazarus poem that resonates ever more strongly with these simple words:

> Give me your tired, your poor,
> Your huddled masses yearning to breathe free

In a recent moment of despondency about everything, I reached out to my friend Farai Chideya, the multimedia writer and thinker. I told her that what was getting me down was the feeling that the bad guys are winning, that it's ultimately hopeless, and that we spend too much energy trying to make things better. As long as the constructs of money and real estate dominate our government, we're doomed. We've built the systems that enslave us. With typical brilliance and quick-wittedness, Chideya responded, "Yes, bad guys win, but truth tellers also win."

A friend of Chideya's, Betty Reid Soskin, has lived through many times of tumult in the United States. When I met her in 2018, she was ninety-seven years old (and the oldest National Park Ranger, assigned to Rosie the Riveter WWII Home Front National Historical Park in Richmond, California). We might think racism, misogyny, and xenophobia are out of control in the twenty-first century, but she's seen them way more out of control. She told me that periods of chaos arise when democracy is redefined, and that we all have access to the reset buttons.

The United States has always been in a tug of war between those who believe in democracy, justice, and equality for all and those who believe in it only for

[6] Michael Paulson, "How 3 Actors Overcame Trump's Travel Ban to Take the New York Stage," *New York Times*, Dec. 2, 2018, https://www.nytimes.com/2018/12/02/theater/the-jungle-st-anns-warehouse.html.

[7] Paulson, "How 3 Actors."

themselves and their friends. Artists and cultural institutions can chip away at the harmful tactics of our government and governments everywhere to fragment us. This involves supporting programming for people from vulnerable communities and taking extra steps to provide platforms for artists from vulnerable communities. We can use art to offer a more representative and inclusive vision of our world, to inspire people to change the world, to provide levity and joy.

As storytellers, artists in all genres have the power to change the picture, to change the narrative, to change the public discourse. When consciousness is transformed and opened up, it is more likely to lead to better choices, whether in the voting booth or the schoolroom, the workplace or the community. When we realize the strong man is a straw man, we can strive to build the world we envision for ourselves.

There are various simple actions that everyone can take to protect and improve democracy:

— Register people to vote. Voter suppression and voter manipulation are some of the most serious threats to our democracy.
— Stand up for and with vulnerable peoples. Wide swaths of communities are vulnerable under the government. Volunteer for or contribute to an organization that works on these issues.
— Support a free press. Your favorite truth-telling publications are dependent on subscriptions to stay afloat.

It's worth noting that Azar Nafisi herself comes from a banned country: Iran. For the epigraph in *The Republic of Imagination*, she chose the Langston Hughes poem "Let America Be America Again." Although he wrote, "America was never America to me," he closes with hope:

And yet I swear this oath—
America will be! ▲

Hassan Hajjaj
artist

Richard Mosse
artist

Tanya Selvaratnam
producer

Isolde Brielmaier   Our conversation revolves around a current and urgent global discussion regarding international movements of people, both voluntary and forced. This type of movement goes beyond political boundaries, calling into question issues of identity; human, legal, and political rights; displacement; the definition of home and what home means to a broad range of people; and citizenship, among other things. Individuals and communities have been put into motion and into exile. They have been moved into spaces of uncertainty, into the so-called shadows, and into what essentially have become states of suspended life or existence.

    This includes undocumented citizens in the United States and Europe, the crisis in Syria, and conditions throughout the Horn of Africa. Historically, we can think about Bosnia, Herzegovina, Rwanda, those who survived Katrina and fled Louisiana, those who fled the terror of the Ku Klux Klan in the United States, or Jewish communities forced to flee their homes in Europe. The list goes on and on. A lot of this calls into question identity, and how people have chosen to represent and identify themselves, and how that isn't always in line with official structures of power.

    Hassan, as an individual and as an artist, you've traversed multiple spaces. Can you talk about being a transnational, someone who's gone from Morocco to Paris to London and back?

Hassan Hajjaj   I was moved to England via my mum and my dad. Along the way, I found myself a misfit in both countries. Growing up in London, I became a Londoner, but I didn't see myself as British because I'd always be reminded that I was not British. Going back to Morocco, I was the person who lived abroad.

    I try to express my journey and my experiences in my work. For example, I have a series called *My Rock Stars* that shows people that I met along the way in London, in Paris, people that had been moved. They call a place home for a moment, but sometimes they don't end up being there all their lives. I have friends who've come from Brazil, got married in London, have documents in London, and the next minute they're living in Paris. This is part of the world that we're living in. There are people who choose to move, and there are people who choose not to be moved but get moved.

    The series includes people I've known or I've grown up with in London, mostly artists or designers. It came to me that when you look at medina images, you see beyond just the pictures; you see the documentation of a city at a time. I thought, okay, it is my turn to continue this form of studio shoots and to go beyond pretty pictures, to document my friends at a certain point of time. It's a journey of myself along with that person.

IB   **Can you talk about the fabrics, the materials, the poses, the adornment in the images?**

HH   It's about having nothing and making something out of nothing, or making something from very cheap materials. For example, in *Mr. J. C.-Hayford*, in the Tang's collection, the fabric in the suit was made from a sun parasol. Using something like this is about trying to be more grand, trying to have a dream life. It's really a journey in my life and the lives of the people around me, and I want these lives to be documented. So when you see Joe Casely-Hayford's photograph, that's when he was in London. If you see Cobra Mansa, he was in London, then he went back to Brazil.

I just met someone from Mali who lives in Canada—this is the way the world is, it's not anything new anymore. But when people choose not to move or somebody's been pressed to move, then it becomes a big problem.

IB **Tanya, you've worked in the creative realm for several decades now in addition to being active with social justice and human rights efforts. You've touched in the past on the idea that borders have many layers to them, and you have questioned—I don't even know if there's an answer—how we keep our cultural borders open.**

Tanya Selvaratnam When I was thinking about the theme of visible and invisible walls, I thought about how sometimes the walls are between us and the people who are right in front of us. We've seen that so much in our country over the last few months, how this lack of understanding and this lack of empathy have led to horrible decisions being made and how important it is to be able to use or to pierce the walls that those in positions of power would seek to erect between us.

I produced the film *Happy Birthday to a Beautiful Woman*, the artist Mickalene Thomas's first film about her mother. Making that film was part of her process of getting to know her mother, from whom she had been estranged, and who had sacrificed so much to give Mickalene the ability to express herself as an artist. This is a way that art has been used to bridge that wall between a mother and a daughter. And I think about how grateful I am to exist in this country today because of the sacrifices of people like my father, who came as an immigrant from Sri Lanka, where he was a minority discriminated against. He came here to seek better opportunities only to find that once he got to the United States, many white people saw him as Black and some Black people saw him as white. I think of how hard he had to fight to exist in this country.

What I've done pretty much my whole adult life is do as much as I can in the limited amount of time I have on this earth to contribute in some small way to making it a better place. For me, a year and a half ago when our current president announced his candidacy, I was terrified that he was going to win. I came from a country that had already experienced the deleterious effect of a narcissistic, jingoistic ruler like Donald Trump; we had the South Asian Donald Trump. And I saw the damage that could be done, so I dedicated myself to producing as much digital content as I could to get out the vote.

As the great Toni Morrison says, "This is precisely the time when artists go to work." Artists are going to be so important moving forward, maybe more important than ever, in shaping public consciousness, because movements come from the ground; they're not going to come from above. The change of consciousness is not going to come from a politician giving a speech.

This is where all the artists really have to get to work and contribute to building empathy and understanding. Although it's a trying time and there's going to be unmitigated damage done to so many vulnerable people, it's also an exciting time because people are so awake in a way that they haven't been in a long time. So while I feel sad for all the damage that is being done, I'm also very optimistic because of how much we can do to pivot public consciousness and hopefully impact policy in a positive way.

IB **Many artists feel a strong sense of responsibility not only to their craft but also to building a groundswell in terms of movements. Richard, where is your point of entry into all of this? Can you share a bit about your work and what you think about the artist's role?**

Richard Mosse I spent the last three years making artwork about the refugee crisis that's been unfolding in Europe, North Africa, and the Middle East. I made this work along various points on two of the busiest and most perilous routes in the European Union. That's taken me from the Persian Gulf to the border of Syria and Turkey, across the Aegean Islands, up the Balkan Corridor to Germany. And the second route, which I've intercepted at various points, is from Sub-Saharan Africa, lands such as Mali and Niger, through the Sahara Desert toward Libya on the route north to Italy, France, and the United Kingdom. I couldn't go to Libya because I'm working with a camera that's classed as weapons grade, so it's sanctioned. I intercepted this route again off the coast of Libya as people traveled on Italian rescue boats.

IB **You're following multiple migrations here?**

RM Yes. Those are the routes, but there are whole different types of people on the routes from so many different countries, fleeing so many different harsh realities. Along the southern route, people are coming from the Horn of Africa, especially Eritrea and Somalia, all the way across to West Africa, countries such as Senegal and Mali, or fleeing Boko Haram and other Islamist groups in places like Nigeria. There's a lot of climate change in the Sahel that's forcing people off their lands. There are also people coming from Sub-Saharan Africa fleeing persecution and conflict, which often has a correlation with climate change. And those on the route from the east are fleeing war in Syria, Iraq, Afghanistan. But I've also met people from Iran, Bangladesh, and Pakistan, fleeing persecution and economic hardship.

The project includes a film and photographs. The film, titled *Incoming*, is a fifty-two-minute video installation with three screens and 7.1 surround sound. It describes actual journeys. In the photographic prints, *Heat Maps*, produced with the same camera technology, I'm documenting camp architecture from a high elevation. So one is about the journey and the other is about the migrant staging sites.

The whole project was produced and made with an extreme-long-range border-enforcement and military-targeting camera. It's thermographic, so it can see day or night, and it can image the human body from about eighteen miles. That doesn't mean we always use it from such a distance, but it has that feature. It's very powerful technology, and it's very much a military tool, not available for consumer use. Since it's weapons grade, it's very hard to travel with legally, and without the correct export documentation, you could be locked away for weapons smuggling.

IB   **Why that specific camera?**

RM   To investigate the medium. It's very much about a European subjectivity—to remind but also to confront the viewer, particularly a European or American audience, that these are the technologies for which our governments—surveillance states—are paying vast sums of money to control our borders against what they describe as "insurgents" but who are usually stateless, dispossessed, and very vulnerable people.

So my project attempts to confront the viewer with that reality, to reveal this, as well as to work against it, to allow the viewer to think through this form of representation, and hopefully allow them to see the refugee's struggle anew, to refresh the subject and provoke the viewer to see in a way that hopefully holds a mirror up to them.

The project is very much about perception. It is also about privacy—the camera depersonalizes and anonymizes the individual—which is both an appropriate yet symptomatic approach to figuring these individuals, due to, for example, the Dublin Convention. (Refugees often wish to conceal their identity from the camera's gaze.) So there are tensions within the work that we are deliberately bringing into collision in order to make the viewer feel these problems and their own complicity.

There are also ways to interpret the work more simply in terms of body heat. If you're a refugee, on a daily basis, you're facing the risk of hypothermia, mortality from the elements, because you are living in tents and risking your life on the cold sea waves. Boats frequently sink and refugees die of hypothermia, something we witnessed many times and which we show in the film itself. To image the refugee's body as heat is a way to allude to that bodily risk, particularly hypothermia.

IB   **One of the things that you're talking about is an alternate mode of creating visibility—not only for the subjects, the people who make up the content of the images, but also a heightened visibility or awareness on the part of the viewer. Hassan, what do you think of the idea of visibility and presence and relationships to people but also in regard to governments and systems of power?**

HH   Thinking of what's happening right now in Europe, I was having a conversation with my friend Miriam, and we figured out that a while back you could be sitting at home watching the news and you could see thirty-eight Iraqis get blown up. And all of a sudden one day you wake up, for example in Germany, and all the Syrians are sleeping in the train station. I was imagining how the German people were probably watching the news yesterday and going to work and now it's on their doorstep. So it's not just their problem, it becomes our problem. And this is happening everywhere.

There's this disconnect between the government and the real people. Governments are splitting countries in two. It's happening in Europe; it's happening over here. It's creating this thing that is kind of good—there's a self-expression from both sides, everybody has the right to say something—but it also creates tension. There can be something positive, but sadly enough, this kind of chaos happens with it.

If you're not really aware of the refugee movements, what Richard said could scare you. The whole of Africa is running into Europe. It's a big problem, and it's a problem for everybody. It's not just "them" or "us." Even my kid, who's thirteen, understands about politics and is aware of what's going on. I was a kid when I heard about the Vietnam War. I had a radio, and the war was far away; it was like another world, but now I think that's changing.

IB **There's an immediacy to crises now with the advent of technology.**

HH This younger generation is living in the moment; they've got the world in their hand even if they don't travel. I don't know about their awareness when it comes to history, because sometimes people only think of the problem that's happening now. But actually you have to sometimes refer back to how it started and not blame just the people who are with it now.

IB **My father says that history is your best weapon. Some of these crises are deeply rooted historically. To talk about what's going on in Europe now and not be fully aware of and engaged with the history of colonialism on the part of the French, on the part of the British, on the part of the Dutch, the Germans, it goes on and on... There's a big disconnect there.**

TS There's also this false construct of what it means to be an original person. There's a delusion that people give themselves about who is an original citizen or inhabitant of a particular place. Those in power have a perplexing need to dehumanize someone—they just change who that someone is at certain points in time. Right now the Mexican and the Muslim—they're the most visible enemies in the United States who have been constructed by those in power. If we go back to earlier in the century, it was the Japanese; if we go back to the nineteenth century, it was the Irish, who came to this country in waves during the Irish Potato Famine. I'm always aware of how much there is this need to dehumanize somebody so that somebody else can consolidate their power and control people.

IB **And define themselves in a way—the way in which we define Americanness, the way in which we define citizenship. Determining who is able to rightly claim those things is often done in opposition to something, along those false binaries.**

TS Power and money are these systems we've set up to enslave ourselves, and those who've mastered the tools of these systems can maintain their power only by creating people who are separate and selfish and scared, which is why it's so important to have artists doing the work to force people *not* to be separate and selfish and scared, to realize that there are a lot of commonalities between us. We know for a fact that most Americans actually feel very similarly about a majority of issues, whether it be climate change or immigration or criminal justice reform. Yet we've been manipulated to think that we are separate.

IB **And that's a wonderful opportunity for artists to step in and change that image—this idea of humanizing, of making more visible individuals or communities that are disenfranchised or pushed to the margins.**

TS   But it's also important to recognize the limitations of art and technology. I was at a talk where a Google executive was saying that somehow technology was going to save the world because there were more people with iPhones and cameras taking images and witnessing things. It was going to make the world a better place because people could film a police officer straddling a young Black girl at a swimming party, because you could see the Syrian refugees, because you could see the warfare. But we're creating disaster porn. Are we changing policy? While we're using art and technology, we must also understand that it's important to take political control, because until we take political control, the issues we care about won't be actionable.

IB   **How do we do that? Where is that bridge between art, technology, the visual realm, culture, and actually impacting policy? That is, effecting change in a way where it can actually be implemented?**

RM   One criticism of the contemporary art world is that it's constantly preaching to the choir. I think art does have this power to move people, including the people who don't necessarily read *Artforum*. We communicate, that's what we do, and our role now is to move people. I have problems when people want art to be didactic or become propaganda. I think art needs to stay in a rather neutral and ambivalent space to be effective, to make people feel, because I feel that human experience and social responsibility is not about likes and followers and angry comments on Facebook—it's far more complex, and the viewer is very often complicit in certain ways. I guess we should ask ourselves what art's task is. Is it to hold a mirror up to society, to confront us with an image of ourselves that is not necessarily comfortable? Or is it to affirm the beliefs and positions to which we already subscribe? Or is it to prescribe, to tell people what to think and how to respond?

HH   It's true. Artists can say something and can change something, but at the end of the day, it has to come from the person. We can only do so much. It's nice when you can communicate with people who don't look at art. I'm doing my best and trying to see if I can touch one person, which is better than none.

IB   **That's creating a sense of responsibility also for your viewer in terms of thinking about reception.**

HH   Exactly. In some of my early work, I'd take pictures of women with camouflage djellabas, which are Moroccan gowns, with Louis Vuitton bags. And I realized that if I put this image in front of the public, there would be two kinds of thoughts. And because I was testing the viewer, I wanted to see what the viewer thinks. It was interesting because some people said, "Oh, look, terrorists, Muslims." Then some say, "This is very cool." Because camouflage was in fashion in Europe then, and they saw the fashion side. Sometimes you have to play around with the viewer's mind—they have to question themselves—you don't have to give it all to them. You want to push them not to be lazy.

IB **Richard, you straddle two realms as a filmmaker and a photographer. In your work, do you go in with specific goals as you're beginning a project?**

RM No, I go in asking questions, and I usually come out the other end asking more questions. I don't go out with a fixed idea that I have to prove "this"; it's not prescriptive in that way. Good art is about asking questions rather than answering them. Also, my work is in a space between documentary reportage photography and contemporary art.

IB **For me, at the crux of what each of you do is storytelling. And there's no one clear path to doing that. All of you are working in multiple mediums to achieve that and going in with a set of questions as opposed to this idea of "this is what I want to achieve."**

HH For me, sometimes you can start with an idea, and then once you start scratching the surface, it goes somewhere else, and then you find yourself thinking on this new level. I have to let myself go and try to see where else it goes. In a sense, it is a way of searching for yourself within the work. I think any artist will probably ask, "What's the next thing to do?" But when you're on a roll, you find many different layers within a layer, and then you're learning as you go along.

TS For me, as a producer facilitating the work of many artists and directors, every project is so different based on the subject matter. There are some projects where we know the story that we want to tell; there are others where the story has to present itself. For instance, one of the most recent films I worked on, *Chavela,* was about the Mexican outlaw/ranchera Chavela Vargas; she was a muse to Pedro Almodóvar. I also produce a lot of social justice PSAs.

I have no interest in politics myself. I don't believe in the two-party political system; I think that the dark-money machine has totally corrupted our government. But because I was terrified of what would happen to this country if it got its version of what I experienced in Sri Lanka, I did as much as I could. On November 9, 2016, I thought I'd be sailing into the sunset and going back to my happy artist life. And instead, like so many people, I sailed into the fire. So one thing that's definitely changed for me is that while I'm doing films like *Chavela* and projects like Mickalene Thomas's film, I will continue to do more social justice work because I won't be able to sleep if I don't.

IB **Is there a way to think about migration, movement, mobility more positively and not necessarily as a plight, even though we are contending with a lot of that, specifically in Europe but also in the United States? That can involve storytelling—a lot of relevant stories are not heard, they're not told, and therefore what's going on right now in terms of the scapegoating, the xenophobia, the dehumanizing is more prevalent.**

TS There's been so much dissecting and analysis of the failure of storytelling as what got us into this place over the past year. So many of the problems that we're dealing with and the siloing of people that's happening right now, not just in the United States but all over the world—which enables people to live with their own isolating perceptions of themselves and the people around them—are because of the way that our popular culture has evolved. There was a time when I was growing up when there were just a couple of television channels that you could watch, there were just a couple of publications that you could read, a couple of radio stations that you could listen to. But now, it really is user's choice, not dealer's choice. That allows people to cherry-pick what they're exposed to. And there's no arbitration or editorializing that goes on.

RM   They don't even choose; the algorithm chooses for you.

TS   That's the corruption. We are all great storytellers, but we're constantly telling stories to people who already know them. How do we pierce through those walls and have the stories reach the people we want? A lot of it is going to boil down to support and money, and it's something that, sadly, evil people figured out many years ago—how to bust the algorithms, how to penetrate and get their stories out there. It's not that our current president is an effective communicator, but he was able to weave the most distorted stories.

IB   **We're seeing this around the globe—messages predicated on very specific narratives, many of which have at their core xenophobia, anti-immigrant ideas, and complete historical amnesia.**

TS   This is where the artists and the people on the ground will really have to seize control. They have to rise up because there's just too much money that's fighting against us. The Murdochs didn't fire Bill O'Reilly from Fox News because they thought it was the morally right thing to do; they made that decision because people freaked out and rose up, and the ratings dropped, and then advertisers pulled their support because people were rising up. Moving forward, it's going to be very important not just to continue to tell stories but to figure out how to have those stories penetrate to the places where we need them. Again, it's not that we actually feel different about most of the issues, it's that we don't realize how similar we feel.

HH   For me, I'm talking about my personal inner situation. Lots of my friends have been touched by what's going on. These are friends I would never have expected to be touched: they can't enter the United States, or in England, Brexit's hit. So sometimes it's difficult to think of the positive side because we're going through moments like this. Even coming to the United States for this event, I was told I can't bring my laptop and my camera because Trump changed the rules. Sorry to say, I almost canceled the trip, but obviously, I wanted to be here. I always felt this land is a free land; I have friends here, I feel at home.

     At this moment, the earth needs to settle. We're going through lots of political changes. I'm a person of the world: I was born in Morocco; I'm Moroccan, and I'm a Londoner, too. But when you have these situations around you, you do question yourself.

Audience   As a storyteller, as an artist, how do you tell the story of people who are extremely vulnerable without objectifying them? There's a fine line between telling the story of the subject and telling the story instead of the subject.

IB **When we talk about individuals, communities who were historically and are currently vulnerable, oftentimes they have been defined by someone else, and they have not had a voice nor been visible. In my own curatorial practice and teaching, it's about creating a platform to allow people to have a voice, to speak for themselves.**

RM A lot of my work is about visibility. So many people in eastern Congo are dispossessed; it is a place that I would argue is in a state of near anarchy. Of course those people have their own voice; I'm not trying to put a voice in their mouths, but the work is trying to challenge some of the conventions of photojournalism and reportage photography, and to try to find an alternate way of communicating that particular story, hopefully one that's more effective.

In my newer projects—*Incoming* and *Heat Maps*—that objectification is embedded in the work on some level, as is the problem that the work is trying to deal with and trying to reveal. The camera becomes the author, and a camera like that portrays people in a way as a heat trace. I like to read that in terms of an idea by Giorgio Agamben, the Italian philosopher. He had a concept of "bare life," and he saw the refugee as the crisis point for liberal democracy. We're seeing that all over the world in Europe and in the United States now, where this perfect storm of refugees, who are coming from different parts of the world for various reasons, is being used by opportunistic politicians to change the system. What Agamben called the "state of exception" is when emergency laws prevail because of emergencies—that's when the law stops working. It's not just the refugee who has no human rights; it's also the citizen who loses rights. So the refugee creates the crisis by which the system of human rights is suspended for all of us.

The camera strips the individual of identity, anonymizes the individual, and portrays people as biological traces rather than as people with colorful clothes and identity, even though of course they are. It felt like an appropriate way to portray the refugee, which is this stateless person. And also the people around him, the volunteers, emergency workers, Frontex officers, search and rescue people, and other aspects of the military humanitarian complex that has formed around this crisis. All of these people—whether citizen or stateless—are living, breathing human organisms; we share the biological fact that we are pools of heat created by cellular combustion. So I hope this work will evoke this sense of shared humanity, which seems to be a very difficult idea in these febrile times.

TS It's often up to debate whether a work of art is exploitative or whether it is giving voice. It is the utmost responsibility of the artist to fuel that responsibility to their subject. In my own work, when I am showing a difficult situation, it's important to connect it to some type of action that might lead to the eradication of that problem or solving that problem or offering greater awareness of that problem.

I find the debate over who has agency to depict people's stories really strange. There are organizations that have been beating the drum of the need to witness for decades because when you have situations without witness, the atrocities are exponentially higher.

You can't really say that only those who are the identity of the people they're filming are allowed to film. That means that I, as a Sri Lankan woman, can only film Sri Lankan women? For me, the ultimate goal has to be highlighting the efforts of others, giving voice to others, and focusing on positivity and inclusion and uplifting people as much as possible. That's where documentarians really can get to work in filling that role so that there is witness. And when they tie it to action, it's even more powerful and potent.

Audience   If you completely give agency to the subject whose story you're trying to tell, how is your work artistic, not documentary? And if you make it artistic and you are putting your own input in it, then how much say does this subject have?

IB   **Think of Malick Sidibé. His images are filled with agency. Sidibé saw himself as an artist, an author. People came to him and commissioned images. But what you see is the result of a back and forth, a conversation, a negotiation. Someone would come into the studio with an idea of how they want to be seen, of how they want to be presented. Through a conversation with Sidibé come these images that stand in stark contrast to previous images of Malians from the 1940s and 1950s.**

   The process is a little bit fluid, but you should come to it with a heightened awareness of the fact that you are an author and the subject is literally providing the content of your work. What are their intentions, what are yours? How can they come together to then create?

TS   Albert Maysles, the documentary filmmaker, was a big inspiration to me. He's written some beautiful things about the role of the documentarian and about his process and how he worked. As a documentarian, he placed his fate and faith in reality—that was his guide. And he preferred to be a fly on the wall rather than the person who was trying to put his imprint on it. He let the story find itself, and that's very important. But I've also seen successful documentary films where there was a strong imprint of the filmmaker and a lot of editing that went into it.

HH   What you said earlier about Malick Sidibé is a good answer in some ways because he was actually a studio photographer for the town. He wasn't looking at himself as an artist in the beginning. He created a studio setup in Bamako where people came to have their pictures taken and sometimes dress up. But somebody later on saw his photos as art, and then he became an artist.

Audience   I'm a professor of anthropology here at Skidmore, and I do a lot of work on Mexican cultures and Mexican migration. In this past year, I've studied refugee and migrant issues in France, Vienna, and Berlin. I found from meeting people from many different countries in Europe that the visual aspect of the migration experience is important to refugees. There's so much that can't be visualized, so in some ways, art is a way to imagine certain forms of suffering and experience. In Europe, I was struck by how much the dominant visual culture is one that creates this image that European or French or German culture is somehow very different from the one the migrants come from. It emphasizes difference and disconnectedness. Yet one aspect of the visual culture that's oftentimes not represented is the humanitarian aid workers, the French and Germans who see themselves as connected to migrants and refugees.

I'm thinking about how much the identity of the migrant is represented, but what I see happening in Europe is that French people are thinking about what it means to be French right now, and Germans are thinking about their identities as well. Those identities also need to be represented visually. In the United States, there are a lot of visual images that separate white Americans from brown Mexicans. What about the images of collaborative cross-cultural relationships that are generational in this country around migration? Art in some ways has the potential to help us imagine and visualize things that are hard to visualize otherwise. How do we visualize not so much cultural differences but cultural connections in a moment where difference and division are almost naturalized or normalized?

TS   The nativist thinking that's happening all over the world is terrifying. It's especially terrifying because it doesn't actually represent the way the majority of people think. But the minority is seizing the mic and taking the platform and their views are taking hold. One of the reasons they're taking hold is this crisis of storytelling and having storytelling penetrate through walls. People don't really understand where they come from; they don't actually understand who they are. That's going to be a real task for artists moving forward: how do we inform people about the commonalities between us, that we are truly human first?

RM   In Europe, it's a product of migration displacement. During World War II, there were tens of millions of people moving around all the time, and that crystallized as Europe. So this nativist idea is just not true. And it's sad.

IB   **You mentioned the term *generational*. I do think that there is quite a bit of difference when you talk in terms of generations. I'll speak about my mother's family, who are Austrian. There's a very clear sense of being Austrian on the part of my grandparents' generation that differs from my cousins' generation and from the younger generation. We can say the same thing here in the States. And that's where culture really plays a role—when we talk about what it means to be American or the issue of race. That intermingling, intersecting of cultures actually does exist.**

TS   I have to remind myself every day of the words of Flo Kennedy, the civil rights radical activist lawyer, who said, "Don't agonize, organize." It's so easy right now to be pessimistic, and it takes real courage to be radically optimistic. But it's so important because I do believe that the long game is ours to win, and when I say "ours," I mean the majority of people who believe in progress and justice and equality. I see what's happening right now, in my optimistic view, as the last gasps of the patriarchy—it's going down screaming. But I do find hope with the younger generations.

It was really hard to watch so many of my friends' kids right after the election. They were distraught and depressed and crying, not knowing if their parents who are immigrants were going to get sent home, not knowing if their friends were still their friends because they looked different from them. We need to reach out to these generations and reach out between different groups of people, because there's hope if we come together and communicate with one another. And I take hope just thinking about all those who weren't awake who are awake now and civically and politically engaged. People that I never thought would have been asking are asking, "What can I do?"

They had a sense of urgency, calling up their senators, showing up at the town halls. There were tens of thousands of women who signed up for leadership training programs after the election. We might not feel it tomorrow, or weeks from now, or months from now, but years from now we will.

Audience   When you were talking about representation and who can represent whom, I thought of the controversy over Dana Schutz at the Whitney Biennial. Can you speak to that?

IB   **Dana Schutz, a white, female artist, painted an image of Emmett Till in an open casket, which was included in this year's Biennial. The curators are both Asian American, young, early thirties. The artist Hannah Black wrote an open letter that set off a huge firestorm—about who has the right to represent whom, who has the right to represent violence, to represent Black death. It brought up issues around censorship, around cultural authority, around appropriation, around monetizing Black bodies and death.**

TS   That was a case of something being handled terribly by everyone on all sides of that conversation. I was having dinner with a friend who is a person of color, and she had just seen the piece and said to me that she'd actually been moved. I was going to the Whitney two days later with another friend who is also a person of color. We walked around and around and couldn't find the painting. I was getting frustrated because I felt like this controversy was a shiny object that was distracting us from the actual problems and the bigger conversations that needed to be had, but I wanted to see this work. And we asked a guard where it was, and she kind of winked. She said, "There was a leak, and so it's been moved to storage for its safety." And we all started laughing, including the guard. And I asked, "When was it moved?" She said, "Last night." I thought, okay, wow, the censors won.

IB   **Well, it's back up now.**

TS   So there was the outrage over it being up, and there was outrage over it being taken away. In the same way that we have to have the courage to put our work out there as artists, we also have to have the compassion to observe the work of others. And we have to be better at having conversations around that work.

A lot of the more open-minded and enlightened people who should have been talking about this didn't want to get their hands dirty; they didn't want to publicly get involved because it had become too hot. But what I feel is important is that when these controversies happen, they shouldn't be things that allow us to slide backward. They must be things that help us push forward with a greater understanding of the problems that might have happened, and how we can work better so that they don't happen in the future. What I worried about with that controversy is that because of the way it transpired, it was used to stifle expression. It is important for artists to be curious and to take risks. I would hate to see any artist be stifled from taking a risk because of what happened around that controversy.

Audience — I'm a senior here at Skidmore College. I'm a visual storyteller, and my medium is interactive web design. I just finished a project on linguistic prejudice among the Puerto Rican community in the United States and in Puerto Rico. I look back on it, and I wonder how I would feel about doing a project that wasn't so personal to me. As storytellers, how do you take a step back from a project that could hurt you and that is personal to you, but that a community out there needs?

HH — There's one piece of film I've done. I'd been taking pictures of this friend of mine for seventeen or eighteen years, on and off. I decided to step aside as a photographer and film her. When I see the film now, it touches me because it's very personal not just for me but for the subject because it was about her. Some things happened within the film that were unexpected, and that made it more interesting and more questionable as a piece of film.

It's about a woman who works in a square in Marrakesh. She's third generation, does henna, and wears a veil. In her group of friends, one of the guys wears a hijab and has makeup on, so it's a real contrast. I had this feeling of, What's going to happen? Will some people say something? Does it have a negative effect? But actually it opened up whole new questions for the work. When I decided to put the film out, I was a bit worried about how people perceived it. But I've had lots of positive feedback, and I was really glad these moments happened.

From my point of view, you just have to know that not everybody's going to like your work. As long as you're happy with it, you have to put your work out there for yourself. If you can touch a few people that have the same feeling as you, you're doing the right thing.

Audience — My parents migrated to the United States in the 1990s. Two weeks ago, I was trying to have a conversation with my father about race. His experience with the United States is very different from mine. He wasn't aware of how he was racialized, so he didn't have anything to contribute to that conversation. How do you make the invisible visible when some people don't even know they're invisible?

HH — In my journey, I'm making myself visible toward my parents, because my parents came from a village. They can't read or write. I was the first one to read and write, so when they needed to go to the dentist, I went with them. For me, I look at myself as the next generation to make myself visible but also to make sure that my parents are visible, too, because they put me in this world.

TS Whether it's dealing with a parent or dealing with an artist and subject, it's important to be able to step back from the assumptions that might prejudice you in viewing somebody in a particular way. Always be gentle and compassionate with somebody else. Don't feel like you have to force somebody to change their opinion because it doesn't coalesce with your opinion. The world is big enough for all those opinions. I have to deal with that with my own family as well.

As an example, I have Sri Lankan relatives, persecuted minorities in their own country, who voted for Donald Trump. Why? Their church told them to (which is actually illegal), because their church is anti-abortion. The most important thing you can do is open up the conversation—but don't expect that you will all agree. Don't expect that you will see eye-to-eye. Beautiful things can emerge from those gaps.

IB **My experience in my family is similar, although I am a post–civil rights 1970s baby. One way I have worked through some of that was to meet my father where he was and hear about his story. Speaking with my grandparents before they passed has also helped me to understand where he comes from. And then I began to see some of the commonalities, some of the places where we overlap. We're like two peas in a pod, and especially along lines of race and gender and class, we think so much alike. But I had to understand what his story was, and understand that although it's very, very different from mine, it's equally valid. And it's a part of mine as well. Throughout our father-daughter relationship, it was a lot of him telling me, "Isolde, you have two ears and one mouth." Keeping that one mouth shut and listening as he began to share his story, I realized, wow, there's so much overlap here.**

Audience I want to share with you my perspective. Half of my family—all my siblings—emigrated from Syria, where I was born and raised, to Europe on boats. Some of them took the Libyan route and some of them took the Greek/Turkish route. Now they're all political refugees in Sweden. When I see work like Richard's work, I become happy because I see people caring. I see people raising awareness about the story of my fellow countrymen and the story of my family members. But sometimes I wonder how much of this is people telling a story and people caring, and how much of this is people looking at us refugees as material or raw content that could potentially evolve into a cool, artistic product? Some of my sisters and brothers who were on those boats back then were photographed. Do you have any thoughts on agency and who is doing what to whom?

RM Artists tell, they communicate. I'm European and the refugees coming to Europe are going to change my country as well, so I do have a stake in it. It's all very complicated, and you're absolutely right: it's all in there, and it's all a problem, and it's not easy. I guess we have to ask ourselves whether art is simply another form of entertainment, cool products for the art fairs, or whether it wields a different, greater power in our society.

TS I think about all the conflicts around the world that don't have witnesses, that we don't hear about, and that are truly invisible. And how tragic those situations are. It's a catch-22: Are we going to solve the war in Syria? No. Is the documenting of the atrocities and the suffering bringing more awareness? Is it convincing people to give to causes like the white Helmets? I think about so many conflicts, including in my own country. The lack of documentation of certain genocides means that the history bank is not there for future generations to learn from. So I feel that it is incredibly important to witness. ▲

MASS INCARCERATION AND THE PRISON INDUSTRIAL COMPLEX

Jeff Sonhouse
A Bipolar Faith Captured in Front of a Microphone
2005
Oil, matchsticks, glove on canvas
84¼ × 78 × 4⅛ inches
Tang Teaching Museum collection, gift of Peter Norton, 2019.48.7

Jeff Sonhouse's improvisational portraits combine art history, popular culture, and current events into unique and iconic images of masked Black men. In this painting, an explosive moment in the 1995 trial of OJ Simpson is invoked through an actual black leather glove affixed to canvas. The Afroed heads of the figure on the stand are made from hundreds of individual matches, which Sonhouse literally set on fire, burning holes in the canvas that in turn reveal the wooden support and wall behind. Sonhouse has said of this process, "When working with matches, the fear of being unable to control the fire and losing the painting is present throughout the entire process; therefore the experience is fraught with caution that leaves little room for symbolism…Fire has a long history. Most people, I suspect, associate fire with life or its beginning. So there's an innate attraction to its power to create as well as destroy."

What I Would Change about Incarceration after Thirteen Years in Prison

Johnny Perez

[1] Peter Wagner and Bernadette Rabuy, "Mass Incarceration: The Whole Pie 2015," Prison Policy Initiative, accessed Jan. 9, 2020, https://www.prisonpolicy.org/reports/pie2015.html.

[2] Timothy Hughes and Doris James Wilson, "Reentry Trends in the United States," Bureau of Justice Statistics, revised Jan. 9, 2020, www.bjs.gov/content/reentry/reentry.cfm.

As a nation, we pride ourselves on holding onto the principles of decency, compassion, and the preservation of humanity. While these values are at the core of our national identity, criminal justice policies in the United States do not reflect them, which communicates to the world that we are willing to compromise our shared values in the name of retribution and punishment.

Walk into any prison and you quickly notice that it is devoid of life. I spent twelve years and ten months in one of these concrete structures, and what was most difficult to bear was the lack of human decency and compassion—it was lacking not only in the team correction officers but also in the oppressive physical and visual environment. A metal toilet/sink combo, no hot water, no windows (so no direct sunlight), gray and dreary colors all serve to break down the human spirit and keep the prisoners from escaping their cages.

I learned a few lessons along my journey of incarceration. These insights are an attempt to bring us closer to a society that is reflective of the shared standards by which we all try to live.

Felonies Are Forever

In theory, the criminal justice system operates under the assumption that defendants are innocent until proven guilty. Television shows such as *Law and Order* and *How to Get Away with Murder* perpetuate this misguided perception. The truth is that the minute a person is arrested, their previous and future life will be negatively impacted for the remainder of their existence: this is the assumption of guilt. Collateral consequences are the legal and regulatory sanctions and restrictions that limit or prohibit people with criminal records from accessing employment, occupational licensing, housing, voting, education, and other opportunities.

According to the Prison Policy Initiative, 636,000 individuals are released from prison each year and over eleven million men, women, and children cycle through local jails each year.[1] In 2012, the Bureau of Justice Statistics reported that at least 95 percent of all people in prison would be released at some point, and nearly 80 percent of people would be released on parole supervision.[2] I was once one of these people returning to a society that had moved on. The first thing my parole officer asked me to do was simply try not to break the law, as if the fact that I applied a criminal solution to poverty as a teenager was something I did compulsively. Society forgets about our humanity while we are incarcerated, but it remembers our transgressions long after we have paid the social price for breaking the law. If we are to be a nation of true second chances, we must eliminate any sanctions that result not from convictions but from a small involvement with the criminal justice system.

Solitary Is Torture

I served three years in solitary confinement. Without question, solitary is torture. Imagine being placed inside a space the size of your arms outstretched. In the summer, the walls get so hot they literally begin to sweat. In the winter, you sleep with your head under the thin covers to keep warm only to be awoken every hour by correction officers tasked with ensuring that no one escapes. You lose a sense of time or day; you even forget what you look like since mirrors are nearly nonexistent in isolation. After years of being able to see no more than six feet in front of me, my vision is permanently impaired. If I hadn't developed a high degree of grit, I may have succumbed to suicidal thoughts. No wonder, then, that over 50 percent of self-harm acts happen while prisoners are in solitary confinement.[3]

Life in solitary means being locked in a cell for twenty-three to twenty-four hours a day for weeks, months, years, even decades. Albert Woodfox was held in solitary confinement for more than forty-three years.[4] I was just one of more than 100,000 people held in solitary cells across the country. The United States leads the world in military spending, medical research, and robotics. It also incarcerates more of its citizens than any other country on the planet: as of 2005, 724 people per 100,000.[5] But no fact is more disturbing than the United States accounting for half the world's isolated prisoners and continuing to do so despite, and in defiance of, international standards for the treatment of prisoners.[6]

I believe we can hold people accountable for their actions and still value their humanity. Solitary is ineffective and costly, and it exacerbates mental illness. Additionally,

[3] Susie Neilson, "How to Survive Solitary Confinement," Nautilus, Jan. 28, 2016, nautil.us/issue/32/space/how-to-survive-solitary-confinement; "Inmates in Solitary Confinement 7 Times More Likely to Harm Themselves: Study," CBS News, Feb. 13, 2014, www.cbsnews.com/news/inmates-in-solitary-confinement-7-times-more-likely-to-harm-themselves-study.

[4] Joanna Ing, "Albert Woodfox: My 43 Years in Solitary Confinement," BBC News, July 19, 2017, www.bbc.com/news/world-40647418.

[5] "World Prison Populations," BBC News, June 20, 2005, news.bbc.co.uk/2/shared/spl/hi/uk/06/prisons/html/nn2page1.stm.

[6] Jean Casella, et al. "Solitary Watch." Solitary Watch, solitarywatch.org; Christopher Zoukis, "What 'The Mandela Rules' Mean for American Prisons," Huffington Post, June 24, 2015, https://www.huffpost.com/entry/what-the-mandela-rules-mean-for-american-risons_b_7649928.

the long-term impacts have not yet been studied in depth. What do our punishments say about our own values, character, and collective identity? In the end, how we treat others is more a reflection of our inner character than of theirs.

Mass Incarceration Is a Symptom of Racism

The United States has a disease called racism, and nowhere does this disease show up more than in our criminal justice system. It is the same racism, though mutated and often strengthened, from the days my ancestors were enslaved. The evolution from slave to criminal was articulated in Michelle Alexander's catalytic 2010 book, *The New Jim Crow*. In prison, I came face to face with white officers whose only interaction with a person of color was in a correctional setting. This disturbing characteristic illuminates just how segregated many parts of our country still are.[7]

The racial disparities in criminal justice, a direct result of a history of systemic racial oppression since the formation of the United States, are well documented. The laws and policies governing every aspect of the justice system—from policing to sentencing—also have a disproportional impact on disenfranchised communities and people of color in particular. This circumstance is a sophisticated and intricate system of subjugation and racial control, which is predicated on the commodification of Black and brown bodies.[8]

In prison, it was difficult not to notice that most people, regardless of the prison (I was held in nine prisons in total), had the same skin color as I do. I left many conversations feeling as if there were larger forces at play. The men I shared space with were from the same neighborhoods.[9] They aspired to the American dream, but many found opportunity not around the corner but on the corner. Poverty and lack of higher education were obvious influencers; less subtle was the frustration with a system that saw only their criminal solutions to life's challenging times, not their unrealized potential.

Years later, as an advocate, I would gain insight into the trends I saw firsthand. The overrepresentation of Black men in the system is the result of Black men being incarcerated at a rate five times greater than that of their

---

[7] Joseph P. Williams, "Segregation's Legacy," US News & World Report, April 20, 2018, www.usnews.com/news/the-report/articles/2018-04-20/us-is-still-segregated-even-after-fair-housing-act.

[8] "An Unjust Burden," Vera Institute of Justice, May 2018, www.vera.org/publications/for-the-record-unjust-burden.

[9] Aaron Marks, "These 5 Neighborhoods Supply over a Third of NYC's Prisoners," *Gothamist*, May 1, 2013, gothamist.com/2013/05/01/these_interactive_charts_show_you_w.php.

10 "Criminal Justice Fact Sheet," NAACP, accessed March 13, 2020, https://www.naacp.org/criminal-justice-fact-sheet.

11 "Children in Single-Parent Families by Race in the United States," Kids Count Data Center," accessed Jan. 9, 2020, datacenter.kidscount.org/data/tables/107-children-in-single-parent-families.

12 "Race and the Drug War," Drug Policy Alliance, accessed Jan. 9, 2020, www.drugpolicy.org/issues/race-and-drug-war.

white counterparts.[10] You don't need to see the inside of a prison to notice that they are filled with Black men: just look at the absence of Black men from their communities and the more than half of Black kids who live in single-parent households in the United States.[11] Multiply this by years of policies aimed at these same Black communities, and then ask: Does the United States value people of color?[12] The truth is that no amount of prison reform will be possible until the United States faces the ongoing transgressions against people of color. Mass incarceration and the policies that herd Black and brown families into cages are fruit from a poisonous tree, and that tree is called racism.

Final Thoughts

If a system is not reflective of our shared values, then we have an ethical obligation to change or end that system. If a disproportionate percentage of our society is held in human cages (and, in the case of private prisons, commodified in the name of capitalism), then our lawmakers should be ashamed of their actions and we should be ashamed of allowing the dissolution of the moral fabric of our society. If we throw away human beings or deem them not worthy of dignity or redemption, then we place ourselves among the ranks of those who have committed some of history's greatest atrocities.

We should not only look at individual responsibility but also hold accountable the systems that increase the likelihood of breaking the law, especially in communities of color. By implementing measures to increase transparency, we can begin to see behind those concrete walls and preserve the dignity of all incarcerated people. Furthermore, appropriate accountability should include a hard look at reentry and ways in which the criminal legal system can facilitate and support newly released people.

As I look into the eyes of my son, I am overwhelmed with love but also with fear. Love, because as a fatherless son, I understand the value of having a father. Fear, because as a Black boy in the United States, he has a one-in-three chance of being incarcerated like his father. So when people ask me why I am devoted to changing the system, I say that it is simple: because it is my responsibility. ▲

Elizabeth Hinton
scholar

Duron Jackson
artist

Johnny Perez
activist

MASS INCARCERATION AND THE PRISON INDUSTRIAL COMPLEX

OCTOBER 6, 2017

Isolde Brielmaier   We're focusing on mass incarceration and ideas of mobility and immobility—the social, political, and economic aspects of mass incarceration—as well as reform of the prison industrial complex.

Let's start with a few statistics. The United States has the largest prison population in the world, and the second-highest per capita incarceration rate behind Seychelles, which in 2015, had a total prison population of 799 per 100,000 people. That year, in the United States, there were 698 people incarcerated per 100,000. In addition, nearly 60,000 juveniles are in detention. A 2014 Human Rights Watch report states: "Over half (53.4 percent) of prisoners in state and federal prisons with a sentence of a year or more are serving time for a non-violent offense," a result of the "tough on crime" laws instated since the 1980s.

Why do you believe that this is such a critical issue, and why should we care if we have no connection with or involvement with the criminal justice system?

Elizabeth Hinton   Mass incarceration affects all elements of our society. It has eroded US democracy; it has shaped our elections. If it wasn't for the systematic disenfranchisement of people who are incarcerated and people with criminal records, the outcome of all elections from Jimmy Carter onward, at least, would be very different. If we look at the 2000 election in Florida, the exclusion of people who were incarcerated or people whose names resembled those of people who were incarcerated shaped the election in that state—the critical state in the election of George W. Bush. So, that in itself has shaped our history.

Mass incarceration also reflects American values that we're coming to terms with in a different way in the Trump era. What does it mean that the "land of the free" is home to the largest prison system on the planet? What does it mean that in Michigan, California, Georgia, and many other states more money is spent on imprisoning young people than on educating young people? This reflects our values in the aftermath of monumental civil rights legislation. The question is at the heart of our society and at the core of the inequality and segregation that we see in the United States today.

Johnny Perez   There are some things about the education piece that really stick out for me. What about how much money we spend on incarceration? For example, on average, the cost to incarcerate one person for one year in New York State is about $68,000. It costs about that much to go to a college like Skidmore, right? Think about that. A person at Rikers Island is about $275,000 for four years, which is equivalent to four years at this school. But it's not only that. Any time we think about money, and we're in the place where we've actually profited or privatized prisons—different states have privatization of prisons—we're in a place where we've actually commodified human beings who are disproportionately people of color. It's not reflective of our shared values, you know?

Duron Jackson   I'm very concerned about how the prison industrial complex pervades every place that we navigate. A lot of the objects that we use, the chair you're sitting on, the clothes you're wearing are touched by the prison industrial complex. It's almost cliché at this point. This is the new slavery, a new form of slavery. When you think about us as consumers, we are literally supporting the enslavement of our fellow Americans.

IB **There's not a lot of specificity in the phrase *made in the USA*.**

DJ *Made in the USA* is almost synonymous with *made in prisons*. That's what keeps me engaged and interested in spreading the word.

IB **We're talking about a system that's been institutionalized. I'm thinking about Elizabeth's book *From the War on Poverty to the War on Crime: The Making of Mass Incarceration in America*; Michelle Alexander's book *The New Jim Crow: Mass Incarceration in the Age of Colorblindness*; Ava DuVernay's documentary *13th*. A compelling argument can be made that links the prison industrial complex directly to institutionalized systems. This reaches from the formal founding of this country, from the enslavement of individuals, to Jim Crow laws, to the war on drugs, the war on poverty, the militarization of the police, and so on.**

EH It's significant that people of African descent came to this country essentially in floating prisons. They were shackled. They were in slave ships where they were confined. The history of African Americans in this country and of many racially marginalized people is one of confinement and bondage and literally being in chains and handcuffs in the late twentieth century. It says something about the nature of American racism that every time citizenship rights extend to African Americans, new forms of incarceration and criminalization immediately arise.

What came after the abolition of slavery was the first mini mass incarceration. There were new laws called the Black Codes, which basically forced formerly enslaved people to return to the plantation and work as sharecroppers for no money or risk going into the convict lease system, where they're essentially worked to death. Then, following the enactment of the Civil Rights Act and the Voting Rights Act, we get new forms of criminalization. That's what I write about in my book—new roles for police and urban social programs and new, targeted enforcement of various laws that leads to the mass incarceration we're facing today.

Every time we move closer to our stated value of equality, there's a new insidious system that forms to keep certain people in bondage. It's important to point out that when we're thinking about mass incarceration today as a form of modern-day slavery, it's not the exact same thing as antebellum slavery. It's historically distinct. But being behind bars, being confined, working without compensation are enduring parts of African American history.

IB **We're talking about Black and brown folks, but we're also talking about poor folks. In one of my previous lives, I worked within prison systems and spent some time in San Quentin and Rikers and in the Tampa County Jail, where there were predominantly poor white people. I'm putting you on the spot—but do you have general numbers for how many people are currently incarcerated and how certain communities are disproportionately impacted?**

JP I believe that there are well over two million people who are currently incarcerated, and another seventy million people who have a criminal record on file. Doubling back to earlier, chances are that you probably know someone who's been affected or touched by the system because of those numbers.

EH One in thirty Americans has some form of criminal record, which is significant, so probably at least a few people in this room. In terms of racial disparities, if current trends continue, one in three Black boys born today will go to prison, one in six Latino boys, and one in thirty white boys. That gives you a sense of the ways in which mass incarceration deeply affects the future life chances of young men of color.

IB **And increasingly women, too.**

EH Right. Black women are the fastest growing group of people who are being incarcerated.

DJ We're here in a museum, which is a receptacle of visual culture. And we're talking about how institutions support mass incarceration. The media creates a narrative through visual culture, and it's continuously perpetuated. What I'm most invested in is visual literacy. I'm an arts educator: I'm an artist and I teach art to high school students. Over the past six or seven years, it's been usual for me to have a first-period class and maybe three or four young men of color come to class late because they've been stopped and frisked on their way to school. There's a macro-narrative that our law enforcement is subjected to that targets Black and brown men and places them in the system.

All I can do is make art about it. The only thing I can do with my resources is to create narratives, re-create narratives around what and who Black and brown men are in society. That hopefully changes someone's perception of who we are.

IB **How does everything that we're talking about then impact policy? We're envisioning this system, right? What is the link now toward criminalization policies? What's the history behind that? Elizabeth, you started out by commenting on policies as far back as Carter. How did these policies become solidified so that we now have laws on the books? Say, a stop-and-frisk law, for example.**

EH I began my research on this topic in the early 2000s, at a moment when people weren't talking about mass incarceration as much. The idea was that this was the product of crime-control policies that came out of Republican election strategies, especially during the Reagan administration. Some people said, "Well, you know, there were some federal crime policies during Nixon." My book is based on archival research in the White House central files of presidential administrations from Kennedy to Reagan, so I locate the origins of these policies even earlier, during the Kennedy administration.

It was actually Lyndon Johnson who called for the war on crime in 1965. It's significant that in the moment, in March 1965, when Johnson signs the Housing and Urban Development Act—which subsidized low-income housing for people for the first time—he also signs the first federal piece of crime-control legislation, which begins this massive investment on the part of the federal government and the militarization of urban police forces. And then the week after he declares the war on crime, he sends the Voting Rights Act to Congress. But the narrative that we often hear is that these policies start with either Nixon or Reagan.

What does it mean that at the height of progressive social change in the United States and the civil rights revolution, we also get the beginnings of the carceral state, the war on crime, the militarization of urban police forces, new roles for police and urban governance, new levels of surveillance for low-income people? When we begin to ask those questions, we come to terms with some of the ways in which even the most liberal and revered policymakers were deeply limited in the possibilities they envisioned for American society because of their own racism and because of their own unwillingness to disrupt some of the social and political hierarchies that have characterized the United States since its founding.

The mass incarceration and the criminalization of low-income Black and Latino Americans is a process. This isn't something that just happened, which I think is what a lot of people assume. This goes into visual representations and cultural assumptions that certain groups of citizens are more violent and more criminal, and that's why they're in prison. But that is not the case. Mass incarceration is the outcome of sets of decisions and a path pursued by policymakers when they had alternatives presented to them. If mass incarceration and the kinds of criminalization we see today are the result of decisions and votes at all levels of government, there was a path to this outcome, and there is a path to undo it. Policy is malleable. It's not static, and it can change.

JP   You walk inside a prison today and you'll find that most of the people there are people of color. There are a lot of people there who are living with mental illness who are coming from poor neighborhoods. Why? Because we've criminalized mental illness. We've criminalized homelessness. We've criminalized poverty. Now we're even criminalizing just being from another country. And somehow this current administration has bamboozled people into voting against their own interests.

DJ   I think that what you're saying and what you're illustrating is intentionality.

JP   I'm on the New York State Advisory Committee to the US Commission on Civil Rights. We looked at New York Police Department practices and policies that have a disparate effect on communities of color. We interviewed about seventy or so people, including advocates, social workers, former police officers, and current police officers. Something that was brought to our attention is how people of color are depicted in police training manuals; they are about 80 percent of the criminals. So if you're trained at the Police Academy that this is what a "criminal" looks like, then no wonder you're trigger-happy once you're inside the neighborhood.

I'm going to make a recommendation that we overhaul the entire police training manual. I understand that sometimes police officers get another training while on the force, which is another part of the conversation. It's like, "Forget what you learned in the academy, this is how we do things out here." But at the very least, it taps the root cause and exact nature of some of these interactions where the end result is a white police officer killing a Black person.

IB **Because he fits the visual profile of the suspect.**

JP It's already in his head.

IB **Training, at least in New York, is far from perfect but has begun to shift to properly educate officers on how you deal with someone who has clear indicators of mental illness. In one case in 2016, an elderly woman in the Bronx, who was schizophrenic and off her meds, was reported to be swinging a bat. She was shot by an officer who, when he was later interviewed, said that he had no idea that she suffered from mental illness. The neighbors knew, everybody knew, but he had no idea. That idea of training, now that we're seeing results around those indicators, is incredibly important.**

JP We're in a place where the criminal justice system has turned into a hammer that responds to everything as though it were a nail. When something's going on in society, we don't call a social worker and say, "Hey, there's a person out here who's disturbed." We call police officers. Police officers are trained to react with force in a lot of different cases and are trained to incarcerate, not to take someone to a hospital. It speaks to how we are really in a place where we respond to damn near everything through this punishment paradigm that says punish, punish, punish—versus rehabilitation or accountability.

I believe that we can reimagine the entire thing. We can look at systems in other countries as a guide, at the very least to say, "Hey, imagine a prison without fences. What does that look like?" There are places in India where police officers don't even have handcuffs. I don't know what that would look like here, but it taps into how we can reimagine the current state of incarceration in this country.

IB **I want to talk about the system and the actual prisons.** *Criminal justice reform* **is a phrase that's thrown around a lot. But what, exactly, does it mean? There's a big push to close Rikers Island. But is that solving the problem? Where are all of the individuals in Rikers and on the barge for Rikers's overflow going to go? When we say reform, can we get a little bit more specific?**

JP To speak to the Rikers piece, the idea is to bring the population down to about five thousand. Judge Jonathan Lippman created a commission of leaders in the field, and they released a report that indicated that if the Rikers population is reduced to that number, it is a number that can be dispersed into smaller jails within the boroughs where people will be closer to their families and closer to services. As a result, they'll be able to have a completely different type of reentry and rehabilitation.

Rikers Island, of course, is only one jail. But all of the things that are wrong with Rikers Island are also a lot of the things that are wrong with the entire system. So think of Rikers Island as a glimpse to the larger system. When it comes to reform, I would warn people against incrementalism, meaning that we change a little part of the system but not the whole system—like the idea that if we change bail, we're good. No, if you change the bail system, we still have a ton of other issues.

I wouldn't argue against closing all prisons in the first place—let's talk about that. But it's important to be really audacious and take risks in what we're asking for. As long as the reform and changes that we want are focused on humanity and compassion and our shared values, that's a good place to start.

DJ   Audacity is the word of the day here. There's not much of an incentive for institutions to change, especially considering the free labor of prisons. I'm thinking about the connection with mass incarceration in my own neighborhood, Bedford-Stuyvesant, Brooklyn. It gentrified probably faster than any neighborhood in the country. And so you think about how families are affected by mass incarceration.

Matt Desmond at Harvard did a study around eviction rates. It highlights the idea that eviction rates are to Black women as mass incarceration is to Black men. When you think about that, you think about the mass migration of people out of communities. And you think about the idea that in most cases, it's the men who are being removed from their families—men who are the prime breadwinners for their families. When you have one family member who's not working, or one family member who is working and a stream of income is lost, then you have to think about food, shelter, real basic things.

IB   **Can we address the privatization of prisons, and then also the privatization of reentry programs?**

JP   New York doesn't have any private prisons, but unfortunately, we do live in a country where there is privatization of prisons, where we actually profiteer off the fact that we're putting people in human cages. In fact, if you Google "privatized immigrant detention jail" or something similar, you would think that whoever's auctioning off this prison is actually selling cars. They're guaranteeing a return on investment. They're guaranteeing an 80 percent occupation rate. There have been instances where the private prisons, either CCA or the GEO Group, have sued the state for not keeping their end of the bargain, that is, keeping the prisons at a certain level of occupancy.

Then I think about the privatization of reentry. Coming home from prison is probably one of the most difficult things that a person would have to overcome. This is coming from a person who spent thirteen years in prison. I've been home for four years now. I acquired an education while I was in prison, and even then, it was difficult. So when you incentivize an organization, and you privatize it, I wonder how much rehabilitation is going to be involved. I wonder how many people are going to slip through the cracks. We have six hundred thousand people every year who are returning back into our societies. What does that look like not only for them but also for their families who have been directly impacted by the system?

IB   **Can you lay out some of those challenges, Johnny? And also touch on recidivism, which is extremely high.**

JP   This is obvious: we need housing. I've had to answer questions about a criminal record dating back to when I was sixteen years old, when I stole a car, in order to live in a building. And then I've had people say, "Do we want this person here or not?"

We need employment. I went on about sixty interviews before actually getting hired for the agency that I'm at now. No one really wants to hire someone with a record because of the paradigm that you can't be trusted.

Meanwhile, while you're in prison, it's drilled into your head that if you change your ways, we'll forgive you, and you'll come back to society with open arms. But like someone has said to me before, actually we face more oppression here than inside, on the other side of that barbed-wire fence. So housing and employment are the obvious challenges, but there are lesser-known challenges, like when I have to come home and hear my daughter call someone else Dad, when I have to go back into a family that has learned to live without me.

And more important, having to start life all over again at thirty-four years old. When my friends are talking about things from when they were twenty-one, twenty-two, and their college life, they say, "How about you, Johnny?" Well, I was in Clinton Correctional when that happened. So it's trying to pick the pieces back up and come back in the middle of things. I've been to neighborhoods that don't look the same, where buildings that were there prior to my incarceration didn't even exist when I was released. And I'm thinking, "Am I in the right neighborhood?" I am; it's just that the world has changed so much—and don't even talk about technology.

DJ   I think about the impact of not having health care for my brother, who suffered from post-traumatic stress, and still does, from being in and out of Rikers, many, many times. Though we're really talking about vagrancy: jumping the turnstile or drinking in public. From all of these small infractions, he wound up right back in jail. This cycle of incarceration takes a huge toll mentally and physically. My brother is fourteen months younger than I am, and he looks like he's maybe ten years older just from the stress of being in and out of jail and having to deal with a lot of the issues that Johnny's talking about.

EH   I would like to say a word on reentry, because I don't think it's talked about enough. As we're thinking about and critiquing incrementalism and some of the limits of reform, it's alarming that the for-profit reentry programs that I've seen—I'm most familiar with the system in California—are increasingly evolving into what is basically a waystation that leads back to a penal institution. We really have to ask ourselves what we mean by second chances, if we really want to give people second chances. Again, so much of the discussion has to do with values.

If you're sent to prison, and if you're going into a for-profit place, people aren't going to give you the services that you need for all the reasons that we're discussing, and you're not going to get education. When you're released from prison, you need a job, your family needs support, you need to be able to get a driver's license, you need housing. None of these kinds of things are handed to you. They're very difficult to get. For-profit reentry programs are basically a form of surveillance where you check in at certain points during the day. And usually, these facilities are located in the same community where you were arrested in the first place.

IB **So you're guaranteeing a certain amount of recidivism, which feeds back to the system.**

EH Right. It becomes another form of incarceration and another form of surveillance. Because you're literally tethered to this place where other people are confronting similar obstacles.

We have become this mass incarceration society. When we think about decarcerating, closing down institutions, that's got to come with a massive infusion of resources. Again, it's rethinking our values. It's rethinking prevention. Why is it that for at least the last fifty years, since the war on poverty, we have decided to respond to mass unemployment, failing public schools, and failing housing with more surveillance, more police, more incarceration? That is a policy choice that people have made. And that is why we're in the mess that we're in today.

Another thing about privatization that doesn't get talked about enough is the immigration detention system. More than half of immigration detention facilities are privatized, which is terrifying. For-profit and private institutions don't have to be accountable to anyone. This system really began to take off in new ways during the Obama administration. But if it becomes completely privatized, what goes on in those institutions in the age of Trump is going to be completely closed to the public.

JP Regarding prisons, there's this lack of accountability because there's a lack of transparency. If we don't know what's going on, then we can't address it. That's number one.

Then there's the recidivism rate—the number that gets thrown around is 66 percent. You don't need to commit another crime to go back to prison when you're going through reentry. If you leave the state without permission, that can land you back in prison. But the public thinks, "Hey, this person committed another crime."

And when it comes to reentry services, some reentry organizations say, "We serve people who are formerly incarcerated or coming home, but we only want people who are convicted of nonviolent offenses or only the juveniles." The most stigmatized are people who have been convicted of sex crimes and violent crimes.

IB **We've all heard the phrase *school-to-prison pipeline*. We've all seen the viral videos of children being disciplined.**

Is it California that just passed a new sexual predator law? According to one writer, if a first grader gives an unwanted hug, that kid could be disciplined in a way that did not exist before. Black children who already fit the notion of being hypersexualized—again, bringing in the visual—are even more at risk. So let's talk about that before we even get to prevention, because the numbers are pretty staggering.

DJ   I work for a charter school. The charter system is actually a conservative premise. Like the for-profit prison, it's school for profit. And the way that children in charter schools are disciplined has a punitive edge to it. And when you have a punitive system that is also employing a population of people who are culturally insensitive, who have been conditioned by society to believe that young Black children and young Black men are hypersexual or violent, it is a keg ready to explode. You have predominantly white young people coming out of programs like Teach for America or some other teacher training program, and they're plopped in this very Black environment with no cultural training or sensitivity to deal with the population that they're there to deal with. So you have this person who has the power to completely change the direction of a child's life based on who they believe that child is.

      Young Black and brown kids are treated like adults in the street, but when they enter school, they're treated like children. The skew in perception for a young man or young woman who is treated like an adult in public spaces and all of a sudden has to switch gears when they come to school creates a dynamic that's hard for everybody. Then you have a population who is given the power to surveil in a punitive way. All of this is recorded and archived and follows children from high school to college and into the public sphere.

      When we talk about visualization, how we visualize this premise is where we start. How do we treat children like children, and how do we, as a society, perceive them as children?

JP   Something you said really struck me. I was thinking about how my seventeen-year-old daughter knows to tell me to take off certain things on my body because it's going to ring in the metal detector. And I've walked through a lot of metal detectors before. But she knew exactly what would ring and what wouldn't ring. And I wonder, how does a seventeen-year-old know how to clear a metal detector more than an adult?

      The NYPD has a thing called Operation Crew Cut where they're surveilling kids as young as eleven years old all the way until the age of twenty-one, who are suspected of committing crimes. They're monitoring their social media. Then they hand down these secret indictments based on conspiracy—based on who you talk to online, whose comment you've liked, etcetera. This has life-altering consequences when you're arrested.

      Last year, this mother testified about how she had to go into the principal's office and see her son handcuffed at the bicep to the wall because the handcuffs were too big to fit his small wrists. He was never Mirandized, never had his rights read to him. And of course, she was up in arms. But the principal's reaction was automatic. It always defaults to "school safety." In reality, it wasn't school safety. These security guards are hired. They are like NYPD officers inside of schools. What does that do to a young mind who every day has to walk into school and go through a magnetometer and see police officers with guns and uniforms?

DJ   It becomes normalized.

IB   **I went to an inner-city public high school and there wasn't a metal detector in sight. They attempted to bring it in, but parents were against it. There** was never a uniformed officer—the guys always wore khakis. But now we've come to this point where all of that is completely normal and "accepted." Not necessarily by the students and their families but…

DJ That's all coming from fear. And it's the fear that's generated by the media's construction of this narrative about who Black and brown children are.

JP It's been normalized in some schools. It's common to see a school in the Bronx with a metal detector. But if I go to, say, Bay Ridge or somewhere that's a "good neighborhood," the families would be up in arms if you dared to put a metal detector in their school.

IB **How does that decision happen, though, from a systems and institutional perspective? Is it based on stats? Is it based on crimes committed by students?**
    Maybe a week ago, there was a kid in the Bronx who stabbed two other kids after facing bullying. And the first thing that people asked was, "Why doesn't the school have a metal detector?"

JP There are instances like that, which are really not common, that are then turned around as the reason to militarize our schools, to have metal detectors, to not have your cell phone at school, to give police officers bigger guns. This is so beyond me. I struggle with the solutions.

DJ Instead of focusing on the bullying, they want to be punitive.

EH What is it about the school itself and the curriculum of this school that isn't engaging the kids so that they're fighting and stabbing one another? Why is it that we respond, "We need more metal detectors"? Maybe we need better teachers. Maybe we need better resources at the school or in the community.

DJ There certainly are instances where I believe young people internalize the idea of who people are telling them they are. That kid stabbed the other kid because he was bullied. But the media was more focused on…

IB **The idea that there needed to be more policing, more surveillance…**
    What are some things that people who may be interested in getting involved can do?

DJ I often get asked this question as an artist. My work is formal and conceptual, and it's not didactic. It's not telling anyone to do anything. For me, what's most important is to stay informed and to stay engaged so that you can navigate around the consumerism that's supported by the prison industrial complex or so that you can be involved with policy. Write your representatives and your senators. Be mindful of how you engage with people who have been released from prison. Think of the stigma and the shame in it. I personally had to overcome a lot of shame attached to my brother being in and out of prison. It wasn't until I started doing the research for my own work that I developed more compassion around him having been caught up in a system, that I even recognized a system. So just be compassionate, engaged, and stay involved.

EH I'm a historian, so I look to history. History shows us that things don't change out of the goodness of people's hearts. It takes organizing, and it takes being informed. It takes building a social movement, and it takes decades. And as much as this past year has been distressing, I'm also inspired by the social movements that are gaining ground and momentum. The fact that we're talking about this is significant. We've got to keep building and look to the past, for the strategies that worked and that didn't, in order to envision and bring to fruition a different kind of society that's rooted in the values we want to see privileged.

JP As a former incarcerated person, I want people to understand that a lot of the injustices that happen not only behind the walls but on both sides of the fences happen because there's an entire class of people that have been systemically dehumanized. And it reflects in the language that we use. Anytime we see someone as a criminal, or convict, or so-called inmate, we give ourselves permission to treat them a certain way. I would compel you to educate those around you. What do people talk about at the dinner table? The next time a friend of yours says something that you know to be inaccurate, you have a burden of responsibility to correct them. Silence is consent. You can't be quiet.

Also, you can retweet an article here and there, that's okay. But retweeting isn't enough. We need more than that. We need people to be audacious. We need people to take risks. We need people to be true to themselves. And not only that: use your imagination to reimagine things that you have always taken for granted. You don't have to reinvent the wheel. There are so many existing efforts that can use more human power, more human resources to move them forward and move the conversation forward. More important, sometimes it's not about pushing the needle. It's about guiding the needle in a completely different direction.

And then, remember this: the system is not broken. The system is working exactly how it's designed to work. What we're seeing right now is intentional, and it's designed to oppress a large segment of the population, a segment that has the same skin color as me.

Audience I'm thinking about representation in visual images and what that does to a culture. Growing up around Black people, I've heard teachers say, "You are a Black man, so you're either going to be in jail or dead." Can you speak to what it means to be in spaces that weren't meant for you? Do I say, "Okay, this wasn't meant for me so I'm just going to fade away into the corners?" Or, "This wasn't meant for me, but what do I do now that I am here?"

JP I would argue that asking that question is exactly where you need to be. It's not easy, and it's not comfortable. But the courageous part is when you're in one of those spaces, and you look around and you don't see a reflection, and you stand strong in your conviction and say, "This is exactly where I need to be." I'm usually in spaces where I'm the only dude who wears a do-rag to sleep. And this is exactly why I need to be here: the more people become siloed, the more it perpetuates what we're talking about. People need to be exposed to your ideas, your thoughts, and have you push back on things that you don't believe to be true. Is it easy, is it comfortable? No, absolutely not. But when you do make that headway, it is so rewarding.

The other day, I had a conversation at a restaurant here in town. The people I was talking to were all Trump supporters. We had a robust conversation. Then we took a selfie and went our separate ways. But I did walk away learning something, and they also walked away learning something. In order to understand and to really change things, we need to be in those spaces.

EH People get complacent because they see how the Black middle class and people of color in the middle class have grown in the past fifty years. But just because these vulnerable spaces are now open to the degree that they are doesn't mean that they're going to stay that way. It's all of our responsibility to continue the fight to keep those spaces open and to bring more people to transform those spaces to reflect the values and to reflect the kind of society that we are and that we want to be.

IB **There's a difference between thinking about a space that wasn't created for you and thinking about a space in which you belong, right? Because many of us in this room, for various reasons, move in spaces that weren't created for us. But I belong there, and I'm telling my seven-year-old daughter that she belongs there. I might feel like a particular space may not have been for me, but I worked my butt off to get here, and now I'm here and I belong here. You belong wherever you want to be.**

DJ Wherever you are, you belong.

Audience I was struck by the fact that most of us here are on the same page as far as our sentiment on this issue. But there is another side to the argument. Can you frame the best parts of the other side of the argument? Where do you draw the line for some of these issues? Is it violent offenders? Yes, we lock them up for the public safety, but maybe not so much in cases like Duron's brother. How would you best define the argument in favor of the present system? What do you have to fight against to achieve change?

EH One of the big conclusions of my book in looking at these policies is that despite all the billions of dollars spent—before Ronald Reagan took office, what amounts to $25 billion in today's dollars had already been spent on local and state law enforcement, not including the billions of dollars that local and state governments spent on programs that didn't work—we are still dealing with the problem of crime. Incarceration has long been proven to not effectively work as a crime deterrent. There's no correlation between crime and incarceration, incarceration and crime.

People say, "Well, violence and crime have gone down in the United States," which is true in a lot of senses. But in certain communities where there are high concentrations of people who are incarcerated, where low-income Black and brown people live, there are still staggering rates of gun violence. Incarceration hasn't worked to keep the most vulnerable Americans safer. It's time for a different set of more preventative approaches to these problems instead of constantly coming up with punitive responses and the stick, the stick, the stick.

DJ We as a society should live up to the idea of reform to assist and help people get back in the game in society. You're talking about reentry, health care, a place to live, some kind of job training, a removal of stigma around reentry. Look at Johnny. He's an exemplar. And he's also telling us he's walking around being stigmatized because he was once incarcerated. I'd love to have him as a colleague, a neighbor… We have to ask ourselves individually what we want this to look like in our own communities.

JP There's this individualistic paradigm of the person—the person, the person, the person—that ignores the environmental factors that influence the person's behavior. I had a client who was released without a coat in twenty-degree weather after being incarcerated for six months. He suffers from mental illness, and he was released without medication. He was released with twenty dollars. His reaction to being cold was to steal a coat. The first thing that the DA said in court was, "This man had a second chance. He's a career criminal. We should lock him up." No one ever asked the obvious question: why is he being released without a coat?

I want to point out that there's a difference between punishing someone and holding someone accountable. One is a punitive paradigm, and the other is based on compassion. If my daughter was to steal something at the store, I'm not going to stick her in a closet and feed her three meals a day, the last meal at 4:00 in the afternoon, and maybe take her out of her cell and beat her up every now and then. I will go to jail for that. But that's exactly what's happening right now. And I say that with a sense of urgency.

Then the other piece is about violence. Would you believe me if I told you that I didn't learn how to pull a gun on someone until someone pulled a gun on me? Would you believe me if I told you that something like 92 percent of people who have committed acts of violence had themselves been victims of violence? When we look at it through that lens, we should look at the environmental factors that play into that.

When I was sixteen years old, I wasn't trying to decide which college I was going to or whether I should go to karate school. I was trying to decide which gang I was going to join. There are twenty-four-hour pawnshops where I grew up, as if people from my low-income neighborhood have gold lying around to pawn at 3:00 in the morning. A Hennessy costs less than a gallon of milk. And what does that do to the decision making of a sixteen-year-old? I always challenge people to really look through a systemic macro lens.

Audience My question is about reentry, but from a poli-sci and economic perspective. If you show somebody, like an employer, your criminal record, do you feel like they have the right to say, "No, you're not allowed a job"? My cousins live in the Bronx, and they've been criminalized. They have criminal records. They've been institutionalized. And they can't find jobs because they jumped over the turnstiles in the New York City subway. Do you think that denying them work is a violation of the Constitution or other laws? It also hurts the economy that they can't get jobs—the unemployment rate drops, but not for a good reason; it's because they're now out of the labor force. They can't look for jobs.

JP On a personal level, some of the most compassionate, most intelligent, most creative people I have met have been inside of prisons. And I've been to nine different prisons in my life, two of them medium correctional facilities—one was recently closed, Mount McGregor—and the rest of them maximum state prisons. I also meet with employers who say, "The best employees that I have are people who have a criminal record. They have gone on to do tremendous things with their jobs and their opportunities." There are huge incentives for an employer hiring someone who has a criminal record.

    The New York City Council passed the Fair Chance Act in 2015. What that means is that employers are not allowed to ask about a person's criminal history or run a background check until they've made a conditional offer. Now, there are different sides of the argument. There are people who say, "Well, now you're just going to automatically assume that I have a record." And other folks say, "You know what? Here's a chance for you to really get to know Johnny outside of the scope or lens of having a criminal record."

    I strongly believe that the most successful people that I have worked with, successful meaning that they have not gone back to prison for five or ten years or more, are people who have been employed. Those first sixty days out are the most critical. And even for myself, with an education, within those sixty days, I thought, "You know what? Maybe I should rob somebody." But as fast as the thought came, it went. I always think about that person who did not have the psychological resilience to say, "I'm not going to do it." So I definitely am for employing people. Is it a violation of a legal right? It does *feel* like a violation.

EH There's a movement to abolish the Thirteenth Amendment, because it basically says that when you're convicted, you lose, formally and informally, basic freedom, citizenship rights, but also basic human dignity even when you're released. Those are part of the collateral consequences of being incarcerated. If you're on parole, and you see somebody getting abused or robbed, you can't do anything to stop it because you can't put yourself in jeopardy of violating parole or being arrested. You just can't live in society in a normal way. The ways that dignity is stripped, we don't talk about.

DJ It also creates a state of fear. My brother and I grew up in a fairly middle-class existence. Middle-class for Black folks is different from middle-class for white folks. But we had a decent upbringing. We went to very good schools. My father and mother are separated. My father lived in a fairly white middle-class enclave on Long Island. So here we are, two young people coming up together. My brother was charismatic. He was smart, talked about math and science. We all thought that he was going to be the banker, the businessman, the doctor. But one small mistake took him to jail, and it became a cycle. And, over the years, I watched how his spirit was whittled away, walking around with that kind of stigma.

Having a brother who has been incarcerated has also created a certain level of traumatic stress for me and my family. I would have never thought that his life would have been as affected by that one mistake. That has a lot to do not only with the fear he had to navigate his life with, but also the fear that other people had for him based on their misperception of who he was. It is a system with intention to keep people in a particular place. If you're interested in this topic, read *Spatializing Blackness* by Rashad Shabazz. It speaks about how policy was created at the turn of the twentieth century and up until now. It focuses on how policy was used to spatialize—to create spaces exclusively for—Black people, to keep them out of general society.

Audience I want to ask about the criminalization of marijuana and how it affects minorities in terms of incarceration. How long people stay in prison seems outrageous for the crime.

JP Right now we're in a place where a lot of states are legalizing marijuana. I think licenses to dispense are $16,000 or something like that versus being in a place where we say, "Hey, you can sell weed now." We built a system that allows some people to profit off the same thing for which we've criminalized another entire class of people. If that doesn't highlight everything that's wrong with the system, then I don't know what does.

IB **And legalization is much different than decriminalization.**

JP Right. I think about places like Colorado where selling recreational marijuana was legalized, but it wasn't retroactive for the people who have gone to prison for selling marijuana. They're still sitting there serving out sentences for a crime that is no longer illegal.

DJ I think about the economics of it all. The "black market" has supported Black families in places like Harlem and the South Side of Chicago where society hasn't been able to support them. Now we have corporations and people who probably thought very poorly of the guy on the corner who was selling weed, and they are now profiting from it. That's what makes me the most angry, when I think of where the money is going now when you have a whole population of young people, or people who probably aren't so young anymore, in prison for doing the very same thing. There doesn't seem to be any effort to roll back verdicts.

Audience I spent seven years as a volunteer at Mount McGregor prison, teaching a class, which is where I met Johnny. I want to ask you to speak more on the question of incrementalism versus disruption, which came up during the discussion.

And back to the earlier question about being in spaces where you're uncomfortable: if you want to be in a space that's uncomfortable, you should go visit an inmate or volunteer in a prison. For a few of the years that I was a volunteer at McGregor, I would take one of Professor David Karp's criminal justice students with me to the class I taught there. I don't know if that was a shock to them, but it was certainly a place they had not seen before. You need to get yourself motivated to be in a place that makes you uncomfortable in order to do anything about these issues even on an incremental basis, which is all we as individuals can really do. We each have a moral responsibility to live our own lives and to try to remove those contradictions from our own values and to do something ourselves about it. So on the question of incrementalism versus disruption, there are a lot of individual choices to be made as well as group choices.

JP Think of the criminal justice, or criminal punishment, system as an elephant. If you grab the tail and you grab a leg and if someone grabs the trunk and we all pull, eventually we'll topple this beast. I don't want to give the impression that you have to take on every single issue. Pick the issue that you're most passionate about according to your level of capacity or level of interest or education, and grab that part of the beast and pull. Do what you can, but definitely do something. Because if enough of us do something, if enough of us pull on this beast, even if it's just a little bit, I believe that eventually we will topple it.

We can't say, "What's the one thing that will change the system right now?" There is no one thing that will change the system right now because it's so vast and so complex. If we only change the bail system, if we only change parole, then we still have a host of other issues. Everybody can't work on everything at the same time, but everyone can grab a little part of this beast. If you have big hands, grab a bigger piece. If you have little hands, well, grab what you can, but grab something and pull.

Audience In my "Political Economy and Poverty" class, we talk a lot about different economic philosophers, what the government can do to help its people, and whether or not increased taxes impact the poor and the relationship between the poor and the rich. On a bigger picture, I'd like to hear what you have to say on the role and responsibility of the government for the people. The point about how the police officers' first response is to take a person into the correctional facility rather than the hospital is really interesting.

EH I'm very critical of the Johnson administration and the war on poverty in a lot of ways, but there is a promising principle within the war on poverty that was introduced in national domestic policy for the first time: "maximum feasible participation." Basically, the federal government, for a brief moment, from 1964 to 1965, was funding small organizations directly. The idea was that poor people can and should solve their own problems on their own terms. I believe that government is important, that a big state is important, but that the state can allocate resources to communities that need it the most. There's no reason, as abundant as the United States is, that we should have people who are living in the kinds of conditions that people live in, and that we should be experiencing the kind of segregation, inequality, and extreme isolation that we are.

It's the government's responsibility to allocate and redistribute resources in order to foster that founding principle of equality. Throughout most of our history, policy has been guided by the idea of liberty. The two moments when we briefly saw equality shine through were during Emancipation, the Civil War, and then briefly during the 1960s. I think we need to return to that as our guiding domestic policy principle.

DJ Fundamentally, I think the approach should be compassion. To what Elizabeth just said, I'm thinking about a place in my neighborhood, Restoration Plaza, which was founded by a community with the help of resources from the federal government. We need, as a culture and society, to function from a place of compassion, period.

JP The government can and has the power to remove the profit motive from incarceration. If there's a warden who's getting paid for every person who's sent to that jail, that's a problem. There was a judge who was arrested for receiving kickbacks for every juvenile they sent to the juvenile facility. Can you imagine? Can you imagine, as a parent, what would happen if you found out your child was sold, literally sold? That's one.

Two, we need to pass policies that increase transparency and therefore increase accountability. If we don't know what's going on, it's hard to hold people accountable. As a person who frequently tries to get information out of the system, I know it's difficult. You can make a Freedom of Information Act request, and you find so many barriers.

The last piece is rethinking our responses to a lot of the things that we call crimes. In New York City, if you are caught sleeping on a park bench, you'll get a $250 ticket. Mind you, if I'm sleeping on a park bench because I'm homeless, I don't have $250 to give you in the first place. Hello, right? If I don't show up at the court, guess what happens? I got a warrant. Now that's a completely different conversation: "Give me $250" versus "No, we need to arrest you." We can rethink why we put people in prison, why we criminalize people, and then try for a larger and deeper understanding about the collateral consequences of having a record.

If you spend a day in jail or even have a booking, a day, a year, or ten years, the collateral consequences of having a record are lifelong, perpetual. I have friends who are fifty, sixty years old who are still responding for crimes that happened in their twenties, who have literally been brought to their knees with tears in their eyes saying, "How much more do you want from me?" A lot of these policies that feed those collateral consequences are codified into our laws.

DJ Like bail, right? We have people who are sitting in jail sometimes up to two to three years waiting for a trial, and they're not even a flight risk. There are so many things that are fundamentally wrong with our system. It's like a black hole; you start to dig and you realize how much intentionality there is behind it. You ask, "How is my government that I voted for doing this to me and my community?" When you think about that, and when you think about it every day as someone who is Black or brown, that in itself can be a bit like post-traumatic stress syndrome.

Our current Congress is not moving anywhere on these issues. It really is our responsibility to become more civically involved, to get out there and vote, which is something so fundamental that a lot of us don't take advantage of. When you think about our last election, you think about how many people decided not to vote, and then you look at what we have…So vote, everyone. ▲

TECHNOLOGY, VISUAL CULTURE, AND THE POLITICS OF REPRESEN- TATION

Michael Joo
Bodhi Obfuscatus (Space-Baby)
2005
Mixed media (sculpted Buddha, Pakistan, Gandhara area, Kushan period, late 2nd to early 3rd century CE, Phyllite; aluminum geodesic structure; surveillance cameras; monitors; mirrors; steel)
Dimensions variable
Installation view, Asia Society
Hong Kong, 2012
Originally commissioned by Asia Society Museum, New York

"A Gandharan Buddha statue is given a geodesic halo of sorts. Forty-eight live surveillance cameras in the suspended 'helmet' examine every square inch of the statue's face. The close-up images, at once representational and abstract, are presented on a dense matrix of monitors, projectors, and mirrors that surround the sculpture, expanding the perception of depth within the space and implicating the viewer's own reflected image(s)." —Michael Joo

Decolonizing "Artificial" Art Making
The Impact of AI on the Art Ecosystem

Amir Baradaran

Artificial intelligence has, in many ways, become an index for our technological dreams and nightmares: our utopian hopes for transcendence as well as our dystopian visions of monstrosity. Fearing the negative potentials of technology is nothing new: Mary Shelley's *Frankenstein*, 1818, is one manifestation, as are more recent concerns about state-sponsored surveillance and robotic warfare. AI brings new dimensions to that fear, both those embodied in well-established science fiction tropes (machine consciousness, annihilation of the human species) and those apparent in concerns about the capacity of new kinds of computers and software to reproduce systems of inequity with previously unimaginable scale, scope, and speed.

Fortunately, we are not without a map for navigating the social complexities posed by AI. Art and art making provide an opportunity to examine AI's unique possibilities while allowing us to remain cognizant of the pressing issues of access and equity. Indeed, we must grapple with the opportunities presented by AI as well as with the dangers it entails, both of which may be fleshed out by art and art making. Decolonization provides a theoretical framework that allows us to imagine the generative role that artists and others involved in the art ecosystem can play in the future of AI.

Priming the Art Ecosystem

I use the expression *art ecosystem* to encompass the numerous multifaceted, overlapping, and diverse institutions, products, processes, and agents involved in the creation and consumption of art. It is an ecosystem in a constant state of flux, and like any system, it does not exist in a vacuum: the forms and dynamics of power that exist at any given social moment also shape the art ecosystem.

Among its components are *gates*: the physical, virtual, and conceptual institutions that govern and ensure the longevity of the art ecosystem, for example, educational institutions, media, and funding bodies. The second aspect is the *art* or *artwork* itself, that is, the physical, conceptual, or virtual body that is produced, selected, or curated by artists. In the past, artworks were understood as static objects—paintings or sculptures—but in the contemporary era, static works have given way to the interactive works of kinetic, performance, relational, and digital art.

[1] Ben Goertzel and Cassio Pennachin, "Contemporary Approaches to Artificial General Intelligence," in *Artificial General Intelligence: Cognitive Technologies*, ed. Goertzel and Pennachin (Berlin: Springer, 2007).

[2] Stuart J. Russell and Peter Norvig, *Artificial Intelligence: A Modern Approach*, 2nd ed. (Upper Saddle River, NJ: Prentice Hall, 2003).

The art ecosystem also incorporates *processes*, which are the actions undertaken, decisions made, and paths followed by its agents. These paths can involve tools, skills, and efforts, to name a few, and can be grouped into the categories of creation (actions or processes enacted through approaches, practices, techniques, methods, and skills); consumption (the act of engaging with a piece of art, whether a museumgoer viewing a painting or a theatergoer watching a play); and gatekeeping (the tasks undertaken by institutions inside the ecosystem, such as establishing a curriculum, deciding whether or not to fund a project, or hosting an exhibition).

The fourth constituent of the art ecosystem is its *agents*: the individuals who enact the processes of the art ecosystem, or those positioned at the two ends of the production-consumption spectrum as well as those in between. Agents include artists, audiences (patrons, spectators, and so on), museum curators, gatekeepers (art teachers, art historians, critics, and institutional funders who ensure that the system is sustained and capable of reproducing itself), and others. In a traditional sense, agents are believed to possess self-awareness and autonomy. An individual can assume many different agent roles at once.

How "General" Can AI Get?

Artificial intelligence can mean many things. I use it as an umbrella term to refer to the machines capable of applying intelligence to solve specific sets of problems. Also known as *narrow AI*, this field marks a difference between AI as it exists now and AI as it might exist in the future— as something general and free from the bonds of its human engineers.[1] *Artificial general intelligence* is the expression used to describe the free-thinking, independently acting machines often portrayed in novels and films. Three main categories of questions must be answered for AGI to become a reality.[2] The first asks about the nature of intelligence and its core components. Does intelligence require creativity, critical thinking, logic, consciousness, self-awareness, agency, and autonomy? The second investigates whether our human-centered understanding of intelligence is enough. There are surely countless more interpretations that invite reflection on the multitude of diverse and alien forms of intelligence that exist currently, but we are mostly unfamiliar or unaware of them. Humans must be decentered in how intelligence is conceptualized and enacted in order to realize AGI. Answers to the first two types of inquiry help guide the third: whether humans have the capacity to create intelligence and, if so, the ways in which it can be achieved. Is our only chance of, or hope for, creating intelligent machines to do so, as George Zarkadakis asked, "in our own image"?[3]

As such questions are prodded forward by the promise of AGI, it is certain that any answers produced will reshape our sense of self and, by extension, art and art making. Intelligence, creativity, and agency are all at the heart of AGI and also of how we understand the essence of artist creation. Beyond attention to who (or what) creates art, AGI offers a complete destabilization of the art ecosystem, from being to becoming, conception to creation, consumption and beyond.

AI + Art Ecosystem

It is common to imagine AI as reshaping the creative process or becoming the creator itself. The true potential of AI, however, lies in its capacity to reform every single aspect of the complex and dynamic art ecosystem in an exciting but potentially dangerous process. AI is, in many ways, already a part of the art ecosystem. Consider AI's role in the creation of art: several artists have already partnered with software engineers to develop and employ AI as a tool of creation, generating, for example, classical music that is indistinguishable from that composed by a human.[4] AI also has the potential to create opportunities for interactivity and audience participation that extend well beyond those of performance and relational art.[5] In both of these examples, AI has played a part in the process of creation, though it is a narrow part: a tool employed by human agents for the consumption of human audiences in shows funded by human institutions run by human gatekeepers.

Another possibility is that AI itself is the artwork, an outcome achievable with our current state of technology. The possibility of AI as the artist, however, is imaginable only in the future of AGI. I make this distinction to stress the diverging implications of AI and AGI for the art

[3] George Zarkadakis, *In Our Own Image: Savior or Destroyer? The History and Future of Artificial Intelligence* (New York: Pegasus Books, 2015).

[4] Bartu Kaleagasi, "A New AI Can Write Music as Well as a Human Composer," *Futurism*, March 9, 2017, https://futurism.com/a-new-ai-can-write-music-as-well-as-a-human-composer.

[5] Ernest Edmonds, "The Art of Interaction," *Digital Creativity* 21, no. 4 (2010): 257–64; Frank Popper, *From Technological to Virtual Art* (Cambridge, MA: MIT Press, 2007).

[6] Ngũgĩ wa Thiong'o, *Decolonising the Mind: The Politics of Language in African Literature* (London: James Currey, 1986).

[7] Walter Mignolo, *The Darker Side of Western Modernity: Global Futures, Decolonial Options* (Durham, NC: Duke University Press, 2011).

[8] Eduardo Beira and Andrew Feenberg, eds., *Technology, Modernity, and Democracy: Essays by Andrew Feenberg* (New York: Rowman & Littlefield, 2018), 30. See also Sara Wachter-Boettcher, *Technically Wrong: Sexist Apps, Biased Algorithms, and Other Threats of Toxic Tech* (New York: W.W. Norton & Company, 2017), and Ricardo Baeza-Yates, "Bias on the Web," *Communications of the ACM* 61, no. 6 (June 2018): 54–61.

ecosystem and in terms of our understanding of agency, consciousness, and creativity. These pivotal questions regarding AGI come into especially sharp focus when examined in the context of the art ecosystem. Indeed, AGI could feasibly choose to embody any or all agent roles within the ecosystem, participating in creation, consumption, and gatekeeping.

Many people have expressed resistance to the idea of nonhuman agents engaging in the process of creation. This resistance may stem from the centrality of creativity in Western cosmologies of the human experience. Alongside agency, creativity has largely been viewed as an exclusively human quality (despite emerging evidence of creative practices in the animal kingdom). Ultimately, contemplating AGI as operating in and from every corner of the art ecosystem returns us to the earlier questions concerning the nature of intelligence and creativity.

Decolonizing AI + Art

Neither AI nor the art ecosystem exists in a vacuum: they are beholden to the same dynamics of power that shape our social world.[6] The presence of those power dynamics necessitates a consideration of access, fairness, and equity in the context of AI and art: What is the process and what might be gained from decentering traditionally privileged epistemologies, ontologies, and cosmologies? How can art and art making support the decolonization of AI more broadly?

Although this examination and implementation are likely to be rewarding, they are also likely to be arduous, exhausting, and often minacious. As Walter Mignolo points out, decolonization requires both thinking and doing, which is why artists are uniquely placed to engage in this space.[7] I propose four interrelated points as one way of giving shape to the journey of decolonizing AI through art. The first is identifying access as power. Who has access to, and benefits from, AI technology? Technology, through the process of production, already incorporates subjective values that cater to "the interests and vision of specific actors, sometimes at the expense of other actors with less power."[8] Given that racial and economic divides often share the same boundaries, access to AI remains in the hands of a privileged few.

9 Cathy O'Neil, *Weapons of Math Destruction: How Big Data Increases Inequality and Threatens Democracy* (New York: Broadway Books, 2016); Meredith Broussard, *Artificial Unintelligence: How Computers Misunderstand the World* (Cambridge, MA: MIT Press, 2018); Virginia Eubanks, *Automating Inequality: How High-Tech Tools Profile, Police, and Punish the Poor* (New York: St. Martin's, 2018).

10 O'Neil, *Weapons of Math Destruction*; Eubanks, *Automating Inequality*.

11 Gilles Deleuze, "Postscript on the Societies of Control," *October* 59 (Winter 1992): 3–7; Michael Hardt and Antonio Negri, *Empire* (Cambridge, MA: Harvard University Press, 2000); Rosi Braidotti, "Posthuman Critical Theory," *Journal of Posthuman Studies* 1, no. 1 (2017): 9–25; Brian Massumi, "The Autonomy of Affect," *Cultural Critique* 31, pt. 2 (Autumn 1995): 83–109.

The second point is attempting to understand the notion of bias by means of debunking the dominant discourse of objectivity. There is a fallacious idea that the mathematical algorithms that compose AI are neutral or objective.[9] In reality, human agents are very present in the development and deployment of AI technologies, which explicitly or implicity introduces biases. While power dynamics already create inequity in the art ecosystem, such inequities threaten to amass exponentially when empowered by the scale, speed, and scope of AI technologies. It is important that we contend with this reality as part of the decolonization process, identifying and critiquing the biases inherent in any product of human engineering.

The next concern is gauging the pervasive impact of AI on disenfranchised communities. As in most facets of life, the brunt of destructive forces of AI's biases and prejudices falls mostly on groups that are already disenfranchised: people of color, immigrants, women, and the poor.[10] As AI continues to shape tools of knowledge creation and dissemination and assists gatekeepers in making decisions about funding distribution and other activities, it is vital to ask who is disempowered through this process and what perspectives are marginalized.

Finally, decolonizing AI requires undoing through unthinking and thinking through doing. We must critique existing modes of thinking and create space for other forms of epistemology, ontology, and cosmology, including those previously rendered invisible by the colonial project as well as those that have yet to be imagined.[11] While efforts have been made to address issues of toxic masculinity, whiteness, technological determinism, and lack of diversity within cultures of technology, they have largely been driven by those within technological communities and have tended to favor the "details" of inequity and injustice rather than addressing the structural forces by which they are sustained.

The disconnect between these kinds of macro and micro analyses reflects the siloing of higher education, which creates a critical distance between, on one side, artists, theorists, and social scientists and, on the other, software developers and engineers. This distance prevents both sides from effecting change, even if their goals are aligned. The education of artists and engineers must be decolonized, allowing ideas and expertise to move more freely between fields of knowledge if there is to be any hope of addressing the limitations and realizing the potential of AI.

Yet undoing the system we have inherited is no less plausible than achieving AGI. These formidable goals may very well support one another through the generative and prodigious processes they require. Indeed, what is the purpose of art and art making if not to seek out the divine, transformative, and improbable beauty of creativity?

A Heterotopian Future

A significant portion of the AI research conducted globally is set to achieve AGI with the humanlike qualities of consciousness, agency, and creativity. This state of affairs positions agents of the art ecosystem in the center of the race toward a thinking machine. Thus we must acknowledge our professional and moral responsibility to engage with AI while simultaneously exercising critical vigilance in shaping the course of its development.

AI is already being used by giant technology companies to craft detailed narratives about each one of us—stories about our habits, likes and dislikes, networks, and more—that are used to make decisions that affect our lives. Alas, these stories, which serve commercial interests almost exclusively, are for the most part unregulated by law or policy and often exist without our knowledge or permission. As an artist and a queer person of color, I am especially attuned to AI's fallacies—but I also believe that AI can offer a uniquely speculative space for examining our very sense of the self.

This inspection will foster philosophical and ethical questions that are aware of but not constrained by the nature of AI. Some of these questions may be uncomfortable: Are Western ontologies useful, sufficient, or perhaps even necessary to take on examining the nature of AI? Do we need to seek guidance from other—and often othered—cosmologies that live outside the temporal, spatial, and bodily sites of knowledge through which AI and art are conceived and produced? If so, how? This exploration may be the perfect opportunity for rethinking anthropocentrism and allowing for the emergence of bodies (of knowledge) that stem from, or live through, the

This essay was produced with support from Denton Callander, Joshua Tendler, Ikaika Ramones, Farbod Honarpisheh, Isolde Brielmaier, George Zarkadakis, and Steven Feiner. I would like to thank the Knight Foundation, the School of Engineering at Columbia University, and the Rockefeller Foundation.

types of cosmologies that have been marginalized or erased by Western ideas of being and ideals of becoming. In this momentous space, perhaps we should foreground the idea of imagining a radical future that may not need to be about AI but, somewhat counterintuitively, about a metanarrative of the self versus the other that gestures toward a more generative process of be(com)ing. ▲

Amir Baradaran

artist-researcher

Farai Chideya

journalist

Michael Joo

artist

Isolde Brielmaier We are going to explore how art and art making, as well as media, intersect with technology, storytelling, and ideas around representation and engagement. I think we can all agree that in the present day, technology is developing at light speed. Technology touches almost every aspect of our lives, and it has critical implications on the sectors of art, art making, and media—and how it intervenes and intersects in these sectors for the artists, storytellers, and creators who work and exist within those spaces.

Michael, your work is grounded in research and is concerned with materials and with the interaction between history, the natural environment, memory, and, of course, science. How has technology impacted or found its way into your practice? Can you speak specifically about your recent work, *Migrated*?

Michael Joo My mobile, *Migrated*, is based on the migration patterns of Japanese red-crowned cranes through the demilitarized zone between North and South Korea. I extracted their flight paths, particularly the sections where they would fly over this no-person land, this unidentified territory, and then made relative lengths for the arms of the mobile. Attached to the arms of the multi-tiered, segmented mobile were volcanic rocks I'd collected from the civilian control zone just below the DMZ. One might speculate that they came from volcanoes; nobody knows about the DMZ or North Korea—these are things that are kind of unverifiable. So you have these very factual, very real things, very real events and urgencies contrasting in linear and cyclical patterns. Then there was a sensor-driven motor to have the viewers potentially trigger and initiate movement of some of the stones along circular paths that would then hit other parts and activations.

IB How did you map out the flight patterns?

MJ With radio-tag research that had already been done. That was a collaboration with ornithologists and people who were doing hard science and observation of these cranes.

IB Amir, can you give us an elevator-pitch definition of some of the technologies that you use?

Amir Baradaran With virtual reality, or VR, imagine if you put a headset on, and you're thrown into a fully imaginary computer-generated world with a butterfly. Augmented reality would use the same kind of headset. And that butterfly would exist and would understand the space in which we all are, and it would come and sit on your shoulder. If you move your shoulder, that jittering would force it to move away because a real butterfly would move away. The juxtaposition of virtual content upon real time streamed live is called *augmented reality*.

For those who know post-production, imagine everything you do to a photo after it has been shot, and then imagine all of that being done live as you see through your camera. Let's say you have a zit, and you don't want to post it on Instagram. So you would place on a little "mask." What does the mask do? It understands the color, texture, and lighting of the contour of that area and then applies that onto the pimple itself and asks, "If the pimple wasn't there, how would it look based on the contour, based on the context?" And it does that. Basically, you add this virtual content as a literal layer onto your image.

Imagine all of that being done live as you see through your camera; this is what you see in Snapchat. You hold your phone and Snapchat recognizes a face, and it recognizes where the eyes are. Based on the filter you choose, it puts brown eye shadow or purple lips on the face—and the lips don't change; a mask goes over the lips.

IB **Can you tell us about your work *Frenchising Mona Lisa* and your thinking behind that piece in relation to augmented reality?**

AB I made the piece at a time when Nicolas Sarkozy, the president of France, was banning the hijab in public areas. I looked at the *Mona Lisa*, and I saw that the woman was painted with a veil over her dress because it was customary at that time for Christian, upper-class ladies who were pregnant or had just given birth. So I said, "Well, that's interesting." You have an immigrant woman—she's Italian—in a foreign land, France, veiled in a public space. What would Sarkozy do? Is Sarkozy going to kick Mona Lisa out of the Louvre?

Based on that, we did this augmented reality piece with Matteo. Every time you would hold your phone in front of the *Mona Lisa* in the Louvre, you would no longer see Mona Lisa, you would see a performance of me made into Mona Lisa as I put a French flag on my face, like the hijab.

In that specific location, visitors saw the performance through their phone. But there are two ways of augmentation. You could take a two- or three-dimensional object and recognize it and replace it with content. Or you can do it by geolocation. So for people who couldn't go to the Louvre, they could place their phone in front of any image of the *Mona Lisa*, and they would see the performance.

IB **Chris Milk, founder and CEO of Within, a VR media company, has argued that VR can be used as an "empathy machine." I'm interested in this notion of technology and empathy and the emotive qualities of technology. Milk says that because he feels that VR has the ability to bring a foreign place or experience or person physically closer to the user, it creates an awareness-raising experience—you might even refer to it as a phenomenological experience that's engaging multiple senses. He stated on Twitter, "In all other mediums, your consciousness interprets the medium. In VR, your consciousness is the medium." With this in mind, we know that the *New York Times*, *Guardian*, *Washington Post*, and other media outlets have been incorporating VR and AR technology as a new tool for storytelling.**

Farai, as a multimedia journalist and storyteller, tell me about your thinking on Milk's quote and how you felt early on about the importance of utilizing technology.

Farai Chideya I'm a fellow at the MIT Media Lab, and I'm studying virtual reality and how it applies to journalism. There are not a lot of women in VR overall, but I find that in VR journalism, there are actually quite a lot.

Lynette Wallworth just won an Emmy this year for her piece about an atomic test on aboriginal lands in Australia—it's a beautiful film. She's now working on one in Latin America that has to do with the first woman to become a shaman in her tribe. It's about gender equity and a return to home. One of the people in the tribe had lived in London and decided to come back to his village, renewing the language and renewing the culture. There's a level of empathic storytelling. You view her work with any number of headsets of varying quality and price that you use with your iPhone. But Nonny de la Peña, another pioneer in VR journalism, creates work that is used on elaborate museum-quality VR with wires going to cables in the ceiling. And it's a much more immersive experience. In one, you can have a much broader audience and it's somewhat less immersive, and in the other, it's super-immersive but you have to go to the museum.

One of the things that Nonny de la Peña did was re-create children's perspectives of a bombing in Syria through, I think, a mix of photographs and satellite footage. What was it like for these kids on the street to experience a bombing? And people are literally falling to the floor because they're wearing the headset and all of a sudden feel like they are there with the concussive sound and their brains transmitting electrical signals. If you can get the right mix of sound and sight and haptics, then your brain says, "Oh crap. I'm being bombed." And it doesn't matter that you're not being bombed. For that instant, it gives a different perspective than watching someone from across a room on TV. She tackles really tough stuff.

The question I have is not, Does this get into questions of empathy? It certainly does. The question, for me, is, What is the role of empathy in news? There's a lot of evidence that shows that people who consume news that provokes momentary empathy don't necessarily have a greater long-term understanding of the issues. You can have momentary empathy for children who have been bombed in Syria and then say, "Okay, what's for dinner?"

AB   There is something to be said about our interaction with the subject matter. If you're reading a book or an article or watching a video or a film, you're engaging with a topic in a particular way. What you are prompted to do as a step after that experience really has to do with how much you were moved, how many tools are around you to take it further, how much you have that desire to take it further.

I don't know if a full-on 360-degree immersive experience is more useful in creating empathy toward action or if it actually inhibits the user from taking that extra step. If you're reading an article, it leaves you almost desiring more. You're unsatiated; you haven't fulfilled that desire. But if you are fully immersed and you have "lived" it, you might think, I'm done. I can move to the next task.

IB   **Getting to the gallery, putting on the headset, and spending time having that experience is much different than reading about a bombing in Syria. For me, that is the disconnect. We talked a little bit about the idea of VR and AR being marketed as an empathy machine. There's marketing behind it as well—if you can bill these technologies as capable of magnifying** people's empathy, then maybe it's an easier sell. But after you've had that empathic moment, where's the call to action?

FC Well, we talked about VR and AR, but there's also immersive, which is similar to VR except that you're not able to fully explore a world—you're taking something akin to a guided tour of a three-dimensional world. People are using that a lot for nonprofits. The group charity: water did an immersive video about a girl in Ethiopia and how she was taking care of her younger siblings and had to spend all this time fetching water from the well and couldn't go to school. Charity: water built a well to aid girls' education. That project was very message-oriented.

What you can't do in a linear-narrative immersive film is explore on your own. Immersive is more geared toward fact-based storytelling.

IB **In your practice as a journalist, is there one technology that you feel is more useful or more effective at telling the kinds of stories that you specifically want to tell?**

FC There's promise in all of it. One thing that strikes me is that the most durable artifact that we have that transmits information is paper or a stone wall. You can keep reproducing and recopying and reformatting, but anything digital that we create is much more likely to become obsolete. Let's be really clear about that. We're living in a moment when we're creating technologies that are going to be obsolete. So let's play in the playground, but let's not think that this is the invention of paper.

IB **I'm smiling because Michael works with fossils. It's interesting because there's nothing obsolete about them—they're still here, right? Unlike the floppy disk.**

MJ A piece of stone or rock, a piece of landscape, in geopolitical terms, has a lot of value and is potentially contested, potentially desirable, but it also means something else to the people who might live on it, to people who might access it. So it has these multiple identities. It's not just a fossil: potentially it's the bedrock under which the layers above it have been built.

Once it's taken out of that status, which is kind of abstract, it's something that goes to an institution. To me, there's something valuable in seeing material through the use of technology—that's how you access this stuff or even find out about it: through GPS locators; technology to get there; technologies to communicate, to negotiate; ultimately, a smile and handshake. But along the way, all of this material is generating or acknowledging its own place in the world.

I'm re-creating a fossil bed that has been buried for five hundred million years. I want people to walk on it. If we piece together all of its parts from collectors, institutions, and places that have desired them and have taken this land piece by piece, and if it's put back together as a field of fossilized flowers and we're allowed to walk on it, are we also transgressing and pushing against the institution? And that's just from a rock. So I think there are still ways that we can look at our space, and the parallel to what's virtual, immersive, or potentially a method for framing and reframing. That's about time. Getting it is about speed. But I think we cut straight to speed and bypass time altogether when we're talking about some of the things around VR.

IB   I was in your studio walking on and touching this thick sprawl of fossil. I imagine that could be re-created in a virtual reality setting. But the live and the virtual experience are two completely different things.

I'm thinking about representation. We're experiencing VR and obviously there's a direct connection to those who are creating it. The space of technology is not particularly diverse; it's made up of predominantly white men. How is that impacting production or what we're seeing? What are the conversations about opening up some of those behind-the-scenes spaces?

FC   Daryle Conners has been a real mentor to me in understanding VR. She has been everything from a news and doc producer, who many years ago worked on a huge documentary series about the Vatican, to a video game designer—and there are very few female video game designers. Now she works as a VR designer on medical application VR, but she also is doing some creative work in VR.

There's a whole group of people who are emerging who have interdisciplinary experience. Anecdotally, I find women tend to be more in that cluster. If you look at the people who are active in VR or in video gaming with strong career interdisciplinary experience across different media platforms, would you see more women? I have various theories about it. One of them is that because of the sometimes-hostile work environments in tech, women and people of color seek higher ground and, often, will take more leaps and move around more. But that also makes you more adaptable.

In terms of representation, I don't know the numbers, but the level of gender bias in the technology industry is grim. The first computers—that was a job title—were women. There's no reason that women shouldn't be well represented in the technology industry. It's become normal for men to dominate programming jobs, but it was not always normal. We don't know how it affects storytelling; we can only surmise.

Harry Potter is a franchise that has really good gender diversity in its fans. But for a lot of video game franchises, they're looking for products that appeal primarily to teenage boys, and they assume that the only people who can make those products are young men, and often young white men. People never ask, "What would a teenage girl want from a video game? What would a Black person, or an Asian American, or an immigrant want?" Maybe not anything different, but shouldn't we ask the question? And there's not consumer-driven research into diverse content development because people just don't ask the question.

AB   The way in which I think about that particular question of representation is through understanding. As a Creative Research Associate at Columbia University, one of the things we do with augmented reality and artificial intelligence is to recognize that it's so new that very few people from different fields are playing with it. So we create as we conceptualize. Then we throw it back to academics, journalists, peers, everybody else, and ask them to respond.

Artificial intelligence is basically when you have the capability of having the machine feel, smell, and absorb data through different sensors. It could be vision, it could be sight, haptics, anything. And then not only see, which means absorb data, but also analyze the data and then respond. Artificial intelligence says, "I'll function like your brain. I'll absorb the data. I'll aggregate it. I'll analyze it. I'll respond back to it."

I call my students—engineers and computer scientists who are doing their PhDs—my poAIts: p-o, capital A, capital I, t-s. It has two goals. One goal is to say that our technologists are also our poets and artists of the day in a way that we forget. The second is to recognize that the language that's being created and the text that's being produced through coding looks like modern poetry. Technologists use syntax, words, which are letters, spacing, symbols, punctuation. All of this together makes up the components of good, modern poetry. The same way poets pour themselves into their texts, so do programmers who put their lived experiences, value systems, and everything that comes with their lives into their texts. Even though it has to do only with zero and one at the end of the day—until we hit quantum computation, which is a little bit down the road—there's nothing neutral or objective about the text that's being produced. And if there's nothing objective about it, then let's talk about the subjective nature of that text and the knowledge that's produced.

I can give you an example. When Pokémon Go came out, it became the most-used app in the world. It's augmented reality. You catch monsters in different places, so you have to be mobile. But here's the thing: as a person of color, if I wear my hoodie, and I want to catch monsters, do I really have that privilege of mobility through my colored body to be able to catch as many monsters as are available to other bodies? Is a female body able to go during the night to places that perhaps are not safe? As a person of color, there are many places that are not safe for me. But the people who wrote those codes had no understanding of that. They didn't even think about that because it was not part of their lived experience.

FC Augmented reality definitely raises questions of safety, not just physical safety but also psychological safety. People are questioning, for example, how young is too young for augmented reality? Because part of the job of childhood is to teach you to distinguish between dreams and reality.

I relate to your code as poetry. I'm not a coder, but I've had coder friends. They can recognize other people's code; they can often recognize what nationality people are from their code; they make little inside jokes in their code; you can pick up the slang in people's code.

We have come to believe that we are living in the modern era and things are just the way they are. We don't really know what the impact would be of having a more race-, gender-, and national-origin-diverse program or pool. Some groups from outside the United States are highly represented in US companies, and some groups are not. But I do think of questions around ethical design.

MJ I'm very interested in that idea of ethical development and programming. To me, it speaks to these ideas of introducing disparate elements from interdisciplinary thinking fields and markets, putting them together in a potent mix, but not really knowing the impact because the research is not being done; it's ahead of itself. This is where technology is ahead of the results and the endgame impact. Anything that has the subjectivity that Amir's talking about is a place I'm interested in. Who can get that content, or who can get access, and what is the potential content delivery, and the goal of that content? This idea of programming being subjective means there is an agenda.

AB For those of us who are working along that intersection of art and technology or humanities and technology, we have had decades of good scholarship and theoretical tools and frameworks that we used to understand bodily movement, gender studies, theater studies, and performance studies. We have a wealth of beautiful, wonderful knowledge that has been created. And the good news is that for everything we have created up to now, we can extract those theories and utilize them to gauge and assess what we have. The technology I'm working with—augmented realities, artificial intelligence—it looks very new. But at the end of the day, there's nothing new about it. We have all the required tools to be able to engage with it in a critical way. The medium itself has created some changes, which I call *choreography of the space*, that makes things a little bit different. But so be it. Let's build on the existing tools to have critical thinking.

Audience In these times, we relate to each other based on how we define ourselves as individuals, as human beings, but also through the collective. How do we coalesce around a central identity as a society, and how can we use technology to foster that? In regard to gender, there's a lot of technology and immersive experiences of war games and violence, and all of that is part of what young males identify with as defining what it means to be male—conflict and aggression and so forth. How do you see our ability to tackle the question of what kind of society do we ultimately want to be?

AB I don't know how much agency we have to define society when it comes to the question of technology. To do the kind of work I do, I need programmers that have their doctorate degree in a specific technology of AI, machine learning, augmented reality, and other areas. Hard-core, heavy-duty hardware is expensive, so there are major financial restrictions to access these things. So who gets the privilege to have access? More and more, the investors in artificial intelligence are the big corporations that can afford it.

We need to make sacrifices to understand what priorities we're going to put forth. If AI is outdoing Moore's Law—an observation from the 1960s that the size of chips is going to shrink by two every two years—we're going to have this constant progress. We are realizing that actually we have outdone Moore's Law, and we have what we call a progressive incremental increase in how technology is moving. That's why you might be feeling as if every six months, there is something new. There's truth to be said about that. There's a progression that's exponential at a fixed rate.

As practitioners, museums, art institutions, educational institutions, we have a responsibility to say, AI is going to take over a lot of the things that we're going to do, and it takes a lot of money to get into. Is it worth getting into? Do we have the capability? And if so, at the expense of what? Or do we leave it to Facebook or Uber?

The real valuation of Uber is based on the fact that they're aggregating so much data to feed to their machines. Then they can create an AI machine that outdoes IBM's Watson based on our information. And it's the simple things: What time of the day do you take Uber? How long do you take from the time you call the car to the time you come down to take it? Are you a late person? Do you make the car wait or not? Do you go from work at night to a bar? Which kind of bar do you go to?

IB **And what are the socioeconomic and demographic stats of the neighborhoods you're coming from and going to?**

FC It's not "our" information. It's being sold even as we speak. Now, paying in cash is considered a flag for terrorism. I covered big data for the *Intercept* and did a bunch of stories on the sale of commercial data. And it's not as if you can pay with a credit card as a private transaction. Information is sold to political marketers, it's sold to pharma companies, it's sold to any number of entities that I have no control over. A credit card is basically a very flat surveillance device. Understand that when you use yours: it's not just about the money. The creation of technology is not value-neutral; there's always money and power going upstream.

IB **And this is not the kind of society that we want, but it's where we live. It's the one we have. So the question then becomes, how do we navigate it? Where do the ethics, the morals come in? Where can the changemakers step in and impact in some way?**

FC I saw a prototype for an AR device where you hold your phone over a can of soup, for example, and you put in your medical needs, and it would say, "This soup has too much salt" or "This brand of cereal has wheat, and you are gluten intolerant." So what about using AR for something like that?

We talk about police accountability—very controversial. But what if you had just a badge number seeker? It doesn't record anything except noting that you see this police officer at this location and this was his or her badge number. If anything happened, you would have a crowdsourced record of where officers were. You're being surveilled by any number of entities that record your presence everywhere. I don't view it as an escalation to be able to surveil back. AR could provide a means for doing that. It's unfortunate to think of equality coming from mutually assured surveillance, but maybe that's the only way to go.

MJ It does speak to the idea of what society we would propose. We are on the consumer part of the collective. The proposal would be: Are you part of the collective that is the consumer part that is uploading, uploading, uploading, or are you able to turn that around and start rethinking yourself as a collective on the other side with a certain amount of agency? In the positions some of us here are in, what do we do with that access? Do we delve deeper into those arenas or places where we can ask questions rather than upload? Do we begin to download, or challenge, or push against, to ask the questions that require us to be on the other side of that collective?

When I did a residency at the Smithsonian, I was given some research access. I wanted to work with digital technologies and imaging and representation across a huge archive of our society: objects, things, parts of visual culture, parts of objects, parts of historic significance, markers of what we've done, our accomplishments, who we are. And I wondered if that archive of who we are as things, as pictures, as images, as a government-verified and -ratified thing, object, identity, has sides that are hidden?

Is it more important to look at that mummy and see its place in a macro sense of history and what place it played in society? Or is it as interesting to say, "Who is that mummy?" If we go in with a CAT scan and explore its guts and see the quality of the removal of organs, would we know more about whether this was a higher-class person, whether or not that particular society had different values? Interrogating things at every level is a possibility to work through and reexamine what role and what part we're on.

Audience   I've seen a lot of different examples of video games being used for therapy or other humanitarian action. I think it's also fair to say that video games are one of our first immersive experiences in terms of technology. What do you think the role of video games will be in the future? Or even the idea of gamification—making incentives as a form of a game—and what that can mean?

FC   I'll give you an example that blends a video game, or at least the gamification strategy, in the VR world. Daryle Conners—I mentioned that she has done video game design and now does medical VR design—has been working on a product that uses beautiful images and storytelling to achieve a measurable medical result. You can use a narrative environment and, in this case, a VR environment, a video game environment, to achieve psychological and medical effects.

There's a whole company being developed now that will program music for people who have clinical depression. Think about it: when you're down, don't you feel better when you find that one song that makes you rally? What if there was an entire arc of music that got you through a day—it would calm you at certain times and it would lift you up at certain times. So there are ways that video gaming is being used as interventions for mental health.

And there's video gaming for education. One of the best platforms in video gaming for education is Scratch, which allows kids to make games by having this almost Lego-type system for programming actions. To teach people how to create is so valuable. It would be great if we can surface more opportunities for kids and adults to engage as creators and not just consumers.

AB   One of the things I'm working on is the notion of spherical narrative formation. To give you a little context, imagine the world of cinema, which has affected us for more than a century. We're used to being seated across from, usually, a two-dimensional plane, and we consume a product that has been set and authored by the director in a very linear way. If you're Hitchcock, you're blocking every scene from A to Z.

You, as the audience, have nothing to say, other than experiencing the narrative in a group. You can't change the narrative. What I call spherical, instead of linear, narrative formation is: Imagine if you were able to put on your augmented reality glasses and watch a 007 movie. The camera moves right behind the actor, and we see what he sees. Instead of watching him come through crazy car moves, get shot, then come out of the car, and be all impeccably dressed—instead of following him where the story is happening, you can follow that other person who went through a door. You would be capable, in a spatial and temporal way, of choosing your own narrative within this larger narrative. In that case, 007 may no longer be your lead character.

Basically, a notion of co-creativity comes into play, and that's something interesting that's being explored within the gaming industry, though in a very limited way. But there are tons of artists who are pushing back, questioning, If artificial intelligence is enabling our characters to engage with the audience and change the narrative spatially and temporally on multiple levels, who is the real author in this space? The whole notion of authorship is challenged. If authorship is challenged, then who's the artist? I believe myself to be the artist because I create, I am the author.

If there's someone on the other side who's creating with me and choosing the path, to whom does the project belong? To whom does the narrative belong? We can go further than that. If art making is changing through AI, we need to retrain our artists, we need to retrain our audiences, because we have learned for over a hundred years that we sit down, and we consume. Continuing that line of thought, we need to retrain our institutions, be it the museums, be it the cinema, be it the theater, to provide space where we can engage with them differently.

And as for the kind of society we want, we'll have to reinvent with new discussions about authorship, art making, artistry, and technology, all woven into one another. ▲

#FEMINISM?
Activism and Agitation in the Digital Age

Natalie Frank
Story of O, exhibition installation at Half Gallery, New York, April 2018
Wallpaper collaboration:
Natalie Frank x Flavor Paper

"I draw and paint about the intersection of women's desire, sexuality, and the violence that surrounds the body through narratives based on literature. I have worked with unsanitized fairy tales, which all began as women's oral tales. *Story of O*—an erotic novel that shocked and aroused millions—was published in 1954 under the pseudonym Pauline Réage; many suspected the book, with its frank descriptions of bondage and desire, must have secretly been written by a man. This book, the first written by a woman about domination, submission, and sexual desire of women, is a contemporary fairy tale. The author, the French intellectual Dominique Aury (born Anne Desclos, 1908–1998) revealed her identity in 2004, in an interview at the age of 86. Upon reading *O*, Camus decried that a woman could not have written it. Women, he said, did not possess erotic imaginations—nor were they capable of such immorality. In my work, I set out to prove the opposite." —Natalie Frank

Considering a New Feminism

Kimberly Drew

[1] Lucille Clifton, interviewed by Hilary Holladay, "She Could Tell You Stories," Poetry Foundation, April 11, 1998, https://www.poetryfoundation.org/articles/68875/she-could-tell-you-stories.

I don't write out of what I know; I write out of what I wonder. —Lucille Clifton

With the advent and acceleration of social media, we have stumbled headstrong into a new, hyperconnected era of #feminism and #feminist thought. As a writer, feminist, and frequent user of social media, I wonder where we are headed as we embark on a new wave of feminism. I wonder how algorithmic groupthink may help or hurt us. I wonder what we have learned from earlier generations and what we can do to avoid some of the same mistakes.

Today's internet provides an increasing number of opportunities for traditionally ignored, underserved, or otherwise discarded groups to take control of their narratives and, by extension, over their own lives. With respect to feminist groupthink, the first-person teachings of #feminists who, like me, use their social media platforms to #author their own #feministutopias infuse current feminist pedagogy. With each scroll or upload, social media–era feminists employ #selfies, #viral quotes, screenshots, and other imagery to map a #feministfuture. In many ways, we are seeing the manifestations of earlier generations' wildest dreams—but we are still far away from an egalitarian utopia.

It is almost impossible to think about what it means to be a woman in the United States in 2020 without considering how much changed on November 8, 2016. I focus especially on that morning—before the election results rolled in and before life, as I had known it, would completely change. On that Tuesday morning, there was a weighted feeling of hope that it might be possible to elect Hillary Clinton; if that had happened, a veiled sense of American idealism and progressivism might have lived on, almost as if through osmosis, without contest. Racism and sexism might have been a thing of the past.

That morning, on social media, women from near and far documented their journeys to the suffragist Susan B. Anthony's funeral plot in Rochester, New York. They paid their respects (and undoubtedly humble-bragged to their online constituencies) by placing "I Voted" stickers on the tombstone. While there is great pride in exercising our right to vote, a long and hard-earned journey, one of the significant benefits of being a feminist in the age of the internet is having more access to broader portraits of our

[2] Beverly Guy-Sheftall, ed., *Words of Fire: An Anthology of African-American Feminist Thought* (New York: New Press: 2011).

heroes and heroines. In a sanitized history, it seems fair to celebrate Anthony's victories; at a deeper glance, however, it's impossible to ignore that she said, "I will cut off this right arm of mine before I will ever work or demand the ballot for the Negro and not the woman." If we've learned anything from the three waves of feminism, it's that we have not figured it all out.

I wanted to keep this sentiment upmost in my mind before heading to a panel on feminism and social media at the Tang Teaching Museum. I remembered how betrayed I felt that morning in November 2016, not only because of my own hesitations about Hillary Clinton but also because it reminded me to keep a critical mind in relation to defining feminism—a concept and identity that was relatively new for me.

Feminism as a concept was delivered to me through the lens of academia. As an undergraduate at Smith College, I studied with Paula Giddings, the premier Ida B. Wells scholar and a catalyst within the Black feminist movement. I enrolled in her Black Feminism course because it met my requirements and fit neatly into my schedule—not because I considered myself a feminist.

Black Feminism, where we learned about Black women from Reconstruction to the war on drugs, was the only seminar where those working in gender studies would find themselves in the same classroom as those working in Africana studies. There was a palpable tension in class as Africana studies students, usually Black, spoke from their personal experience and gender studies students, usually non-Black, spoke from their interpretations of our coursework. The students had no choice but to engage with a microcommunity generated by what seemed to be a similar interest in a singular subject. It was in that classroom that I cemented my understanding that sharing a gender does not guarantee that any two people will align ideologically. I also learned the incredible history of Black feminists and acquired a copy of the anthology *Words of Fire*, a collection of texts that changed who I knew myself to be as a Black woman and newly minted feminist.[2]

During the conversation at the Tang, which also included Amy Richards and Natalie Frank, we discovered a chasm—an unsurprising one—between how we define feminism for ourselves and how we utilize feminist thought or create new feminist realities for those in our networks. As organizers, practitioners, and artists, we define our own identities from different vantage points. I initially found this possibility daunting, but in practice, it was refreshing to revel in the multiplicity of what being a feminist means today. It is so much deeper than a single definition. Feminism as a concept has matured and now serves many more of us than it did in the past.

In the 2018 Netflix documentary *Feminists: What Were They Thinking?*, filmmaker Johanna Demetrakas draws ties between the feminist movement of the 1970s and the women who were depicted in or inspired by the 1977 book *Emergence*, a volume of photographs by the lesbian artist Cynthia MacAdams. The book arrived at a critical time in the women's movement: just three years after it became legal for women to open their own line of credit and about a year before it became illegal to fire a woman because of pregnancy. MacAdams captured the women of this era, emphasizing what she felt was their distinct look.

In the introduction to *Emergence*, Kate Millett, MacAdams's partner and the author of *Sexual Politics*, wrote, "They're a new kind of woman. You haven't seen them before. Neither have I. At least not in pictures. A new breed of us just coming into being, never recorded until now, never noticed, given a name, allied into a continuity... the lot of them. They with the new thing in their eyes. Looking back at you. And beyond."[3] In the book, feminists of the day posed nude, behind cameras, in front of mirrors—all representing a new dawn for women. Photography, a medium that has been used for good and evil in somewhat equal measure, is used to invite us into the psyche of the time. Forty years later, Demetrakas's film deepened our understanding of the story behind each image.

Watching the documentary, I found immediate parallels between what MacAdams accomplished in *Emergence* and what many emerging feminist artists are accomplishing today. I thought especially of what Petra Collins and Toyin Ojih Odutola have added to the feminist canon. Their portraits of women are characterized by the piercing gaze and unwavering power of their subjects. Then and now, feminists utilize media to tell our stories for ourselves and to define a self-possession that has often been denied to us. It is this media-making that illustrates our stories and helps shape our collective understanding of the era.

[3] Kate Millett, introduction to *Emergence*, by Cynthia MacAdams (New York: Chelsea House, 1977).

A cataclysmic shift in how activism was viewed in the public eye and in the media occurred shortly after the 2016 election. In coastal cities in the United States, there was an urgency to take to the streets and make our voices heard. We saw the rise of the new *Teen Vogue*, and, during the Women's March of 2017, pink pussy hats and signs made for the revolution were plastered all over Instagram. The energy and acceptance of this era of women's rights was an unprecedented force. It was both amazing and deeply saddening to see generations of women marching arm in arm and demanding equality. Today, things are quite different.

To illustrate this contrast, I think of the 2018 book *Together We Rise: Behind the Scenes at the Protest Heard around the World*, published a year after the Women's March. *Together We Rise* is very different from a book like *Emergence*. While *Emergence* was panned by critics in the late 1970s, *Together We Rise* (and other similar books) is now heralded. The roles of women in media have shifted considerably. Women are now at the helm of mainstream publications, in political office, and using the power of social media to take more control. It may be cheesy, but the old adage almost demands to return: "With great power comes great responsibility." What is our fight now, and how do we make it an inclusive one for women globally?

Perhaps the most incredible gift of being a feminist today is awareness. We know that we're a part of a larger history. We know that our fight is a legitimate one. And hopefully, we know that we are responsible for making the world a better place for future generations. With this in mind, I am left wondering what the fruits of this next era will be. I watched online as nearly five million women in Kerala, India's southern peninsula, locked arms to demand equality. But I have also watched as women have excluded trans women from notions of feminism time and time again. I wonder, How will we take charge of this triumphant moment? How will we document ourselves? Most important, how will we all hold ourselves accountable? ▲

Kimberly Drew
writer

Natalie Frank
artist

Amy Richards
producer

Isolde Brielmaier — **This conversation explores feminism. Let's kick things off by defining some terms—especially fourth-wave feminism and #feminism—and look specifically at the implications of technology for these movements.**

Natalie, you've been continuously dealing with feminism, sexuality, and representation, and you consistently engage your viewers with various feminist ideologies and thought. Can you start by telling us about your art practice?

Natalie Frank — My work focuses on women, the body, sexuality, violence, and narrative. In the past five years, I've started to look at unsanitized fairy tales, primarily with drawing. Right now, I'm working on a book of Madame d'Aulnoy, who was the first feminist literary fairy teller, from the 1690s. Because she's a woman, her work has been somewhat overlooked: never illustrated or collected in full. She wrote early versions of many of the stories we know, such as "Cinderella" and "The Beauty and the Beast," though we might not recognize hers; our versions have been Disney-fied.

What's drawn me to these fairy tales has been the fact that they all began as women's oral tales, which I think a lot of people don't know. Some of them are protofeminist; they represent life at the time for women, whether it's the nineteenth-century tales by the Brothers Grimm or Madame d'Aulnoy's seventeenth-century stories. It was interesting to discover that fairy tales and literature were a place that women, when they were censored in everyday life by the church or the state, could express their fears and anxieties and desires.

IB — **Kimberly, you occupy several spaces, both public and private, overseeing the Metropolitan Museum of Art's social media, and you have an influential Instagram account of your own: @museummammy. Could you talk about what you're working on?**

Kimberly Drew — I have a book called *Black Futures* that I'm working on with Jenna Wortham, who's an amazing writer at the *New York Times*. For this book, we are creating an anthology that looks at Black cultural production since the advent of social media. And in the process of bookmaking, I've taken on fifteen other projects, which include moonlighting as a journalist and doing panel talks every chance I get.

Within my work at the Met, one of the creative challenges that I've taken on is how to use social media as a vehicle for access and accessibility. I'm thinking about how a platform like Facebook Live could be a useful platform for people who are hearing impaired. Or, for example, if you close your eyes and think about the Met, most people think of the steps. How can we change the entry point of the museum from being something that's literally inaccessible into something that people feel they have access to and then, much more, feel they have ownership over?

IB — **Amy, in the 1990s, you cofounded the Third Wave Foundation. It was a godsend for so many young women at the time, because we felt disconnected from the feminist and women's movements of our mothers or grandmothers. That's not to disregard those movements, but it didn't feel as if there was a space for something that was a bit broader, a bit** more diverse. You had this incredible idea to cofound the foundation. And now you're writing and producing.

Amy Richards Third Wave started as a cross-country voter registration drive. That work took us out into the community and showed me the real obstacles to voter participation and an engaged citizenship. I learned a very valuable lesson on that trip: I thought I was doing it for people who didn't have ready access to the system, but I realized that if I was living in a democracy that was not fulfilling its promise, that that was doing me a disservice. It was an early and very important shift. I went from being out in the community, talking to young activists, to founding this organization, funding projects that young people were starting, to writing books and spending a lot of time on college campuses to producing documentaries.

One of the most satisfying things I do is run Feminist Camp, which hosts immersive experiences in feminism. When I was spending time on college campuses, I realized that what was more readily accessible to a campus environment, in terms of studying feminism, was already outdated and limited because of whose voices were accessible to a classroom. And it became a much more generic interpretation, not bad or good, just limited, and so I wanted to create an experience that took people, like I did on Freedom Summer, to a community of feminism to show rather than to tell what feminism looks like.

Feminist Camp happens multiple times a year, in multiple places, but our signature program is in New York with days featuring different themes. For instance, on a justice day, you might start in the courtroom of a judge who's working around sex trafficking. I watch students have strong opinions about the police officers who are in the courtroom. And within a short amount of time, they realize that the police officers are often there to defend the women because they don't want the women to be criminalized for something they've been involved in. And we might go from there to a meeting with sex workers who have a very different experience, and then we might go to a group like Equality Now, who are looking at this topic globally. It's meant to show the depth of what feminism means.

IB **How do you each define feminism, or a range of feminisms?**

AR The definition has evolved for me. Even being able to take ownership over that word was hard for me because it felt like it was locked in a box and I needed certain clues to get into the box or accomplish certain tasks. I started defining it as the dictionary does, which is the movement for full social and political equality for women, but that means something and at the same time it means nothing. I've realized, more recently, that feminism to me is about a recognition that we are intentionally meant to be divided on the things that make us different, and there's a desire to keep us from unifying. And that's intentional because we don't all have the *same* thing that makes us different but we all have *something* that makes us different.

To realize that difference as a strength and not as a deficiency would be a powerful moment. So, feminism to me is the recognition that those are moments of value. Forces are trying to keep us divided, and feminism is the movement to try to bring us together even with those differences.

KD I grapple with feminism all the time because I think, in any circumstance, the invisible labels set upon us can be difficult to navigate. I also think feminism is a flawed concept because it's about equality, and I feel like equality is not imaginative. I think so much about the radical possibility of what women can do, and that's largely because I went to a women's college that was very rah-rah woman all the time.

So when I think about feminism or women-specific spaces, I think about it as a space for empowerment, but at the same time, I'm going through this deep thought process about what gender even means and whether it's relevant or important. If I'm thinking about feminism retrospectively, it's a useful label. But when I think about future forward, I wonder if feminism has a place in the future, considering the ways in which we're conceptualizing around larger issues that feminism in many ways tackles but then sometimes shies away from historically, too. So it's a word and label. It's useful and not useful, and it's one that I'm happy to continue to interrogate.

IB **Continual interrogation is important. There's been a lot of critique over the idea that the term is structured around a heteronormative notion of gender and what it means to be a woman within a strict binary. If we're talking about intersectionality and being forward-thinking, to your point, Kimberly, we may need new terms. We may need to add different terms, or maybe we don't need terms at all.**

NF For me, feminism has always been a subset of humanism. It's about respecting individuals' ability to express themselves and their own narratives. I've always made work about that, whether it's going into dungeons in New York and photographing dominatrixes or bringing back seventeenth-century women who have been overlooked, who are fairy tellers and historians. I was drawn into art by artists who use personal narrative and make it political. It was never just about women for me.

I grew up in the repressive South. I think I was fifteen when they called me a pornographer and tried to kick me out of high school for drawing nude figures. So I was very aware that there were outdated ideas of who has access and who doesn't. I remember coming across Linda Nochlin's work for the first time: that really ignited for me these ideas of who has access, who is allowed to speak, and how that manifests.

IB **What are some of the key challenges you feel we're confronting right now with feminism? And what strategies are we using? Are there new strategies because of the digital platform?**

AR I would say the fourth wave of feminism, happening now, is about imagining a way forward. The first wave was about the right to citizenship, just to be counted as a citizen in the United States. The next wave was about legal equality. And I always thought the third wave was about changing behavior. Rape was made illegal in the second wave, but it still happened. How do you change behavior to combat something that the law didn't exclusively take care of? If there's a fourth wave, it's about going beyond confronting a system to creating a system. That's why I agree with you, Kimberly, that the equality frame doesn't work. There are a bunch of equality campaigns right now: 50/50 by 2020, for example. It doesn't work because what we're going to do is rush to fill placements and we're just going to put people into systems that are oppressive. It's not going to change culture.

KD Regarding the issues to be tackled—I think we're in this moment where there's an issue everywhere we look. They change every day. I live in Brooklyn, and I take the subway to work every day, and there was this amazing sticker project that showed where Rikers was on the subway map. There are so many systems that are oppressive that we don't even acknowledge or see. The thing, for me, that's really important is digital technologies—one of the strategies that's been amazing and helpful is just acknowledging the issues.

Some people are quick to critique the way that digital technology and activism intersect—as if knowledge and awareness aren't forms of activism. When I think about the future of feminism, it's about acknowledging how many things are wrong. If there's anything that ties together the last year, it is that there has been a lot that we've been quiet on and now people are having this moment of awakening. But at the same time, there's so much that I'm deeply frustrated by. Even just thinking about the Harriet Tubman pussy hat thing…

On January 20, there was a Women's March, and someone knit a pussy hat for the Harriet Tubman Memorial in Harlem. I don't know how they got it up there, but I can only imagine that someone climbed up Harriet Tubman and put the hat on her. That image disturbs me so deeply and makes me so sad. It very much echoes the voting stickers that people applied to Susan B. Anthony's tombstone, despite the fact that Susan B. Anthony was a wild racist. There are these ways in which we are not properly learning from the past, and in many ways, digital technology allows us to not necessarily do a revisionist look at everything but just to get real.

People talk about social media as this vacuum that accelerates issues. But because we're taking in so much, it slows us down to a certain degree, and perhaps that slowing down is what can, if there is a fourth wave, be a part of where we actually just stop and say, "Okay, is there a group that's doing this work that I want to be doing? Is there someone I could be a thought partner with where I don't have to go and be public immediately about the thing I want but actually have space for critical dialogue and interiority, because it's not about grand statements?" It's not about having the best sign at the protest, because being at the protest can be dangerous. Do you have people you can call if you get arrested? These things are slow work and, I hope, for the fourth wave, that at least we're being more critical.

IB **If we think about social media in terms of access, we're talking about a transnational platform, one that has the potential to cross borders and reach a broad range of people.**

NF For me, through working with books and these oral tales, I've started to think about using social media as a means of access, as a means to have a direct voice into a large and instant community, and I've started writing for art publications. I wrote an opinion piece for *ARTnews* when the Harvey Weinstein scandal was breaking about my ten years of experiencing sexual harassment. It was the first time I wrote something personal and put it immediately into the public.

It was called "For Women Artists, the Art World Can Be a Minefield." I was interested in the real-world effects a personal essay could have. There were probably a dozen women who contacted me after I wrote this piece. For some, it was the first time they recognized or verbalized their own situations, and it opened up a dialogue. Real change happened afterward—within days. It was staggering to see that speaking out via personal essay could have a real-time effect.

IB **Did you give a lot of thought to the repercussions? Many women contend with what calling out or naming someone means for their livelihood, their careers.**

NF I did. I really thought about it. There's a necessity for nuance: what constitutes good sex, bad sex, harassment, rape, legality, illegality. But when you start to lob accusations, it's important to take seriously what the effects can be and to have certainty.

AR There was an important piece in the *Times* yesterday about the first US gymnast to report sex abuse in USA Gymnastics and other programs. She said that the last year has been hell because of the number of people trying to take down her story. I have spoken publicly about abortion and sexual assault, and you can have 90 percent hostility, but then 10 percent of people saying thank you.

NF It's worth it.

AR Totally worth it.

There's an initiative in New York City right now to have the first sculpture of real women in Central Park—to honor Susan B. Anthony and Elizabeth Cady Stanton. I have been against this statue. If we're going to have our first testament to real women, it can't be to white women. The response I got from the women who are leading this campaign, well-respected women, was "Don't worry; we're going to put other women's names at the bottom of the sculpture, Harriet Tubman, Sojourner Truth." I said, "That's not acceptable." The whole thing is terrible, and I say this because we now know better. We can't write a narrative that is not an attempt at a more accurate narrative. I won't feel good if we look back and I did not speak out against that. There are some things we all have to speak out against.

KD One of the things about this moment that I love—because I love messiness—is that we're in a moment of crisis. We're all crisis managing. For me personally, I have a history of sexual violence in my life, and trying to navigate that every day, when every day there's a story, every day there's someone who's doubting someone...I live on the internet, that's my job. I can't *not* look at Twitter; I can't unplug. Crisis management is something that can be difficult to manage. You get into this fight or flight response mode. We're all called to this moment of responsibility and really understanding that our silence is complicity. That's where feminism is right now, at least to me.

IB **You each mentioned the word *responsibility*, and this dovetails with a slightly overused word, *intersectionality*. I had a conversation yesterday with a museum colleague who said that she felt a lot of women of color were very critical of "today's feminism" and of white women because they feel that many white women are able to engage with the issue of gender only as it affected them. This is something that women of color don't have a choice in: you're not Black or a woman, you're a Black woman, and there are a multitude of issues that affect you.**

However we see ourselves, what is our responsibility to engage with women of different races or constructed social categories of difference? What about issues relating to members of the LGBTQIA+ community? While I may not be of that community, I see those issues as integral to my existence in this world. What is our responsibility for engaging, for calling out, for being allies to things, people, communities that are outside of how we see ourselves?

AR When I'm telling the story of feminism to different audiences, I have to work hard because there are names and resources that are more available to me than other names or resources, which is contributing to this problem. Barbara Smith started Kitchen Table: Women of Color Press, and that was the most poignant press, and that gave voice to women who didn't have voice. And Byllye Avery was doing health care not just for Black women but for all women. But I have to remember to write into the narrative people who have been excluded.

When I'm at my Feminist Camp, it's most likely a trans-identified person who says, "Say your pronouns, say your pronouns," and who offers their pronouns up more readily than others. At the same time, I run Feminist Camps in Zambia and we'll have these exercises with schoolgirls there and we'll talk about gender roles and sex roles. In Zambia, I'm mostly around people who are not white, adding another element of realizing that race and gender are fabrications. When we go back in time, race and gender were creations that were meant to divide us.

KD When I was thinking about having this conversation, I was also thinking about why I love art: it's because art is so much a record of a time. Art is something that we all, in some way, participate in because we are alive in a moment. We all bear witness to something, and then some people are courageous enough to make things that respond to those moments.

NF Asking questions and listening to the answer is a big thing. Then if you see something that's not right, you speak out about it. You write about it. You talk about it. You correct someone. You paint about it. I feel an urgency now, which I had not felt before Trump was elected, to speak out about things that I feel and see every day. It's an onslaught. Perhaps that's the only positive thing that's come out of this administration: that we feel that push to speak out and to correct.

AR I think of the metaphor of the stairs that Kimberly was talking about at the Met, because that is an intimidating space. When I run the Feminist Camps, I mentally note which demographic will ask me for a recommendation, or ask me for a connection, or ask for the internship. I identify the privileged group of people, and I prove myself right every single time. I have to be intentional about finding the silent people and saying, "I want to introduce you to somebody." And then do that.

A lot of campers want to go into the publishing industry, which is incredibly elitist and white. They recognize this as a limitation, and so when I meet with editors, I say, "If you want to change what books you're producing, you have to change who the editors are." As much as it's great to have six million out there marching, the change happens one by one, by means of the invitation or introduction to somebody new.

IB **How do you see digital space allowing us to bring more people to the table so that we're not just preaching to the choir?**

KD I think the most important thing that I do, as a social media manager for an institution like the Met, is to give people a vocabulary. Oftentimes, a huge barrier to access in museums is that people don't feel like they know what's inside. If I say, "Here are five works of art from these five different countries," at least you know them. Then perhaps there's a familiarity and maybe you want to go see them—it's an opportunity for people to be able to build their own art historical relationships. Whether they like something or not, they know that it's a thing they can visit. I am twenty-seven and the Met is a hundred and fifty. And it contains five thousand years of art.

Social media, at its very best, is an opportunity for gaining information. Sometimes that information can be emotional, and sometimes it is matter of fact. I'm trying to give people something that they can take away.

Audience Each of you mentioned a balance between being in a position of privilege as well as sometimes being in a minority or underrepresented group. You also talked about the importance of speaking out. How do you balance the responsibility for speaking with the responsibility to allow for other unrepresented voices?

NF I've been thinking about this a lot recently. I was meant to have a show in about two months with fifteen drawings based on the erotic book *Story of O*. The book is an icon of sex-positive feminism. The woman dealer called me up and said, "In this climate of sexual harassment, I will not show your work." And I thought, Wow. This is something I want to speak out about for myself and also for others. I've come to a few ideas about how to speak about this experience. One is in the press; another is through a publication that will accompany the exhibition, which will now take place elsewhere and which will talk about the history of the work, the history of the book, why the book is important, what sex-positive feminism is, and what feminism is. So these real-world events have given me an access point to speak out loudly, either through my work or around my work, about things I care about deeply.

KD Speaking out means submitting to journals and speaking at conferences, if that's available to you, or organizing a conference if you work for an institution that will support such ventures. There is a keen responsibility because we are in a moment when speaking on behalf of others is something you can benefit from. So when I think about feminism as a concept, or how our feminism and our activism can be sold in this moment, it's also important to think about generosity, that when you're doing something for someone else, there isn't an immediate return.

That gesture and that understanding should come from a pure place. Ego can be so dangerous. I have a large following on social media, not just through the Met, and I can shine light on things, but sometimes people don't want light to shine. We have to think critically about what our good gestures are. I'm sure it was a well-intentioned person who put the pussy hat on the Harriet Tubman statue. But there's something important about doing gestures more slowly and being responsive in the ways in which we're showing up or speaking out.

AR Last year, in the weeks after the election, I was an organizer for an Annie Leibovitz exhibit at Bayview Correctional Facility, a former women's correctional facility in New York. Annie wanted an unusual space, and I suggested the facility. But being there after the election, with many women who had been in that space when it was a prison, I heard a lot of talk about how they couldn't speak out. They couldn't risk being arrested. They couldn't risk having a spotlight on them, but their issues needed a spotlight more than ever.

It was a nice reminder to ask that community, who can't speak as readily, how I might be able to leverage my privilege or my power for their community. That's a muscle that you have to practice all the time, because we can get lazy about it. You always have to remind yourself to ask, How do I step outside of my comfort zone? Bryan Stevenson, who wrote the book *Just Mercy*, says that as a culture we have become conditioned to stay away from communities that feel dangerous or marginalized or different. In fact, if we want to be part of disrupting society and systems, we have to go to those places.

I live near tons of public housing in New York. What are you taught to do around those places? To circumvent, to go around. What if, instead, I walk through and actually see what it means to live on this block that we avoid. It is important to go toward the things that you care about and see which populations can't speak up.

IB **We can make statements. We can call out. But asking questions is also important. When something is said that I find offensive, I take a deep breath and I ask a question, like, "Wow, that kind of rubs me the wrong way. Where are you getting that information? Have you had that experience before?" It's a nice way to throw the ball back to somebody, and then just sit and let people chew on the issue without calling them out. Sometimes a simple question makes people reflect.**

Audience — I find that I get easily overwhelmed by all the images—especially the negative images—that we subconsciously take into our bodies. How do you take a step back and find your inner peace again when you are constantly battling these big, overwhelming issues? How can you step forward feeling refreshed and able?

NF — I've been thinking about reading things in the press that are erroneous and to the detriment of people doing meaningful work. I find value in speaking out, writing, to set the record straight. I'm a member of the Council for Feminist Art at the Brooklyn Museum, and I care deeply about the work they're doing. I kept seeing articles implicating the founder of the Center for Feminist Art, Elizabeth Sackler, because of the role of a portion of the Sackler family in the opioid crisis.

It was a matter of activists and journalists not getting the facts right, and then certain claims getting repeated over Twitter and Instagram and then going into the mainstream press from one article to another with seemingly no fact-checking, and it really upset me. So I sat down and wrote an op-ed for Artnet that showed that Elizabeth's side of the Sackler family was completely different from the side of the family that engaged in the opioid crisis. I care about her and the institution she built—the only feminist art center in the world shouldn't be clouded by sloppy lies in the press or by someone else's agenda.

And so, it's self-care and attention to people and institutions that you care about. I'm not going to stop making sex-positive work because someone tells me that she's not going to show it. Or stay silent when I can add my voice.

Building a community where you have each other's backs, especially women with other women, is another positive practice. And if there are inaccuracies being reported and repeated, it feels responsible to speak up and support the people in your community.

AR — Action is my self-care. I had this online advice column for years, and I realized—back to the theme of listening—that a lot of times people wrote to me about sexual abuse and sexual harassment. There was a doctor who every day would say goodbye to this nurse and stick his fingers in her vagina and say, "See you tomorrow." And she said, "I needed my job. I can't not go to work." I would have said, "You have to leave that job. Any self-respecting woman would leave her job." But my response was, "I am so sorry that's happening to you. It's not your fault. And if you want to leave your job, I'm sure there are resources in your community, and I'd be happy to do that research for you."

Years ago, I remember that somebody said to me, "Can I be a feminist and be pro-life?" I responded, "Absolutely not. That's not feminist," because I heard it as, "Can I go shooting abortion doctors?" Then I realized what they were really saying was, "Can I have my own complications around this issue?" And absolutely, yes. So it's about not only listening but really hearing what people are saying and validating other people's truths.

Audience — If we're in the fourth wave of feminism, I missed the third wave. When was that? Can you explain?

AR The third wave was active from the 1990s. A lot of it percolated around the Anita Hill–Clarence Thomas hearing where a surge of women were running for office and speaking out and speaking their truths. It was also the time of the William Kennedy Smith date rape trial and the Rodney King verdict. What made it a third wave were the younger voices who had never lived in a time without feminism, and there were new spokespeople and new vehicles that weren't just about political and legal change, but creating publications or new organizations. Some people still identify as third wave, so I wouldn't say that it's fully gone. And I have always thought that third wave was "you're coming to feminism regardless of your age," even though mainly young people dominated the conversation.

Playwright Eve Ensler, who wrote *The Vagina Monologues* a bit later, in 1996, was very prolific and out there, but she hadn't made the connection to feminism explicitly. Then all of a sudden, her light bulb went off. She was an example of the third-wave experience, and she used art as her expression of it. She was not afraid of putting women's sexual pleasure in the same conversation as women's sexual pain.

That was unique to third-wave feminism. Previously, feminism was practiced more in exclusively feminist spaces and fighting a space that was not feminist. Third wave tried to make the feminists a little bit more mainstream and the mainstream a little bit more feminist.

KD It's also a matter of the way that the media functions. The ways in which we gathered information within that time period were really rapid—that's how I think about my feminism. It's not necessarily what people thought, but it's how people could get access to information. Then within art there were the culture wars with exhibitions like the Whitney's *Black Male* from 1994. It was a moment of intense identity art.

Women artists at that time were working within a feminist politic, and many were also within a queer politic. So there was a way in which we interpreted and were able to receive information—that's how I mark third wave. And then perhaps we're in the fourth wave now because information is everywhere.

Audience In reference to female sexual pleasure and agency and sex positivity, Natalie, I'm curious about your series about dominatrixes. That's a topic that can anger both sides of the spectrum, but it speaks a lot to the power of choice. What were your takeaways and observations in terms of empathy?

NF I spent probably four or five months going into different dungeons all around New York, and I learned so much. My favorite experience was going to a dungeon called the Parthenon, run by a woman named Ariana. It's the only female-run dungeon in New York—so much of the industry is dominated by men. It's also the only fair-pay dungeon that exists.

I went in not knowing a lot about the S&M world but asked a lot of questions. I took oral histories of everyone I met, both the submissives and the dominants. I was really interested in how their interests and desires developed as they aged and went through life. That was one aspect.

Another aspect was sitting in sessions. I was enthralled by how performative it is and also the dynamic that all of these sessions were requested by men and delineated by men. They would set the specifications of what the woman would wear, what they would do. In the relationship between the dominatrix and the submissive, it was the woman outwardly assuming the position of authority. It was a complicated relationship, so I made a series of paintings of these constructs, and I paired them with images of ballet dancers. This idea of storytelling through the body, and contortions, and who has the agency as an artist—whose story are you telling?—was interesting to me.

Audience I want to say how much I appreciate you saying, "If you see something, say something." It sounds like a subway slogan, but finding it within yourself is important because there is so much chatter online. At some point, saying something can actually make a difference. I would love to hear more from you about the kind of vocabulary we can use to have an impact, make a difference.

KD It is tailored to particular experiences. For me, one phrase that I've avoided in the last year is "standing up for a cause." Some people can't stand. There's a circular way that we need to look at our word choices.

The way that Isolde started the conversation around defining feminism is another example. Questioning readily accepted terminologies is powerful. That involves trying to democratize or make more accessible the way in which we talk about certain themes, and finding within a room what may be the lowest common denominator of information.

AR As a parent, I'm often in a position of filling out forms and I try to be very intentional. It's a subtle thing to say "parent" and not "mother," or "child" and not "son," but these terms limit us. Similarly, when I wrote my first book, I was deliberate about not *only* identifying people who were not white and not straight, because that's often what we have been conditioned to read. In the news and in the press, everything is white until we know otherwise. So I tried to name white people as white. But to this day it is so fascinating to me that if you don't say the race or the gender, or don't say sexuality, people assume the default.

When we were creating the Third Wave Foundation, we were very intentional about our board structure. It would be no more than 50 percent heterosexual, and we put the difference on the dominant group, not on the group that had historically not been a part of that. I'm not married, and forms ask, "Married or single"; I say, "Well, I'm neither. I'm not married or unmarried." It doesn't make any sense. Why do you need to know if I'm married, legally or not? Pointing out those things, even if you change just one person's mind, that's enough. Challenging the things we take for granted every single day is important.

NF I grew up with patronizing language in the South. I encountered it a lot in the art world, almost always from men, and I tend to call out being named "little lady" or "miss." For me, it's related to the subject matter of my work and the assumptions that men usually make about me because of my work. I try to use specificity in language and in how I present myself and my work.

I did an interview for my *Story of O* exhibition. The interviewer said, "It's so surprising the way that you look because you would never expect someone like you to go into dungeons or to make this kind of work." I corrected him on the type of language he might want to think about using—language that isn't so reductive—reducing women or reducing our interior lives or our capacity.

Audience There is a lot of talk about feminism in higher education and academia. Do you believe that feminism has become more accessible to folks outside of these institutions? If not, how can we make feminism more accessible? Because it's one thing to speak about feminism in college or in our classrooms, but what about with sex workers? What about with people who work in the restaurant industry? Sometimes it's hard to have those conversations—there's a dissonance there.

IB **It's important to acknowledge our own subject positions, acknowledge who we are and how we frame ourselves in relation to the world around us. Feminism is this ambiguous, fluid, ever-evolving notion. I recognize that I may have my notion of feminism, but it may be different from these women on stage and different from women occupying spaces beyond arts institutions. We have to be able to have a conversation about that while at the same time listening and acknowledging people's experiences and perspectives on themselves.**

Technology comes into play because of its ability to transcend and move across borders. Access is incredibly important.

KD Even the word *access*, when it comes to information, can fail. There are so many ways in which feminism can be misread or misnamed—and we all have our own relationship to the pure definition of feminism. If you're encountering it outside of an academic context, you may not know that you can ask questions of an ideology. The grandest privilege that a formal education can give you is the power to ask questions and the power and tools to critique.

Social media and digital technology puts a lot of stuff in front of us, but how we engage with and interrogate it and how we further the discourse doesn't always succeed because it is such a delicate place. Tumblr is why I'm here right now. I think so much about the conversations I had about identity within that sphere. We didn't have much power then, but there was something in being able to find a community to have these sensitive dialogues with outside of the people I was in class with. These types of conversations have been so much a part of my life and a grand privilege of mine, but for others, that isn't necessarily the case.

So there is a real difference between the weight with which we interpret things and the power and privilege we have around language. How slippery language is in the digital age is an important question to ask.

AR I think most people connect with feminism; they just don't have the label for what they're connecting with. I look at my own experience. From my youngest years, I watched my mother at a time when she couldn't get a credit card. She had to have her father sign for her credit card. When

I was born, the choice on my birth certificate was to have "illegitimate" or to have my father's last name. She gave me my father's last name so that I wouldn't be called illegitimate.

When I was six, I had to go to court and fight to get my mom's name. Think about being a six-year-old in court: "Why do we have to do this, Mom? Why do I have to get your name?" Right now I'm doing something with ROC United, which advocates for restaurant workers. They're paid unfairly and subjected to sexual harassment. They say, "This is unjust, and I want something that's going to lead me to a fairer place and lead this whole industry to a place of fairness." That process is widespread, globally, whether or not you label it feminism. ▲

MEMORY AND MONUMENTS
(Re) Claiming Public Space

Karyn Olivier
The Battle Is Joined
2017
Acrylic mirror, wood, screws, adhesive
Installation view, Vernon Park, Philadelphia

Karyn Olivier's *The Battle Is Joined* is an acrylic mirror encasing the Battle of Germantown Memorial, built in 1903 and dedicated to that American-British Revolutionary War battle in a former colonial settlement, and situated in what today is Vernon Park, Philadelphia, a predominantly African American, working-class neighborhood. Olivier says, "My reinterpretation of the Battle of Germantown Memorial asks the monument to serve as a conductor of sorts. It transports, transmits, expresses, and literally reflects the landscape, people, and activities that surround it. We are reminded that this memorial can be an instrument and we, too, are instruments—the keepers and protectors of the monument, and in that role, sometimes we become the very monument itself."

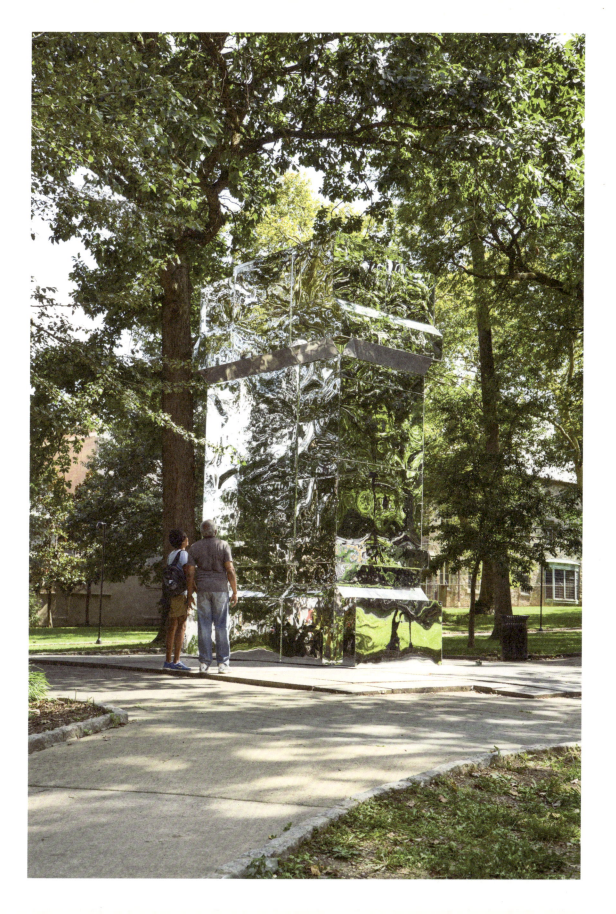

The Questions That Answers Hide

Karyn Olivier

Rome is a city where monuments confront passersby at every turn. Maybe the word *confront* is too strong, but we certainly can't ignore the physical, cultural, and psychological space these monuments occupy. I decided to walk the twelve-mile-long Aurelian Walls, built in the late third century to fend off attacks by Germanic tribes. (Full disclosure: I didn't finish.) This border wall is a monument—the largest ancient Roman monument in the city. It traverses the city in mundane and unexpected ways, incorporating (in effect, protecting) the other monuments it passes. It is simultaneously colossal, invisible, beautiful, politically charged, commonplace, a hindrance, and obsolete.

I am constantly struck by this city, so flooded in history, where new iterations and evidence of the past are continually unearthed. How do Romans reconcile these markers of the past and the meaning and impact they have on Roman society today? How do they function? And what new lens do they offer to investigate and reimagine the much shorter history of monuments in the United States? One thing my time in Rome has done is to reconfirm what we already know: that historical narratives are layered, conflicting, and simultaneous; that a viewer must be willing to dig through the overbearing complexity of the past to grasp its ramifications today and, in the process, unearth a possible glimpse into the future.

I have been thinking about monuments for some time now—about what they represent and what they can become. During this time, I have had to face (arguably) the most contested monuments in the United States—those dedicated to the Confederacy. Proponents often present oversimplified justifications for the preservation of these monuments ("removal would be akin to erasing history"; "we should defend white heritage"; "demolition would equal censorship"). Any cursory investigation, however, reveals the complex role that racism, power, privilege, money, access, and the fight for civil rights have played in their proliferation. Confederate monuments were initially erected in cemeteries, at the gravesites of the people being remembered. Their construction was instigated by a small segment of the elite white population. (For example, United Daughters of the Confederacy began raising money immediately following the Civil War; Paul Goodloe

1 Dell Upton, "Confederate Monuments and Civic Values in the Wake of Charlottesville," *Society of Architectural Historians*, Sept. 13, 2017, https://www.sah.org/publications-and-research/sah-blog/sah-blog/2017/09/13/confederate-monuments-and-civic-values-in-the-wake-of-charlottesville.

2 Robert Musil, *Posthumous Papers of a Living Author*, trans. Peter Wortsman (Hygiene, CO: Eridanos Press, 1987), 61.

McIntire commissioned and funded the controversial Robert E. Lee statue in Charlottesville, Virginia.) These monuments were unequivocally assertions of power, and the hierarchical system welcomed them. Architectural historian Dell Upton notes, "Siting[s] in cemeteries were meant to disguise their political meaning as signs of continued allegiance to the Confederacy. After the end of Reconstruction and federal supervision, the monuments moved to the metaphorical public square and became more openly pro-Confederate."[1]

Debates continue on what to do with these monuments—remove and destroy, remove and reassign (in general, to museums), create monument parks akin to Memento Park in Budapest (dedicated to statues from the Communist regime). In the course of looking at these memorials, I have assembled thoughts, worries, and hopes for our interpretation and reimagining of monuments today.

Our complicated histories need to be wrestled with, even when they can't be resolved. How do we reconcile dissent, multiplicity, complicity? Simultaneity and paradox, which are embedded in our country's history? What do we say to assertions like one in 1936 from philosopher Robert Musil: "There is nothing in this world as invisible as a monument. They are no doubt erected to be seen—indeed, to attract attention. But at the same time they are impregnated with something that repels attention. Like a drop of water on an oilskin, attention runs down them without stopping for a moment"?[2] What about the notion that their inevitable "invisibility" is intentional? The monument starts to feel like a natural part of the landscape—something we don't question. Status quo at best, an implicit or explicit sign of repression at worst.

I believe, though, that monuments should be catalysts that create spaces for discourse. They can commemorate but also allow a viewer to investigate and interrogate America's complicated histories from multiple perspectives. A monument should offer an opportunity to pose questions about our country's past and its impact now, in all of its complexity and messiness. It should let each of us see and imagine our critical role in the ever-evolving American story. The best monuments are instruments that offer a mirror to see ourselves, our community, our city, our country, that implore us to be active, engaged citizens in the world. The talking statues of Rome, installed in public areas of the city in the sixteenth century, are a model I return to. Citizens attached anonymous messages to these statues, reinventing them as sites for protest, political dissent, and critique and commentary on the religious and political authorities of the time. The effigies became the spokespeople of Rome. At times, messages were posted between two statues, creating an ongoing dialogue among multiple histories and shifting authors. The statuary became active, unfixed, mutable, temporal, and contemporary; works of art were transformed into tools and guardians—the keepers and protectors of democracy.

So what is the role of memory in monuments? How do we ensure that they don't do the memory work for us? How do we keep them active? As James E. Young articulates in his seminal text "The Counter-Monument: Memory against Itself in Germany Today," "The surest engagement with memory lies in its perpetual irresolution. In fact, the best German memorial to the Fascist era and its victims may not be a single memorial at all, but simply the never to be resolved debate over which kind of memory to preserve, how to do it, in whose name, and to what end. Instead of a fixed figure for memory, the debate itself—perpetually unresolved amid ever-changing conditions—might be enshrined."[3] This temporal, non-concrete approach is an interesting one to consider.

I believe in objects, however, and the authority that material, mass, form, content, context, and the haptic hold. These monuments, these sculptures, are symbolic, but they are also imbued with the power to craft American history and determine which narratives become our collective "heritage." I am intrigued by the many monument projects that extend and expand the stories told, revealing the complexity of what it means to be a citizen, to be human. These projects can be classified as temporal monuments, space-clearing gestures—ones that mine absence and reuse content.

Temporality and Ephemerality

At times, I think the very idea of permanence—whether in meaning or in physicality—is somewhat absurd. The

[3] James E. Young, "The Counter-Monument: Memory against Itself in Germany Today," *Critical Inquiry* 18, no. 2 (winter 1992): 270.

Berlin Wall loomed for so many years as a stark symbol of division not just between ideologies but between families…and then it took on a whole new meaning as it was dismantled block by block. The same physical walls held completely different meanings depending on the side and era from which they were viewed. And wouldn't it have been something to witness the statue of Saddam Hussein going up and then coming down? This has led me to wonder whether the inverse of permanence is the ideal state for monuments to exist in—fleeting gestures, brief exchanges that become the building blocks for culture. Perhaps we should highlight these moments: they may have more permanence as memories, forever seared into our brains. A piece of marble, a wall of stone: these are ultimately as ephemeral as what we absorb, indelibly, in a moment of connection, emotion, or understanding. These short-lived experiences, ironically, may address our mortality, our need to make something matter in our brief time here, more lastingly than the so-called permanent monument. Felix Gonzalez-Torres's works can be considered to be monuments: he offers pieces of candy (*Untitled*), a fleeting gesture made eternal by its limitlessness— an endless supply to fill our need, our desire. Rudolf Herz's *Lenin on Tour* is another example: a decommissioned statue of Lenin, placed on the back of a flatbed truck, spent the summer of 2004 traveling around Europe. Each night Herz and the Communist-era monument would stop in a new city where artists, sociologists, economists, and passersby were asked for their current views on Lenin.

Clearing and Making Space
The Stolpersteine project, initiated by Gunter Demnig, is comprised of small brass cobblestones, bricks really, embedded into the sidewalk. The information included in the inscription for each stone is the same: "Here lived" followed by the name, date of birth, and fate (usually deportation or murder) of a Holocaust victim. More than seventy thousand stones have been installed, making this the largest decentralized memorial in the world.

    THE TIMES, 2017, was a monument to empowerment, hope, and self-realization in the Kensington section of Philadelphia, a neighborhood struggling through a

[4] See page 171 of this book.

horrific drug epidemic. Artist Tyree Guyton invited residents from Impact Services, a transitional housing facility, to paint cartoonish clocks all over the facade of a colossal former factory. The simple act of collectively painting the building "opened up" the area and created space—psychological and emotional—for those living nearby. There was an urgency to this monument, a calling attention to the possibilities of recovery in the face of adversity. The work had real consequences: drug activity on the block lessened and dealers took their business elsewhere.

Absence and Invisibility

Dan Borelli's *Ashland-Nyanza Project* spotlights a hidden story in his hometown of Ashland, Massachusetts—the dumping of more than forty-five thousand tons of chemicals into its land, air, and water by Nyanza Color & Chemical Co., a dye factory. The area surrounding the plant, deemed a Superfund site by the US government, was capped to prevent more toxins from leaching. Borelli placed colored gels over the streetlights in town to mimic the dye colors produced by Nyanza and to reflect the actual underground concentration of toxins that still exists. He led locals on walks around the neighborhood, using the map created by the colored lights, an ephemeral representation of the scientific evidence. "I [moved] from [thinking about] color phenomenology to color ecology, from color as seducer to color as carcinogen, as cancer," Borelli has said.[4]

In 2017, I installed *The Battle Is Joined* in Vernon Park, a historic park in Philadelphia. In this public work, I created my own version of Rome's talking statues by "initiating" a conversation between two monuments in the park: one honoring Francis Daniel Pastorius, the German settler who led the first Quaker protest against slavery in 1688, and the other the Battle of Germantown Memorial, honoring the failed George Washington–led Revolutionary War battle. The Pastorius monument was boxed over during World Wars I and II because the look of the monument was perceived to be "too Germanic." I thought about the paradox of Pastorius, an immigrant fighting for Blacks' freedom from slavery, and Washington, fighting for the freedom of America from British rule while owning enslaved people. I replicated the concealment of the Pastorius monument but transcribed it to the Germantown memorial. A mirrored facade reflected in real time the present-day viewers and the ever-changing landscape. The reflection reproduced the neighborhood's current demographic, which is predominantly African American (at one time it was a German immigrant stronghold). The mirror encasement made the structure "disappear" from certain vantage points, thus participating in the ongoing debate on the removal of Confederate monuments. As viewers approached the piece, it transitioned from being invisible to being larger than life. Up close, seeing our own reflections, we acknowledge our literal presence and, in essence, *become* the monument. I hoped to summon what was hidden and spotlight a community—one that has one of the highest poverty rates in Philadelphia—in all of its beauty.

Reuse and Displacement

I created *Witness*, a site-specific installation and memorial at the University of Kentucky, in 2018. My intention was to honor Black and brown Kentuckians and deepen the dialogue around a controversial New Deal–era fresco depicting a history of Kentucky. The mural sanitized the portrayal of slavery and presented stereotypes and caricatures of people of color. I gold-leafed the dome to reference sacred paintings, churches, and Byzantine and Renaissance cathedrals. Then I appropriated and reproduced the African American and Native American figures in the painting, inserting the reproductions onto the domed ceiling of the vestibule. This treatment effectively transported and repositioned these anonymous figures into a heavenly space. The gold leaf elevated the oppressed figures—those deemed lowly—to the divine.

The mural depicts subjugated people performing mundane chores and activities but does not reveal their depth of servitude or the range of horrific acts that kept them there. The same figures, transported to a gilded ceiling, reinforce the notion or possibility of rebirth—perhaps spiritually, but more immediately through the viewer's re-investigation, interrogation, and reckoning with our country's complex histories. Around the base of the dome I inscribed a Frederick Douglass quotation: "There is not a man beneath the canopy of heaven that does not know that slavery is wrong for him." This quote addressed the anonymous figures in the original mural as well as my relocated ones by calling out by name the historical sin of slavery.

Artists who work in the public realm and (re)imagine monuments, memorials, and objects of memory know well that we must dissect and critique our histories, shed light on what is hidden, and lay out the complicated landscape for all to examine and question. I often think of a statement by James Baldwin as it relates to my responsibility as an artist and a citizen: "The artist cannot and must not take anything for granted, but must drive to the heart of every answer and expose the question the answer hides."[5] ▲

Dan Borelli

artist

Titus Kaphar

artist

Karyn Olivier

artist

Isolde Brielmaier How do we construct and contend with our history, specifically here in the United States? How have these histories been visualized, concretized, and memorialized? By whom and for whom? What events and communities have been commemorated in the United States? What or who has been overlooked? When commemorative monuments and symbols, in the form of statues, plaques, flags, and other objects, are removed, are we erasing histories or are we clearing space to lay open new ground for inclusion and for the rewriting and expanding of our historical narratives?

James Grossman, the Executive Director of the American Historical Association, states, "Commemoration is complicated and communal work." Titus, you have consistently engaged with ideas of traditional art history and the European canon as well as with history, memory, and representation—specifically with the rewriting, reclamation, and appropriation of narratives. Can you tell us a little bit about this work and about your practice?

Titus Kaphar There is a body of work that I'm doing now, *Monumental Inversions*, which speaks directly to what we're talking about. My work has always been about narratives and the characters in existing compositions who are not the central figures. I'm trying to represent folks who often didn't get represented.

I give myself the freedom to explore and investigate without any sense of obligation to the original or, in some cases, even to the facts or the origin of a particular piece. I take an existing work as a foundation, and wherever the piece takes me, that's where I end up going. I give myself that freedom because I recognize that in all painting, in all representation, there is fiction. As I say, "All depiction is fiction; it's only a question of degree." If that is true, then I can give myself the freedom to explore in any way.

Emanuel Leutze's *Washington Crossing the Delaware* from 1851 is not a historical painting, but we treat it like one. When we think of the signing of the Declaration of Independence, we look at paintings by John Trumbull, and those paintings become the visual representations of those moments—but those moments didn't look like that. All of those folks in Trumbull's *The Declaration of Independence, July 4, 1776* made in the late eighteenth or early nineteenth century weren't in the room when it was signed. But in order to tell this narrative in the way that Trumbull wanted it to be told, he altered the facts a little bit.

When I say, "All depiction is fiction," I'm not the first person to say it. Magritte was saying that in his *The Treachery of Images*, which reads, "This is not a pipe"—this is a representation of the thing; this is not the thing itself. Even our memories function this way. When we remember things, we're not remembering the incident itself, we're remembering the last time we remembered that thing, and we pull it out of our file case and begin to have a conversation about it, and we don't realize how we've altered that original memory.

Karyn Olivier The past is legitimate and real, but your history or memory of it is going to be subjective.

IB It's constructed. Karyn, could you share a little bit about your work?

KO   I have a pretty disparate practice. But over the last five years, I've been thinking about how to intersect and collapse conflicting histories, and what those histories mean in the present moment. I think about blind spots or the underconsidered spaces that exist and how I can insert something into that. I think about rearticulating spaces that could allow for a claiming or reclaiming of narratives: new publics that can claim something as their own. I think about invisibility and how I can use invisibility to actually reveal—I don't want to say "truth" because *truth* is such a bad word—but to reveal what we didn't want to see or didn't want to recognize. How can invisibility allow us to see?

This fall, I was invited to participate in Philadelphia's Mural Arts project Monument Lab, where the city tries to reckon with what's an appropriate monument for the city of Philadelphia. I live in Germantown, which is a historic neighborhood—it used to be German, but now is predominately African American. There's a monument in the far corner of Vernon Park dedicated to Francis Daniel Pastorius, a German settler who led the first Quaker protest against slavery back in 1688—so almost two hundred years before the United States abolished slavery. I found out that during World Wars I and II, the monument was boxed over. It was about the same things we're dealing with today—ideas of the foreign, the other, fear.

Then, at the center of the park is another monument, the Battle of Germantown Memorial, which is dedicated to George Washington. The Battle of Germantown was the only Revolutionary War battle that was actually fought in Philadelphia, and it was a failed battle, but power structures allow for monuments to exist based on a person. I thought it was interesting that George Washington was fighting for America's freedom while owning slaves; you also have this immigrant, Pastorius, fighting against slavery and asking, "Blacks are American, so how could they not be treated as citizens?"

I wanted to engage that history and these different time periods. I decided to box over the Battle of Germantown Memorial, which on some level was irreverent. But I knew in the act of boxing or shrouding and making it invisible, people would remember that it was there. All of a sudden, they had to be aware.

Even though I was putting history into the present, it didn't seem enough. So I thought, How can I deal with what's here now? By boxing the monument with mirrors, it reflects the current landscape and is always shifting. Now instead of white faces, Black faces are shown. If no one's in the park, the landscape, the trees are changing; it's never sitting still. I like the idea of the monument having this certain verticality and static nature, then all of a sudden, it dissolves. Or the idea that when you're looking at it, it's not just about the vertical axis—what's above, below, around you is being reflected. Often the monument is made out of stone and marble and is heavy, static, impenetrable. It's almost like the period at the end of the sentence. Monuments can never be the periods of a sentence—that's where we go wrong.

It was spotless; people took care of the work. Someone said, "If they're spending money on this piece, they must realize we're still here, because it's a pretty poor Black neighborhood." The community took the piece over, and it became theirs in a way. I had a vet from the neighborhood say to me when I was installing it, "How much is this piece costing? Twenty-five thousand?" I said, "Close." He replied, "How can we be building this when people are starving a couple of blocks away?" I said, "I live four blocks from here, and I know people are starving. I know people need basic necessities, I know we can't survive without them, but are you saying that we can't have beauty?"

If you think that's okay, fine, but I think we deserve beauty. I don't think this type of project should exist just in the downtown area, where it's upper-middle-class and rich; we deserve to have a moment to see ourselves reflected, to see ourselves and see our beauty, to see this beautiful park that we take for granted. Yes, you may be right that this $25,000 could have gone to something else, but I believe that we need this. And what's better than to see yourself reflected, and to see an evolving, changing, constantly shifting narrative of what America is and what it means to be American?

IB **And creating conversations among people on a community level—that goes back to that space-clearing gesture, right? Where we clear the space for people to engage and consider history differently. Dan, your work around this topic?**

Dan Borelli   I'm from Ashland, Massachusetts, the second town on the Boston Marathon route. As runners go by, just off to their left in the center of town is one of the first Superfund sites, part of the Environmental Protection Agency's program to remediate contaminated sites. It literally means that it's going to require super funding to clean up an area—it's that nasty. There are about 1,400 Superfund sites in the United States.

I was working on developing my own color theory and mapping the history of color and how color has fallen out of architectural discourse when I discovered that the source of contamination in my hometown was color. Ashland is the site of one of the first color plants in the United States to produce synthetic dye for the textile-manufacturing industry. All of a sudden, I jump from color phenomenology to color ecology, from color as seducer to color as carcinogen, as cancer. Specific chemicals that were dumped in the town manifested themselves as an angiosarcoma cluster. I grew up with friends who passed away from the pollutants of color. In response, I created *The Ashland-Nyanza Project*. It's a multiyear, three-part project, and I'm on year seven. I started the project by going to people whom I came to call the culture of loss: the moms, the sisters, the siblings, and I said, "How would you feel, in your gut, if I were to treat this artistically?" Not what do you think, but how do you feel? And this is where I think artists thrive; we get to the "how you feel" and we make that feeling public. I needed to tell the story of the history of the contaminated. If a place like Ashland forgets about the people they have lost, then we have created social amnesia.

One part of the project is inside of the Ashland Public Library, which is the only place where this narrative is made public by default. The EPA's documents showing the history of the contaminants reside there. The negative impact, the cancer cluster, the deaths are not marked anywhere else in the town. I restaged the library with interviews, with people giving testimonials. I recontextualized this narrative; I made physical models; I made an interactive sequence of mappings; I used every representational trick I could. Then, I used EPA documentation to map where the contaminants are today to the nearest streetlight. I put gels over the streetlights, and I lit up the entire town with color for a month so people could walk and viscerally feel where the contamination is today.

IB **It's like a living, breathing memorial. At the center is loss rather than victory. This goes back to Karyn's point around power. Even though the Battle of Germantown was lost, there's this power there around which we commemorate and build monuments.**

DB It was really a gut punch to people who had, for years, been ignoring it. Contaminants had dumped right into the Sudbury River, which is the river where Henry David Thoreau canoed. The sight of contamination, the hill, is named after a Native American inhabitation site.

I was asked by the culture of loss to make something permanent. They gave me a two-acre parcel that they called a "healing garden." I teamed up with the Laborers' International Union of North America; they have a training facility a mile from the site. I designed a color sundial, because I wanted to get people off the concept of electric time and back to ceremonial time, which is what Native Americans called it. It's a more naturalistic way of looking at time.

The color sundial is twenty feet wide and twelve feet tall. I wanted to make color back into something positive and have it wash over your body. The Nipmuc tribe, who used to reside there, came to do a healing ceremony. The moms go there and pray and reconnect with their lost loved ones.

About a year into it, a group of middle-class/upper-class white kids broke the pavilion. Each of the twelve panels consisted of four unique custom-cut pieces, so a total of forty-eight pieces. Close to thirty were broken. There's honestly no reason why they did that.

IB **Why now? We saw this big ramp-up in 2015 after nine African American churchgoers were murdered at the Mother Emanuel AME Church in Charleston, South Carolina, by a domestic terrorist who had posted numerous images of himself donning the Confederate flag. About a week and a half later, filmmaker, activist, artist, and producer Bree Newsome climbed up a flag pole and removed the Confederate flag from the grounds of the South Carolina State House. She was arrested for that action, and that was one of the first instances where we really saw this debate take center stage. So why now, and why is there such a heavy focus on the South?**

KO I'm going to say something that will sound crazy: I think it's partly Beyoncé. I'm being dead serious. It's a conflation of things: I think it's Beyoncé, and her *Lemonade* video and the Black Panther Superbowl performance. I think it's Black Lives Matter and Black Girl Magic and Trump. It's the combination that's allowing this to happen.

IB **It's actually not that crazy in the sense that, in order for these discussions and debates to take off, they need to extend into the realm of popular culture.**

TK It's important to recognize that this is not just happening right now. There are folks down South who have been having this conversation for decades.

IB **But it's so visible and loud right now.**

TK What is different about this particular moment is how an individual voice can spread so quickly. Technology can take these inside-the-community conversations outside the community instantly.

I made a piece that spoke to the sculpture outside of New York's American Museum of Natural History, and that received a whole bunch of attention. But David Hammons had addressed that sculpture decades ago. As an artist who looks up to David Hammons, I always say, "Yes, I did that, but you need to know what my source was, where it came from." It's important for us to recognize that there are a lot of people who were doing this work who haven't been heard until now, but they still have been in the trenches.

IB **Let's talk about this idea of existing monuments: what do we do? I've seen on social media the option to "Check yes or no" and the question "Do we remove or don't we remove?" How do we get out of that binary conversation? How do we see the role of the historian and the artist in that equation?**

TK It's interesting that we're having this conversation; often, decision makers are not talking to artists. We're talking about sculptures, we're talking about artworks, but by and large politicians are making these decisions. They're not addressing makers—that's the first thing. The second thing is that I don't understand why "keep it" or "take it down" are the only two options. We limit ourselves by keeping it to a binary conversation. Artists of this moment, of this time, need to make new works that address older monuments and other public works. And those artists, myself included, must recognize that in our making, there are things we're going to miss.

As Karyn said earlier, these monuments shouldn't be a period, they should be open. Because in twenty years someone is going to come to a work that I've made and say, "Titus, this was nice, but you completely forgot about the transgender community or the Indigenous community." So then I'd need to come back in and engage the work in a way that speaks to that community, too. And we need to recognize that a monument shouldn't be concrete, it shouldn't be a period at the end of the sentence, it should be many, many, many commas.

IB **That's a critique of history itself, right? There is this inflexible traditional canon that history has been constructed within, and it is considered truth.**

DB People conflate history and the archive as being like a pastoral painting from the Hudson River School or "pure," untouchable. They're not recognizing that there are very specific choices about what is included and what is intentionally excluded.

KO   But what to do with monuments? Sometimes it would make sense to make something else that's in conversation with an existing monument. Another time, maybe it makes sense to put it in a museum. But if we say it has to be one thing, we're going to fail.

TK   I think we get out of our binary by going to artists; we let the people who make things address these questions. If the options are just to keep it or take it down, then take it down. But that's not enough: that doesn't even begin to address the problem.

IB   **There's still the history and what led to the culture in which these monuments exist.**

TK   There's something about monument making itself that we're buying into by thinking that these things are powerful simply because they are where they are. In other words, just because an object is on a pedestal doesn't mean that it deserves to be esteemed, or that it's a valuable piece of art. The truth is that most of these monuments, unfortunately, are not made by our national Berninis. We're not looking at Donatello sculptures and saying, "Oh God, this is such a hard decision because this is so amazing." Most of the time, these sculptures are made by second-, third-, fourth-tier artists.

     If you give contemporary artists the opportunity to say, "Let's do battle. You put yours up, and I'll put mine up," I guarantee that the contemporary conversation will be stronger. Because as contemporary artists, we have a whole arsenal of materials that weren't available in the past, and we have the ability to speak to the people in our communities directly. I'm not scared of the sculpture. I'm not intimidated. It doesn't frighten me. I'm not upset about it. What I'm upset about is that we're not making opportunities for our living artists to step in and engage the conversation.

KO   If we're looking at the model of a traditional monument, sure. But I make temporary monuments, and, for me, the idea of permanent monuments just makes no sense anymore.

     I keep thinking about the talking statues of Rome. In the sixteenth century, there were these six statues, and people would put notes on them. And they became a site for protests. The statues themselves weren't particularly provocative, but someone decided to transform them into these other beings, to have another meaning. It's temporary to me because it's living and breathing and not sitting still.

IB   **Think about the notion of power and structures of power and history and how they are intricately bound up in one another. So many people hold on to that painting of George Washington crossing the Delaware as a monument to this man, to the founding of this country.**

DB   I'm starting a project on the Plymouth Rock in Plymouth, Massachusetts, and its relationship to the Pilgrim Nuclear Power Station. The power plant is the same plant, same design, same maker, same year as Fukushima. It's sitting right on the edge of the Atlantic Ocean, and it's a mile south of the Plymouth Rock. The first claim that the Pilgrims landed there was made in 1741, but on the rock, they wrote, "1620." My point is that when we go back, we see that our predecessors have put these completely staged objects in public spaces.

KO   But do you think part of it was wanting us to have something that we all can believe in? I don't think it was malice; some of it was citizens needing a story.

IB   **Of course. That's part of national identity.**

DB   There's a creationist story by the Pilgrims, and then their successors, to make the claim that they own this land. It's interesting that we project our national identity onto geological formations. Never mind the fact that the rock is in pieces, and that there's even a chunk of it at a church in Brooklyn Heights. But there's an attitude that you can't question certain founding myths.

TK   This is part of the challenge. We're questioning all kinds of things: what we held as truth yesterday, we question today—that's a given. In terms of addressing monuments, we have to be able to hold in our hands two opposite things at the same time. George Washington was an important historic figure; George Washington enslaved people. Thomas Jefferson was an articulate, poetic, amazing individual; Thomas Jefferson stole liberty from hundreds and hundreds of people. We have to figure out how to have these monuments, whether they're temporary or permanent—I like temporary better—hold these two diametrically opposing ideas in balance.

DB   What's missing around the object of the monument is a discursive space.

TK   In a museum and in teaching, you can reframe, recontextualize, and pluralize history. There's not a capital "H."

KO   Absolutely. It's that single perspective. It's not necessarily false, but it's only one perspective.

IB   **That's "the danger of a single story."**

Audience   There's a new archive created by scholars at John Jay College of Criminal Justice that documents the presence of enslaved people in the Capital Region. We've known that there were enslaved people in the Capital Region, but there hasn't been easy public access to these histories. My question is: Wouldn't we want a more permanent monument to the enslaved people, that is, lest we forget? In Germany, there are brass bricks in front of the houses where Jewish families lived. I'm fascinated by what you're saying about temporary monuments, but I also have a hunger for something more permanent, and I wonder if you might comment on that.

DB   The House of the Wannsee Conference in Berlin is easily the most powerful exhibition experience I've personally had. Villa Wannsee's role in the Nazi government is the same as Camp David: it was where high-level politicians went to retreat and strategize. There's now a permanent exhibition that makes public all of these government papers and memos that showed just who was involved in decisions about the Holocaust. When I went, there were photographs of the individuals at the table, listing the types of decisions they made.

The United States hasn't made public this insane archive of the founding fathers, the bureaucratization of enslavement. That's what I think is so brave about what the Germans did: they showed the methodology and the depth and the bureaucratization of the Holocaust, and it blows you away.

KO I did a project in Central Park with Creative Time. I found out that Seneca Village was near the site of my piece. It was one of the only communities of free Black property owners in the United States. It existed for about thirty years, and then, all of a sudden, the property was claimed in order to build Central Park, and the residents were scattered wholesale throughout the city. Little evidence of them remains. It turned out that City College completed a dig with graduate students, and they found remnants from Seneca Village. I was thinking about the Wisconsin ice sheet coming through New York twenty thousand years ago and how it affected the terrain of the city and the park. This evidence is in plain view, but we don't see it.

So I thought of making this lenticular billboard with one image of the glacier, to make reference to this history of twenty thousand years ago; one image of a pottery shard from Seneca Village in the 1800s; and one image to refer to the present landscape. It was almost like twenty thousand years were being compressed, and you control time by how you see it. All there is at the site of Seneca Village is this little plaque, so I felt I had to do something more. If the history of Seneca Village was on display, that would be a memorial. That would indicate a statement of dealing with our own terrorism.

IB **Before you can commemorate or memorialize, you have to actually acknowledge. I'm half-Austrian, so I've grown up with this history lingering. I went recently to Berlin with my mother, who had not been there since she was a child of the war. It was incredibly moving to walk on the street and see eight bronze stones—*Stolpersteine* or "stumbling stones"—with the names of the parents and six children who were taken from that house, then murdered at Auschwitz or Bergen-Belsen. In the center of the city, you've got the Holocaust Memorial and the Memorial to the Sinti and Roma Victims of National Socialism. There is rich text that fully acknowledges and implicates Germany in this history.**

We have yet to do that here in the United States. When you walk into our Capitol in Washington, DC, there is a specific historical narrative that is laid out and, in my opinion, fed to people. Now we have the new National Museum of African American History and Culture and the memorial to Martin Luther King Jr., but there is no history of enslaved individuals, there is no history of the Indigenous communities on whose land the Mall

actually sits. As a nation, we haven't done the work to contend with and acknowledge our history. It's incredibly difficult work.

I like the temporary idea, but I, too, hunger for that monument that says, "We implicate ourselves. We exist on the backs of many, many people, and we are paying homage to them."

TK There's a distinction between the kinds of memorials or monuments that remember individuals and try to deify individuals and the kinds of monuments or memorials that talk about a moment in time where many people were affected by a particular thing. Whether we're talking about the Holocaust or Indigenous people or the enslavement of Black people, those are different kinds of things. Maybe the memorials where we're trying to reckon with our tragic history and its impact on hundreds and hundreds and hundreds of people are the spaces where these things are permanent. But this idea that we glorify a single individual, that we put George Washington on a pedestal, maybe that we get rid of. Maybe we decide we're not going to do that anymore.

Audience In terms of both people and places, do you recognize any place that should have outstanding recognition paid to it? Let's say that the Colosseum in Rome should stay exactly as it is. We have to lock on to some things, even things that were bad, because they served important purposes for many who were there at the time.

TK I wonder if there's a space for believing in democracy to work. To what degree do the people who live in a community have a say as to whether something stays or goes? Is there some way to engage that? It's important to give folks the opportunity to say, "This is my community. I live here. I want to have a say." Right now, these decisions are made from up high, and the people on the ground aren't really asked for their opinions.

DB I want to talk about ruination in response to the example that you brought forth. Lots of cultures have a history of staging architecture as emblematic of a previous social structure. In the case of Rome, it signifies a political system and a political ideology that failed. There's something really interesting about using architecture in identity shaping, and in particular for architectural ruination once the object is no longer in use.

For *The Ashland-Nyanza Project*, I proposed to the town to name the large remediated landscape, a cap—it looks like natural green grass—as a ruin. So long as it remains useless, it has cultural use—it can teach you. Once it goes back into human use and flow, and we reinhabit it, we'll forget. To the point about permanence, I made this argument that the remediated cap—one of the first built in this country—has cultural significance while it remains without use. It signifies the failure of a system of unregulated industrial markets. It needs to stay as it is so that we can learn, because we're about to dismantle the regulatory systems by which citizens are able to hold the industrial economies accountable.

Audience I have a theory that the reason we think about these monuments as permanent has to do with the materials used to make them. I'm interested in hearing from you as makers. How might you incorporate new materials, and how might those materials interact with the old? How do we break down this historically constructed idea of materials like metal and stone and bronze to make them less intimidating?

KO — I don't think we shouldn't use those materials, but if the monument doesn't activate, doesn't engage, doesn't allow a space for discourse, then it's failing. The material doesn't matter. But I believe that those materials are so weighted and so loaded that you read them as something other, something from another time, something that may have just a tangential relationship to who you are and what your life is today. If those materials could find a way to bring about engagement, keep them. But if they can't, the materials are a problem.

When I was covering over the monument in Vernon Park, Philadelphia, there were questions like, "Is this going to damage the stone?" I said, "I hope it does something to shift it, maybe." To what end is there preservation? What does it mean to preserve anything? Let it be stone and see what happens over time. I'm not sure how preservation serves a monument conceptually, or serves us in having a dialogue. Monuments can't stay what they are because we keep changing, our culture keeps changing. Let a piece evolve.

Audience — I'm the Executive Director of the Preservation Foundation here in Saratoga. One of our most recent projects was a four-year restoration of *The Spirit of Life*, a Daniel Chester French bronze sculpture in Congress Park in Saratoga Springs. It's a hundred years old, and we organized a restoration effort. The bronze was a memorial to one specific person who was responsible for preserving our spring waters, which our community still identifies with—but it's not an image of that person. We did consider how it is used in the park today, and how it's evolved and been used throughout time.

KO — Has the signage changed at all? How do you make that relevant, both what it meant back then for French to do that, and what it means today?

Audience (same) — The inscription talks about giving back to your community to make it a better place. It still serves that purpose, and it's a very uplifting sculpture.

KO — But would people pay attention to it as opposed to if there was a current dialogue? Someone could speak about what the sculpture means today when, in New York and other places, we're talking about fracking. Our water might be ruined.

Audience (same) — We are a tiny nonprofit, staff of two, and it was a $750,000 restoration. We probably fell short on permanent signage.

KO — But what about adding that permanent signage? What if, every year, you ask someone in the community to write about what the sculpture means to them now? That would be a way for that monument to have permanence but also be a current subject. You can have the community do the work.

Audience   Is it the responsibility of the person who commissions the art or the artist themselves to speak to the future, to try to perceive how a work might be translated generations later? How does that change the meaning? Most of the things I have seen in my life have a context of what was happening at that time.

TK   That's challenging—I think it's virtually impossible. I think about what my kids' world is going to look like when I'm dead and gone, and I'm convinced it will look nothing like what I think it will. The best we can do as contemporary artists is to attempt to speak to the people that exist with us in this moment in time. We'll fail, but we'll do the best we can. Then maybe, if we're lucky, something of that will connect to the generation that follows. But that in itself speaks to the reason for talking about this impermanence—it's actually humility. It's recognizing that my ability goes only so far, that I am going to miss some marks. I want to keep space open for somebody else to say, "You know what, Titus missed the mark here, but I'm going to follow up. This is going to be a conversation."

    Now we have a dialogue instead of a monologue—that's what most of our monuments are, these little monologues. In my own work, I try not to think about forever and permanence, or even this idea of marble and stone. When you put marble floors in your bathroom, do you feel like that can never go away? No—you think, Next season, I might change that. So there's an opportunity for us to rethink all of this, to stop with the idea that something being made in stone or bronze makes it permanent. And stop with the idea that that's what gives it value. If you do something like having people in the community write, it might last for a moment, but it might also impact somebody deeply. How is the bronze sculpture more significant, more permanent, than that impact? ▲

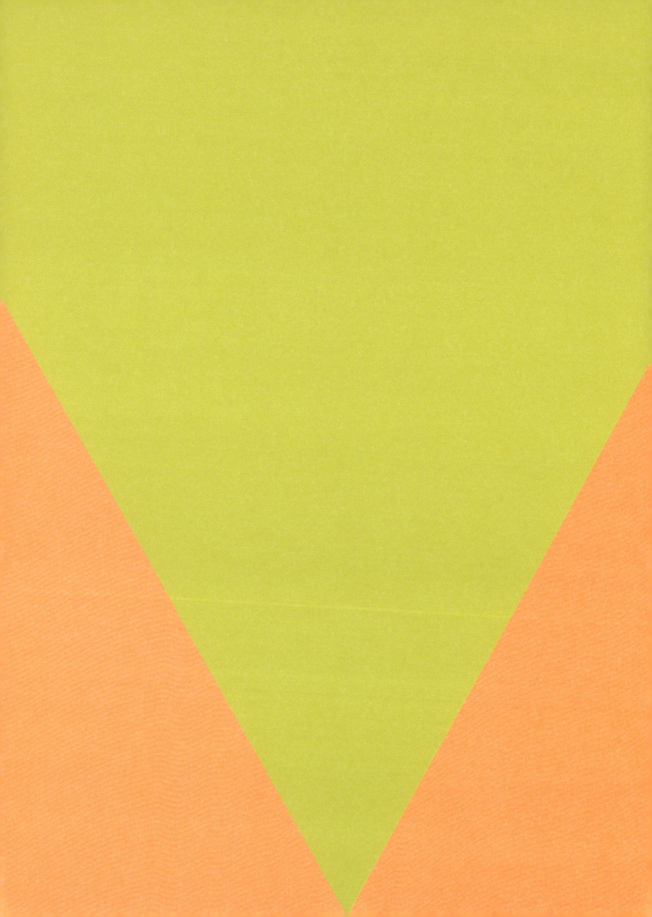

GET UP, STAND UP
Rights and Responsibilities of Citizenship

Sam Durant
"Every spirit builds itself a house, and beyond its house a world… Build therefore your own world"
2017
Wood, vinyl text
167½ × 539¾ × 377 inches
Installation view, Blum & Poe, Los Angeles

Sam Durant's deconstructed house references the first houses built by and for the first freed Africans in Revolutionary Massachusetts. Its wooden boards, originally used in the artist's 2016 outdoor installation *Meeting House*, in Concord, Massachusetts, include texts by prominent African American contemporary writers and poets while the work's title is based on an 1836 essay by abolitionist and transcendental philosopher Ralph Waldo Emerson. Durant has said of this work, "I've always been attached to different types of language…From vernacular signage like handmade protest signs that are so loaded with different kinds of meaning to mom and pop stores that advertise by hand lettering their windows to poetry and the power of words that aren't said and read between the lines."

Immigration, Discrimination, and the Journey to Citizenship

Minita Sanghvi

[1] Alan Houston, "Population Politics: Benjamin Franklin and the Peopling of North America" (working paper, Center for Comparative Immigration Studies Research Seminar, Dec. 2, 2003), https://escholarship.org/uc/item/6ps3x4fh.

[2] Catherine Rampell, "America Has Always Been Hostile to Immigrants," *Washington Post*, Aug. 27, 2015, https://www.washingtonpost.com/opinions/from-benjamin-franklin-to-trump-the-history-of-americas-nativist-streak/2015/08/27/d41f9f26-4cf9-11e5-84df-923b3ef1a64b_story.html.

For me, as for many immigrants, citizenship has been a destination, not a right. It is a long, arduous, and expensive journey. And during this time, one has the responsibilities of being a good citizen, but one definitely does not have many of the rights or even some of the aspirations of a citizen by birth. In the United States, we often consider ourselves the nation of immigrants. Yet discrimination and violence against immigrants and people of color have been woven into the very fabric of the American tapestry—from the early roots of our nation to the present day, and especially during the Trump administration. But this is not just a Trump problem: this is an American problem.

The Trump administration has focused on immigration issues in a rather harsh manner and has created a climate of fear among immigrants. However, one can find, at almost any time in the history of the United States, stories of discrimination and violence against immigrants, especially those of color or perceived to be of color. In fact, in many cases, Trump's present-day policies originated all the way back to our founding fathers.

Take, for example, the attitude toward immigrants entering the United States in the 1750s. Benjamin Franklin complained of the scourge of German immigrants polluting America and described Spanish, Italian, French, Russian, and Swedish people as having a "swarthy" complexion.[1] He wondered aloud, "Why should we, in the Sight of Superior Beings, darken its People?" While many European immigrants were not considered "white" at the time of their arrival in the United States (they were instead marked by their ethnicity), over time they have been folded into the Caucasian/white group—and many are proud to belong to that group. Today, the Trump administration believes that brown people from across the border are "infesting" the country like vermin. While he may be the only one to say it out loud, several politicians have used racial dog whistles on the issue of immigration. Often the discussion and debate about immigration is really about having the *right kind* of immigrants. Most politicians hide behind "procedural legalese of having the right 'papers,'" but the real message is that anyone "who doesn't look sufficiently white or sound sufficiently Anglophonic is presumed illegal until proven otherwise," says Catherine Rampell in her *Washington Post* op-ed "America Has Always Been Hostile to Immigrants."[2]

Another critical issue pertaining to immigrants today is often framed around the idea of "their culture and ideals versus ours." Benjamin Franklin's opinions toward immigration were largely based on the color of America; those of another founding father, Alexander Hamilton, were more focused on the ideals of the United States being polluted by immigrants. Hamilton, himself an immigrant from the Caribbean islands, noted, "The influx of foreigners [would] change and corrupt the national spirit;… complicate and confound public opinion; [and] introduce foreign propensities" into the American Republic.[3] Many people consider Hamilton a popular hero among immigrants, thanks in part to Lin-Manuel Miranda's famous Broadway musical, which valorizes the life journey of Hamilton from a bastard orphan in the Caribbean to a war hero and founder of the US Treasury. While Miranda's line "Immigrants, we get the job done!" sparks applause on Broadway, Hamilton in reality had a more checkered perspective on immigrants.

Apart from color and ideals, religion has also been a point of contention and a reason to discriminate against immigrants. While Trump's Muslim ban is a glaring example of present-day intolerance enshrined in policy, the Know Nothings, a national political party in the mid-nineteenth century, canvassed on the basis that Irish Catholic immigrants would threaten the livelihood and liberties of native-born Protestants.[4] In her op-ed, Rampell notes that Emma Lazarus's sonnet "The New Colossus" ("Give me your tired, your poor, / Your huddled masses yearning to breathe free"), mounted on a bronze plaque on the Statue of Liberty, was written "when the United States began implementing strict laws to keep the huddled masses out." She refers to the Chinese Exclusion Act, passed by Congress in 1882, as the "first major immigration law to restrict entry of a specific ethnic group, after complaints that the Chinese were polluting American culture and appropriating American jobs."[5] So it should come as no surprise that in January 2019, a professor at Duke University asked Chinese students not to talk in Chinese in the hallway, threatening them with withholding internships and awards.[6]

From the internment of Japanese Americans in World War II to the current ban on Muslims, from Benjamin Franklin's apprehension about the darkening of America

[3] "The Examination Number VIII," Jan. 12, 1802, Founders Online, National Archives, https://founders.archives.gov/documents/Hamilton/01-25-02-0282.

[4] Richard Carwardine, "The Know-Nothing Party, the Protestant Evangelical Community and American National Identity," *Studies in Church History* 18: 449–63.

[5] Rampell, "America Has Always Been Hostile."

[6] Harmeet Kaur, "A Duke Professor Warned Chinese Students to Speak English," CNN, Jan. 29, 2019, https://www.cnn.com/2019/01/28/health/duke-professor-warns-chinese-students-speak-english-trnd/index.html.

[7] Carrie Jung, "Harvard Discrimination Trial Is Ending but the Lawsuit Is Far from Over," NPR, Nov. 2, 2018, https://www.npr.org/2018/11/02/660734399/harvard-discrimination-trial-is-ending-but-lawsuit-is-far-from-over.

to Donald Trump's designation of Mexicans as "rapists" and Haiti, El Salvador, and African lands as "shithole countries," there is a long and mostly evident history of discrimination against immigrants woven into the fabric of the United States. And yet people continue to come.

I came in 2001. I came because, as a lesbian in India, I couldn't possibly exist under tyrannical Section 377, which deems homosexuality a crime. My dreams of a family, a healthy, productive life, and an ability to live as my honest, true self were impossible in India. So I came. I've lived, studied, worked, paid taxes, voted in elections once I became eligible, and fulfilled all my duties as a responsible citizen. In turn, I've been told to "go back home" several times. I've been told Asians are stealing "our" jobs, "our" spots at universities, "our" scholarships in med schools. In recent years, Asian Americans have sued universities like Harvard, claiming that they discriminate against Asian American applicants and assign too much significance to race, which forces Asian Americans to face a higher bar than other candidates.[7]

I've been asked to show ID on a trip within the United States to confirm that I'm here lawfully. I've been told that I speak very good English. (To which I politely respond that India, a former British colony, is second only to the United States in the number of people who speak English.) Some may describe these incidents as discrimination, others as micro-aggressions. Many believe it is just part of the path to citizenship. None of these experiences deterred me from applying for US citizenship the moment I became eligible, at a cost of $725 (nonrefundable) and two days of work, during one of which I renounced my Indian citizenship and pledged allegiance to the American flag.

But these expenses of time and money are just the tip of the iceberg for many immigrants. Numerous young people come here as students, and to apply for a student visa, they must be enrolled in a full-time academic program. To work in the United States, an immigrant must be sponsored for an H-1B visa. To apply for a green card, allowing permanent residency, the immigrant must then hope to win a lottery. Finally, after five years of being a green card holder, an immigrant will be asked to take a test to showcase their knowledge of the history of the United States, geography, and civics.

8 Clark Mindock, "US Workplace Immigration Raids Surge 400% in 2018," *Independent*, Dec. 12, 2018, https://www.independent.co.uk/news/world/americas/us-politics/ice-immigration-workplace-migrants-undocumented-immigrants-raids-trump-obama-2018-a8678746.html.

9 Tess Bonn, "Trump's Immigration Rhetoric Has 'Chilling Effect' on Families, Says Children's Advocacy Group Director," *The Hill*, Dec. 20, 2018, https://thehill.com/hilltv/rising/422371-childrens-advocacy-group-director-says-trumps-immigration-rhetoric-has-chilling.

10 Helena Bottemiller Evich, "Immigrant Families Appear to Be Dropping Out of Food Stamps," *Politico*, Nov. 14, 2018, https://www.politico.com/story/2018/11/14/immigrant-families-dropping-out-food-stamps-966256.

These regulated processes don't even scratch the surface of the trials and tribulations imposed upon illegal immigrants, refugees, and asylum seekers, or of those crossing the border who are separated from their children for months at a time. The Trump administration has weaponized US Immigration and Customs Enforcement, casting fear into the hearts of immigrants across the country. The number of workplace immigration raids—designed to find and arrest undocumented immigrants—surged 400 percent in 2018.[8] Immigration raid arrests declined during the administration of Barack Obama but have risen sharply since Donald Trump took office in 2017. So many communities are devastated by these raids, so many households torn apart. Families are scared of seeking medical help or of accessing government programs for fear of deportation. In 2017, for the first time in a decade, the number of children in the United States living without health insurance increased—from 3.6 million to 3.9 million, according to a recent report by Georgetown University's Center for Children and Families. Marylee Allen, the Director of the Children's Defense Fund, says that this increase is found especially in states like Texas, and squarely because of Donald Trump.[9] The CDF found that immigrant parents, especially those who are residing illegally in the United States, were hesitant to enroll their children in health care because of Trump's escalating rhetoric toward immigrants. For the same reason, many low-income immigrant families have stopped accessing governmental programs such as food stamps.[10] These are the harsh realities on the ground.

In contrast, it is easy, or thought to be easy, for citizens by birth to expect the rights provided to them in the constitution—unless of course you are Black, brown, LGBTQIA+, Native American. The rights of these groups have been trampled upon in numerous instances since the eighteenth century. Some have found justice; many have not.

Naturalized citizens like me are still figuring out where we stand. What is our place in the United States? What price do we pay for our citizenship? What benefits do we accrue from it, and do the benefits outweigh the costs? Indian American comedian Hasan Minhaj appropriately calls it the American Dream tax. Minhaj has captured the experience of an immigrant or naturalized citizen in a visceral way in his stand-up special *Homecoming King*. He relates to the audience an incident his Muslim family suffered after 9/11. They received an anonymous threatening phone call, and immediately afterward, someone broke the windows of their family car. While Minhaj ran out on the streets to figure out who had done this to his family, his father started "sweeping glass out of the road like he work[ed] at a hate crime barbershop."

In his stand-up routine, Minhaj says he ran to his father and asked, "Dad, why aren't you saying something?" To which his father looks at him and responds, "These things happen, and these things will continue to happen." Minhaj continues, saying that his father believes that this is the price an immigrant pays for being in the United States. He says, "My dad's from that generation like a lot of immigrants where he feels like if you come to this country, you pay this thing like the American Dream tax, right? Like you're going to endure some racism, and if it doesn't cost you your life, well, hey, you lucked out. Pay it. There you go, Uncle Sam. But for me, like a lot of us, I was born here, so I actually have the audacity of equality."

Perhaps it is appropriate, then, that this generation is "woke," becoming allies to their immigrant brothers and sisters, parents and grandparents, neighbors and friends. Citizenship can become a right only when there is equality. America is built on the dream of a more perfect union. And so the fight continues. ▲

Sam Durant

artist

Eric Gottesman

artist

Minita Sanghvi

professor

SEPTEMBER 24, 2018

Isolde Brielmaier — **There are various ways in which we conceive citizenship, and likewise there are various rights and responsibilities that citizenship may or may not encompass. We will engage those issues and consider visual culture's role in citizenship.**

   How would each of you define citizenship? And how do you think we, as a society here in the United States, generally define it? Is it a social right, a form of agency, a practice, a relationship of accountability between public service providers and their users, all of the above, and/or more?

Eric Gottesman — Yes to all of that. When I think of citizenship at the basic level, I think of belonging. Something that we've been saying as part of For Freedoms, an organization I cofounded that uses art to provoke civic engagement, is that citizenship is defined not through status, not through ideology, but through participating—whether you're a professor in a college or a student in a society or a citizen in a community or a member of a family. I think of citizenship as a form of active participation.

Minita Sanghvi — I'm going to differ from Eric. To me, citizenship was $640. That's the price one pays for the N-400 form to get naturalized, plus $85 for the biometrics test. That $725 is not necessarily accessible to all. And these costs do not include lawyers' fees, the two days that you have to take off work—one day for the interview and test and another day, once you're approved, to go and say the Pledge of Allegiance and become a citizen—or the business-casual clothes or business clothes that you have to buy to stand in front of a judge. A lot of people would want to actively participate and become citizens and cannot.

   For immigrants, there's this thing called "US citizenship" that you aspire to. My parents already had green cards, so it was a given that I was going to become a citizen; it was just a matter of time. But for a lot of people who come here as students or refugees or asylum seekers, it's a long path. It's a frustrating path, and it's an aspiration. We are participating in America in every single way all through that process, but we are not citizens. When we go talk to our representatives, we are aware that our voice means little to them because we are constituents but not citizens, and so we don't have the vote to say, "In November, I'm going to show you."

IB — **It's interesting that you boil it down to purely transactional terms. There are multiple layers here: point of access, privilege, and, for some people, the journey to get here. Even when you break it down in that way, it becomes quite a feat to tackle for many people.**

Sam Durant — In general, the idea of citizenship is different from the idea of rights, particularly the idea of human rights. Citizenship is something that can be given and taken away. Citizenship comes with obligations and responsibilities as well as rights. And we owe it to one another to live up to the ideals of what it means to be a citizen, to participate in the society that we have, fully, to give as well as take. If we don't, then we're going along with something that, especially these days, we might not be too happy with.

IB **It's one thing to hear about something, but it's another thing to actually see it. Images concretize a lot of what we think we know. In what ways does each of you feel that art or visual culture plays an important role? For example, Eric creates art and social interventions that address nationalism, migration, structural violence, and colonialism, among other themes. Sam's work frequently references US history and relationships between culture and politics. Minita's book** Gender and Political Marketing in the United States and the 2016 Presidential Election **looks to marketing, which includes the visual. Why choose to focus on art or visual culture as an essential vehicle to engage and inform people?**

EG Participation as a form of citizenship is aspirational, but participation and criticism can and should coexist. A lot of times, artists think about whether we are part of a system or outside of it. Participation can be a baseline of entry into something, but it doesn't necessarily suspend critical faculties or critical judgment. In fact, criticality is a fundamental part of being a citizen, whether or not that status is granted by some other authority.

For Freedoms is an artist-run initiative to increase civic participation and direct action on behalf of artists and arts institutions. In 2015, my project partner, artist Hank Willis Thomas, and I started the first ever artist-run super PAC to engage directly in the political process. We put our skin in the game in a real way: we were registered with the FEC and the IRS. But we were also acting as artists and performing the role of political strategists.

Over the last few years, we've run a number of different events and activations, hundreds at this point. We're in the midst of the 50 State Initiative, where we are working with two hundred arts institutions, museums, galleries, colleges, and universities and over eight hundred artists, including Sam and many others, who are doing billboards, exhibitions, and town hall meetings.

One of the goals is to make the claim that all art is political. Art is politics. And all arts institutions are in fact civic institutions. Why draw a line between them? It's all part of the same thing. Art can be a gateway for participation in society so that even people who are left out for one reason or another are making things. They are laboring and they are producing; and that is a way of valuing. If we expand the notion of what we consider to be citizenship to include creativity, then we start to get a clearer picture of what citizenship actually could mean.

IB **You're asserting that art has multiple points of entry. Accessibility is a vehicle, right?**

EG Yes. My practice prior to For Freedoms was very much about working within communities slowly. Over time, ideas would bubble up in various forms of creative actions. Sometimes, exhibitions look like so-called activism or political action, and sometimes I create other types of actions.

SD The work that For Freedoms does is a great example of why art is important. It's bringing imagination and creativity into everyday life—where it always is and it always was. If we think historically, art, making, expressing are fundamental human needs. The United States, only a little more than two hundred years old, is an anomaly in history. It's a completely commercial society, and it has sidelined creativity and culture and different kinds of expression and made us feel like they're not important and we have to constantly justify them, answering questions: Why art? Who needs art? I think it's the other way around, actually.

IB **Sam, you frame this culture as a commercial society and offer this idea that, in certain contexts, art constantly requires ongoing justification: maybe because it's hard to prove its return on investment. But your projects often engage and activate community and spark discussion and debate. That may not be a tangible return that you can deposit in a bank, but it has real ramifications and impact.**

Minita, can you talk about how you place emphasis on the importance of the visual as well as messaging and storytelling?

MS Politics is all visual. If Christine Blasey Ford decides to testify about how she was assaulted several years ago, you're going to have her and an all-male panel. That visual is something that's reminiscent of Anita Hill and her testimony from the 1990s. Those are the image bites that we talk about. They remind women, again and again, that they're second-class citizens. The year 1992 was called the Year of the Woman, but we haven't come very far. Especially in politics, and especially when it comes to gender, visual culture is critical in explaining and uncovering the layers of bias and sexism that still pervade institutions.

IB **That's relevant not only to the discussion on citizenship but also in a consideration of how individuals craft particular images of themselves. That image is often critiqued and pulled apart, especially when that visual is not upholding what we conceive of as proper or what a woman or person of color is supposed to project.**

When we think about individual political figures, and the way in which they impact our view of who is entitled to engage in citizenship or who is entitled to a voice, how do you think that impacts our view of particular issues?

MS One of the reasons that Donald Trump won was that he had a better marketing campaign. He was masterful. Hillary Clinton was doing political science; Donald Trump was doing political marketing. There's a difference between the push-and-pull strategies. She was doing more sales, a get-out-the-vote approach; he was pulling people in in a sort of blitz or branding media. When he said, "Build the wall," it was a very visual statement. You can immediately visualize exactly what he means.

And in some ways, for some people, it was picturesque. His notion "Make America Great Again" builds into nostalgia. He never tells us when America was great and for whom it was great. We all imagine this America that was great at whatever time we want it to be. The campaign and the marketing and the slogan were visual and so catchy. That was really good branding. Hillary Clinton's slogan was "Stronger Together." That's great, and I thought it was a better slogan, but it doesn't have the same impact.

Politicians who succeed are able to give this awesome visual to the people that's full of promise and hope. Barack Obama offered a "new, sunny day of hope" vision. It was visual; everybody could see themselves together with him. Hillary Clinton, unfortunately, just couldn't do it.

SD The amazing linguist George Lakoff has been very helpful in understanding how we communicate our values. He shows that we don't think rationally: we think in terms of metaphors; our thought is 90 percent emotional and unconscious. His book *Don't Think of an Elephant* is an example: just try not thinking of an elephant right now. When we refute an argument by using the same words, we are actually strengthening the idea we are trying to dispute. We need to use new language that reflects our values and just forget about arguing.

EG What is amazing about what happened with Trump's campaign is that people reacting against it made it stronger. The reaction against Trump became a political marketing tool. It made me think that he was a brilliant marketer. I was talking about this with Cuban artist Tania Bruguera, who says that he's *not* a brilliant marketer. In Cuba, people love Fidel Castro, but nobody loves Donald Trump. He just won. Her point is that there's a difference between winning our hearts and minds and winning a calculated game.

A lot of art is reactive, and I wonder if that's the power of what we have as a creative community, as an arts community. Is that where the value lies?

SD I completely agree. Another thing that Lakoff shows is how you strengthen the neural pathways in the brain when you repeat something. It gets stronger and stronger and stronger. The more you try to argue against another argument, the more you strengthen that argument. Lakoff says that we need to have our own vision and our own images, if you're a visual artist; or our own metaphors, if you're a writer.

MS That's one of the biggest problems the Democratic Party has today. They're struggling to find that vision. The big branding they had recently, trying to build off the New Deal and the Four Freedoms, was "A Better Deal," and I'm thinking, really?

IB **This notion of citizenship can impact particular communities. How do different political parties, specifically Republicans and Democrats, define citizenship? How are their ideas articulated visually within the political sphere?**

MS Shirley Chisholm, a Democrat, was the first Black woman to get elected to Congress. This was in 1968. The first Black woman to get elected from the Republican Party, Mia Love from Utah, was in 2014. The chasm between 1968 and 2014 tells you the story of race relations and the two parties.

One of my colleagues often says that Black and white are the only races that matter. But I see myself as a brown person. And he says, "No, no, race in America is just Black and white. If you're not Black, you're white." In the South, especially in the Bible Belt, that opinion does hold true. Bobby Jindal in Louisiana and Nikki Haley in South Carolina have managed that idea well. They were thought to be not-white enough to gain the Black population's vote, and they were white enough for the white population's vote.

"Morning in America" was one of the iconic images of Ronald Reagan's campaign. It was "morning in America" for some, but not for gay people—this was during the AIDS crisis. There's definitely a way these parties handle women, race, and minorities of different sorts. The reason why white people, including the white working class, Trump's base, get so agitated about immigrants is because of this notion that immigrants are getting more rights through citizenship and that this is somehow diluting their citizenship, and it's taking away their power as a citizen. Citizenship is about equal rights. It's about active participation for everybody, and both parties don't believe that.

EG It gets even more complicated when we look at the history of the parties and the fact that this president is not necessarily of the party that he won the presidency with nor is the party itself holding the same relationship to values pertaining to race as it was in the 1950s.

SD What do you think about the recent, highly publicized victories of young women of color? Are you optimistic?

MS Isn't it great that we have all these fresh and diverse voices? It's almost like we flipped the script. Fundraising is so much harder for women of color, but Alexandria Ocasio-Cortez is like an ATM machine. People are just sending her money.

EG A lot of these candidates—Stacey Abrams, Andrew Gillum—are coming out of a longer-term strategy on the part of progressives, through organizations like People For the American Way and others, to start building the kinds of pathways that the conservative movement has been building for decades. As artists, what are the ways we can build beyond the structures that we're mired in? That kind of creative thinking is a part of political marketing as well.

IB **Where do you identify the shortcomings of the United States in ensuring that citizenship means the same thing across political, economic, culture, class, or race lines? It's twofold: building these long-term pathways but at the same time recognizing that we have this notion of citizenship and whether you are or aren't one.**

MS The word *build* is interesting. These candidates—Ayanna Pressley or Alexandria Ocasio-Cortez or Gillum or Abrams—are winning almost despite the Democratic Party. They are winning because the people are saying, "We're no longer going with establishment politics." The Democratic Party is not building them; the Democratic Party is not allowing all voices to get on the stage. Right here in New York State, the party bosses chose incumbents in the elections. Then people got together and asked, "Why?" And they signed their own petition, and got signatures, and elected their own people. Across the country, people are finally fed up with party bosses deciding who wins. Eric, I disagree with you: the Democratic Party is not building candidates as a party; the people are building and making those pathways. That's where the real power is: that the citizens are wide awake. And the citizens are participating by creating pathways for these diverse voices that otherwise would not be heard.

IB **When you have these independent candidates who are building their own structures and pathways, it's not dissimilar from what artists are doing as they move beyond a reaction or response to create and execute a new vision and new contexts.**

SD The ability to solicit large numbers of small donations has allowed this phenomenon to become visible and have success. I've been spending a lot of time thinking about the effects of social media. It's such a powerful phenomenon in US culture now. I have a number of younger students at CalArts who don't have smartphones and don't do any social media. I think that's a good sign for our culture, and for our visual culture.

EG It's kind of a radical act now.

SD Jaron Lanier is a Silicon Valley pioneer; he started virtual reality back in the 1980s. His most recent book is called *Ten Arguments for Deleting Your Social Media Accounts Right Now*. A lot of things we know about—Cambridge Analytica and that kind of manipulation—but he goes into the details of how much you're being manipulated, even if you think you're just using social media for your professional life or as a convenience.

Grassroots politicians can raise a lot of money. Kids can donate a dollar. If you're really passionate about a candidate, you could donate a dollar by text message. If millions do it, that's a lot of money.

EG What if voting was available on your phone? That would change things. Even voting rights are being taken away and being restricted and battled over.

MS In June 2018, we found that your citizenship can be taken away, too. Trump and the US Citizenship and Immigration Services have started the denaturalization process. They can say, "Well, you are naturalized, but guess what? Not so much." In terms of voting rights, we consider New York a superprogressive state. But here in Saratoga, our polling booths don't open until noon. That's not access. Access is early voting. Access is polling booths open from 7:00 a.m. to 9:00 p.m. There are lots of different ways to participate for people who want to, but they don't have access. I would have liked to drop my son off at school and then go vote, but I couldn't do that because the booths were not open.

Active citizenship is an effort even in a place like New York. Forget places like North Carolina, where they're actively taking away voting rights, or counties where voting records are getting lost. Stuff like that only happened, by the way, in Black counties, not so much in white counties. There are so many pieces to the puzzle in terms of active participation and what that means and what people can and cannot do.

IB I also think of what we presume when we say *citizenship*. What the notion of citizenship actually encompasses varies. It's fluid.

SD If you look at other countries in the world and how they handle voting, there are some interesting examples. For instance, in Mexico, they vote on Sunday, so you don't have to worry so much about people being at work. In many countries, voting takes place over a week. In many countries, voting is mandatory and you're given a fine and a misdemeanor charge if you don't vote, including in Mexico. So there are a lot of better ways to handle voting. We probably have one of the worst systems possible in terms of empowering our citizens. But that's what you are saying: let's envision something better and try to fix this system in which voting only happens on Tuesdays.

MS It fundamentally changes American politics if everybody votes.

SD We have to figure out a message for that. A visual, a metaphor: we have to put our values out there in a way that captures people's attention and imagination.

EG As artists, that's where we're situated. I think of Joseph Beuys with Free International University. This radically open university was intended for, at times, combative discourse. Talk about feeling uncomfortable! But it was never sustainable. It was intended as a prototype for a potential participatory, democratic education. We can experiment with and carve out space for these things because we're creative or we're artists. Maybe this is the upside to the sad separation in American culture between artists as individuals apart from society: it carves out space for us to be subversive.

Audience Many museums aim to be a place for everyone but lean very clearly toward progressive thought. Are there any museums or cultural institutions that are doing things that lean more toward the conservative? What does that look like?

EG I read a statistic that Wyoming has the largest per capita ratio of museums to people. I think that's because there aren't a lot of people in Wyoming, but the state traffics in nostalgia—cowboy museums and so on.

IB If you cast your net wide in terms of how we conceive museums, you would probably find much more variation. But when you're talking about today's art and living artists right now, it's fairly safe to say, in general, that many artists tend to be more on the progressive side.
   Political leanings and ideologies may shift as you move further off the ground level in institutions, that is, when you start talking about leadership and the gatekeeping community, where decisions are made about what work to show or what exhibition will never be shown. We've seen that throughout history. But if you think about it, there are a lot of historically controversial exhibitions and institutional decisions that lean more heavily toward the conservative.

MS If you go to the Perot Museum of Nature and Science in Dallas and look at the fossil fuel section, it is not progressive at all. Texas is an oil-drilling state, and the museum is bending science. In Kentucky, there is a museum that promotes intelligent design. So there are museums that have a conservative viewpoint.

Audience   I'd like to add to that. It's not just what the leanings of the museum are, it's how the collections are used. I work at the Metropolitan Museum of Art, and we have people who come into the museum specifically to use the collections for a conservative bent. Even though things might be presented in a certain way by the institution, the public or the people who come in to do their own tours use the museum in ways that are more conservative-leaning.

IB   **Thank you for that insight. Any other questions?**

Audience   I'm a curator here at the Tang, and one thing I think about is the impact various projects I work on have on people. In participating in the For Freedoms activations, we're asked to measure the impact of our different programs. That's really hard to do. How do you measure the impact of the different projects that you engage in, whether that's art or writing or activism or something else?

MS   I'm a management and business person. The only way we measure impact is: Where's the money? Sales, profits, return on investment.

SD   As an artist, it's hard to make a quantitative judgment about the impact of your own artwork. Public art is a little easier to assess in terms of impact or feedback from larger groups; things like that are often built into the structure of the project. It takes mechanisms, it takes infrastructure, staffing to gather feedback. As an artist, I do it anecdotally and informally. Oftentimes other artists are the toughest audience. If you think that other artists respect what you did, or think it's valuable, that's pretty great.

     The artist Adrian Piper comes to mind. She's very clear about the impact that she wants to have with her work, which is to help people overcome xenophobia and racism. It's about trying to get you to step outside yourself and help you to see the fiction of race or of xenophobia. I don't know how she measures that, but the fact that she has these clear-cut goals for her work has always been inspiring for me.

EG   I feel strongly that the artist shouldn't be held responsible for measuring the impact of his or her work. It's an alchemical thing that happens, and it would be difficult to have to be accountable to explain that. But it's interesting when institutions start to engage in that conversation. What would the question be? In For Freedoms, we're trying to figure out how to frame a question for our partner institutions to ask. Maybe: When you walk out of this room, how are you different from when you walked into it?

IB   **The evaluation component for institutions, specifically museums, with regard to issues of reception and audience is incredibly important. We see ourselves as public institutions and, in a way, as similar to artists. You all don't create work to shove in the back of a closet; you create work to put it out there in the world. It's our job to help make that happen. But** our funding in many ways is contingent upon impact. If we're trying to get funding from public programming or exhibitions, we need to show that *x* number of people came through and engaged in a particular way. Measuring impact becomes trickier with some of the programming and presentations that have more of an ephemeral or temporal aspect to them. That's something that's nebulous in a way, but it is important for institutions, nonprofits, and others to be able to measure that.

Audience What's the difference between art and branding? Both can be visual. To me, it feels like branding is something where you have a specific goal, and you want to be able to measure it in some quantitative way. With art, maybe that's not necessarily the goal. As an artist, you wouldn't want someone to walk away from your piece thinking, Oh, this means I need to vote for this person because they are good and the other person is bad. You're not hoping that people will come away with such a direct message.

Sometimes I worry that those simple messages are the ones that get across more easily. And when we're talking about political campaigns, it can get you into this pessimistic state of mind because you think we can only talk about simplistic ideas. I like that you are talking about art going beyond that and not trying to combat simple ideas with other simple ideas. So where do you think the intersection between branding and art lies, and is that a correct dichotomy or distinction?

SD I think they're two totally different things. I mean, it's like apples and oranges. They're done for different reasons by different people. Not to say that artists don't use branding and branders don't use art. They do, definitely.

EG I agree with that in the sense that art is intended to open up questions. That's why this idea of measuring is a hard thing for an artist: maybe they'll go somewhere I didn't intend, and maybe that's better. Whereas branding is supposed to direct you to something—that's how advertising works. Do this, buy this, vote for this. In the context of labels and political brands—conservative, progressive—are artists progressive? Why are artists progressive? These are interesting questions.

I also want to challenge some of those brands as an artist and as somebody who believes that brands are constructed and that they don't really exist. It is getting increasingly hard to define what "conservative" means now or what "progressive" means now. A lot of those brands are used in politics to simplify and group us.

MS My wife, Megan, would say branding executives are artists who have sold their souls. And I guess that's the way I see it, too. ▲

CULTURE NOW
Appreciate/ Appropriate

Renee Cox
Missy at Home
(from *The Discreet Charm of the Bougies*)
2009
Digital ink-jet print on watercolor paper
31¼ × 40 inches
Tang Teaching Museum collection, purchase, 2019.9

"*The Discreet Charm of the Bougies* is a psychodrama. The star's name is Missy. She lives a very privileged life. She is very much self-aware, but she is very much alone. She's got a white maid, but she's blasé about it. It's expected, in a way. Throughout this series, you see her going from living in this depressive, unconscious state to becoming enlightened and realizing she can live a life of joy. Obviously, it's my own personal journey. Because for me, one of the key things was when I realized I didn't need anybody to validate me except myself." —Renee Cox

Exploring the Limits of Cultural Appropriation in Popular Music

Matthew D. Morrison

As long as cultures have (co)existed, there has been cultural appropriation. Since the 1980s, however, the term has emerged in popular discourse as a critique of the misuse of the cultural attributes or performances of one community by those who do not belong or cannot claim an immediate connection to that group. Many of these criticisms developed in response to the appropriation of Indigenous American culture by non-Indigenous people, such as the coopting of the Native headdress (which has specific ritual and communal meanings) by a sports mascot in a decontextualized or exploitative context (for instance, the NFL's Washington Redskins). Appropriation itself is an act that involves one entity taking possession or making use of the cultural property of another with or without their permission. Today, *appropriation* is a buzzword that is frequently used to suggest that the culture of a marginalized group has been "stolen" by a dominant one, generally in fashion, art, language, or music. But cultural appropriation is complex, and the implications of the term get especially murky when considering how popular music is made, performed, and consumed. I am interested in wading through a bit of this murkiness by drawing connections between the legacy of blackface minstrelsy and the current understanding of the impact and meaning of cultural appropriation within the history of popular music in the United States. Focusing on this history is my attempt to provide some clarity about what is at stake when we talk about cultural appropriation, as well as what is at stake when cultural appropriation occurs in the commercialization of popular music—a multibillion-dollar industry that continues to be shaped by Black innovative and creative practices.

  Within the exchange of culture, appropriation is unavoidable. Once one group begins to interact with another, language, food, customs, and other aspects of culture are impacted over time. But when we talk about cultural appropriation in the context of popular entertainment in the United States, we must also consider the history of colonialism and slavery that created the unequal conditions and power structures in which early Indigenous, African, and European traditions were "exchanged" in the development of US culture. Enslaved African Americans were considered property, and Indigenous people suffered genocide and were mostly stripped of their land and

1 It is also important to note that blackface minstrelsy was the United States' first export of popular entertainment internationally. In the mid-nineteenth century, the custom of blackface reached as far as Japan and Australia. Many other forms of American and Black popular music developed out of blackface (vaudeville, Tin Pan Alley, Broadway, blues, country, and so on), and these styles came to influence the development of popular music and identity worldwide.

2 Film, popular records, and radio programming all developed out of the economic and aesthetic impact of blackface performance. *Birth of a Nation* (produced by D. W. Griffith) was the first full-length US film and featured whites in blackface portraying stereotypes of Black people; "race" and "hillbilly" records were among the first commercial records marketed to audiences in the early twentieth century and developed their aesthetic and marketing practices out of blackface; "Amos & Andy" was one of the first comedy radio shows and became one of the longest-running and most popular of its type. This radio show (which became a TV show that featured the first all-Black TV cast performing in these roles) featured white men using blackface tropes and its sounds to perform stereotyped Black roles on the radio.

3 Perry A. Hall, "African-American Music: Dynamics of Appropriation and Innovation," in *Borrowed Power: Essays on Cultural Appropriation*, ed. Bruce Ziff (New Brunswick, NJ: Rutgers University Press, 1997), 32.

personal rights; thus European-descended Americans were able to engage with the culture of "others" from a position of authority that left them unaccountable for their appropriative acts. The structures of white supremacy that developed within slavery are the context out of which blackface minstrelsy, the first original form of American popular music, laid the foundation for the US entertainment industry in the 1820s.

Blackface began with white, mostly Irish American, men blackening their faces with burnt cork, dancing to tunes of British folk origin ("Jump Jim Crow," of about 1827, is one of the first popular blackface tunes), and performing their stereotyped interpretations of Black movement and dialect. Blackface minstrelsy continued to influence the growth of American popular music throughout the nineteenth century as other white ethnicities donned blackface and performed stereotyped roles like Jim Crow (enslaved "darky"), Zip Coon (urban "dandy"), and Lucy Long (cross-dressed "wench"). After Emancipation, women, African Americans, and other marginalized groups who wanted to enter into popular music were economically and structurally pressured to do so through this dominant commercial form of entertainment.[1] It is difficult to determine to what extent the earliest of these blackface performances contained actual representations of Black aesthetics, but it is clear that these minstrels performed and were often received (especially by white audiences) as though the performances reproduced accurate cultural (music, dance, language) aspects of Blackness. Black people were largely unable to challenge these racist caricatures or represent themselves on the popular stage in large numbers until the turn of the twentieth century, almost seventy years after blackface had already established itself as the driving force of American popular entertainment.[2] Black Americans were also largely denied awards (recognition) or rewards (compensation) for any contributions to popular music despite the counterfeit or real imitations of Black aesthetics that laid the foundation for the music industry.[3]

Within our cultural and legal understanding of property, we have not yet graduated from the idea that the aesthetic and creative contributions of African Americans and other minoritized groups belong to the public domain. In fact, copyright laws and notions of intellectual property are founded directly upon the belief that they do. The fact that Black people were considered property and had no ownership over their aesthetic innovations, during either the development of blackface during slavery or the Jim Crow segregation era, continues to impact how we think of cultural appropriation in the context of US popular music. These aesthetic innovations—which involve sounds, movements, and performance practices that are ephemeral but key in popular-music-making practices (such as the twelve-bar blues or the blues scale)—were deemed to be in the public domain and outside of copyright protection because they were interpreted by modern intellectual property laws as unfixed "ideas" and not as tangible "original works of authorship."[4] In short, the aesthetic innovations of Black cultural production often find their way into popular consumption through commercialization. This process takes place within an industry that was founded on the exploitation of Black performativity and the negation of Black aesthetic practices as forms of intellectual property under copyright law. It is important to note that this process occurs within the context of actual Black people being under- or devalued as humans and citizens, within the racist systems that have shaped society since slavery and the invention of blackface. Furthermore, non-Black people—particularly white people—are often rewarded and awarded for engaging in these exploitative practices by a market that is itself made up of customers with the financial and technological access to purchase and consume popular entertainment produced by a commercial music industry that is based in our unequal and racist societal structures—economically, socially, and culturally.

This is not to suggest that African Americans or other marginalized groups cannot culturally appropriate, that white people are the only ones who engage in this act, nor to argue that all cultural appropriation is, by default, a negative act. I raise these considerations to emphasize that cultural appropriation or exchange occurs within structures of power that must be considered when determining impact and meaning. Appropriative acts of cultural exchange can be reciprocal or exploitative or a mixture of the two, depending on who is appropriating whose material, the power relations among these groups, the channels through which the appropriation is disseminated, and who is doing the consuming.[5] When we speak of cultural

[4] The sheet music of the nineteenth century and the sound recordings of the early twentieth century are examples of "tangible" works that might be protected under copyright law. For more on this topic, see Gerald Carr, "Protecting Intangible Cultural Resources: Alternatives to Intellectual Property Law," *Michigan Journal of Race and Law* 18, no. 2 (2013): 364.

[5] Richard A. Rogers, "From Cultural Exchange to Transculturation: A Review and Reconceptualization of Cultural Appropriation," *Communication Theory* 16, no. 4 (Nov. 2006): 477.

[6] Hall, "African-American Music," 33.

appropriation in popular music, specifically, it does not always imply theft. But to act as though this exchange occurs outside of the history of cultural exploitation of marginalized groups by the popular music industry is to be complicit in a system in which, as African American studies scholar Perry A. Hall has written, "white-dominated wider culture absorbs aesthetic innovation, [as] it continues to avoid engaging or embracing the human reality, the very humanity, of those whose shared lived experiences collectively create the context in which such innovation is nurtured, maintained, and supported."[6]

The goal of the commercial music industry, from its founding until now, is to sell music. The players (executives, producers, artists, marketers) in this industry have relied heavily on the appropriation of Black aesthetic practices since the origins of blackface minstrelsy within a context of unequal societal structures and copyright/property laws that typically exploit Black innovation. It is up to consumers and creators to give careful thought to how their listening, purchasing, and borrowing practices are informed by a reciprocal or exploitative engagement with the actual people who are often the creative arbiters of popular culture in the United States yet who continue to fight for equal rights, representation, and justice within a system that has, since its founding, capitalized on and exploited its most marginalized people for economic, cultural, and political gain. As long as we (as a popular audience) continue to conspicuously consume popular music and entertainment without giving careful thought to our purchasing practices or to who/what we are consuming, the industry and its actors will continue to blur the lines between reciprocal exchange and exploitation. In this case, African American and other marginalized groups will continuously suffer grave and often life-threatening structural inequities throughout society while their cultural products lay the foundation for our collective sources of enjoyment and commercial entertainment. ▲

Jessica Andrews

writer

Renee Cox

artist

Matthew D. Morrison

scholar

Isolde Brielmaier **In an age where images, ideas, and sounds are widely accessible, the topic of cultural appropriation, particularly within popular culture, is a hot-button issue. How do we define cultural appropriation? To get to that, we have to define or identify how cultural appropriation does or doesn't differ from cultural appreciation. Do we have to even talk about who owns culture, or if somebody owns culture?**

Jessica Andrews I've written about cultural appropriation at *Teen Vogue*, and a lot of people look at me as the cultural appropriation police. I'm not at Coachella running behind people telling them to take off their feather headdresses— I don't do that. It's actually a really nuanced conversation. In the fashion industry specifically, it's about respecting other cultures and giving them credit when they inspire you. A lot of designers take inspiration from other cultures or marginalized groups and then won't acknowledge them. I say respect is the minimum. That's a basic courtesy.

And secondly, give who inspired you a seat at the table. When you're taking from a culture that you aren't a part of, it's not going to seem authentic when you don't have anyone in the room who represents that culture.

Lastly, you see a lot of stereotypes in fashion. That's a big part of how cultural appropriation offends. Designers will pull from African fashion, but it's safari with people running around in animal prints and the idea that they're all in jungles. If you've been to Africa or even read about it or Google-searched it, you know that's not the truth. It's a dehumanizing stereotype. And we've seen it happen over and over again in fashion. There was Gucci and Dapper Dan. And Dapper Dan wanted to be a part of the fashion industry.

IB **Can you give a quick snapshot about Dapper Dan?**

JA In the 1980s, he was embracing the logo trend that we see resurfacing now, and he'd do custom designs for affluent shoppers, who were mostly of color. He'd take logos from Louis Vuitton or from Gucci and incorporate them in such imaginative ways—nothing like what was on the runway. He's really a genius, and as someone outside of the fashion industry, he had a loyal following and so much support. But when the fashion industry got wind of his work, instead of embracing him and giving him an opportunity, they sued him and put him out of business. He was out of work for about three decades.

Fast forward to this year, Gucci puts a look on the runway in their Resort collection that is a clear copy of what Dapper Dan was doing decades before. And because social media gives a voice to people who didn't formerly have one in the industry, people called them out. You're saying his work is good enough to steal but not good enough to get him a job.

Once they were called out, to their credit, Gucci reached out to him and sponsored his atelier, which is now back up and running in Harlem. So it is a success story, it does have a positive ending, but you wonder, without social media, would that have happened? Those are the kinds of things that we are fighting for at *Teen Vogue*: to give marginalized people a platform and to hold designers accountable and make sure they give credit and make sure they're giving opportunities rather than cherry-picking from cultures and making money off of them while shutting us all out.

Matthew D. Morrison   I'm going to draw on the work of Richard A. Rogers, a media theorist who gives a basic definition of cultural appropriation that speaks to what Jessica has already pointed out. Rogers describes cultural appropriation as "the use of a culture's symbols, artifacts, genres, rituals, or technologies by members of another culture." We could think about cultural appropriation, as Rogers points out, in a number of ways. Often, we think about it as a system of exchange where there's some type of reciprocity being offered. As you said, after thirty years, Gucci is in conversation with Dapper Dan, and they have a reciprocal relationship now. Then there's cultural dominance. Those who are marginalized are retooling, or finding other ways to use, the tools of those who are dominating them for their own purposes. This is what Dapper Dan was doing prior to being admitted into the structures of the fashion houses.

And then there's cultural exploitation, which is what we are having the most direct conversation about today, where those who are marginalized, often Black and brown people in the context of the United States, are not only *not* given credit for work, but are seen as being *less than* by enacting their own cultural creations. It's this idea of appropriation to the extent of taking on that of what bell hooks calls "eating the Other," absorbing another's culture, another's practice, without dealing with the humanity and personhood of those folks.

There is not a way to talk about appropriation without thinking about the dynamics of power involved in that exchange since the moment of development of the West, which was developed out of the transatlantic slave trade and the genocide of Native peoples. Because of the globalization of American culture and entertainment in particular, appropriation is always on the table when we think about how things are absorbed in popular culture at large.

IB   **Even before we can talk about cultural appropriation, it's important to think about ideas of privilege and power—history, capitalism, imperialism, assimilation, how those come into the creation of culture, the consumption of culture, the spotlighting or upholding of one culture over another. Renee, I'm thinking of your work from the late 1990s, particularly the series that takes back the visual identities of superheroes.**

Renee Cox   When I was shooting for *Essence* magazine, they had me shoot somebody called Sunman, a superhero they were trying to develop. I shot him and it was great, and then I never heard about Sunman ever again. Fast forward, I'm in Toys "R" Us, I have two little kids, and I'm climbing over people and fighting with them to get Power Rangers. I'm walking around the store, and I realize there are no superheroes of color. What happened?

In my art practice, when I see there's a void, I feel like I've got to go in and do something. I'm really into the notion of revisionist history because, as we know, the victors have written the history books. If that's the case, then I should be able to go in there and write my own history. But I can't just pull it out of the sky. In order to give it credence, I went and did my research, and I came across the fact that back in the 1970s, there was a Black Wonder Woman named Nubia who appeared on two or three covers. I thought, perfect. This is the license for me to expand on Nubia. My character is Rajé, who is actually named Rage, but I knew if I named her Rage, I would cut off a lot of people because they'd see some angry Black woman.

I created scenarios and stories that I could illustrate using this character that I portrayed. There was an image I did called *Taxi*. Why? Because Black people couldn't get taxis in New York at the time. So I decided that I'm going to have this superhero actually picking up taxis in the middle of Times Square.

There's a reactionary point as well. Another work in that series is called *Liberation of Aunt Jemima and Uncle B*. Why was this needed? Because Aunt Jemima and Uncle Ben were the desexualized slaves that lived up at the big house. My superhero goes in there and restores them, and they become Roshumba, who was a supermodel at the time, and Rodney Charles, an actor. I drag them off of the box, and they join forces with me to cure the ills of the world.

In terms of appropriation, I consider it more about revisionism. I got the idea for *Liberation of Aunt Jemima and Uncle B* from Betye Saar because she did a liberation of Aunt Jemima. But I changed it around entirely. I can be inspired by other artists, I can have those same thoughts, but I can bring the idea into my time frame or my generation. That's when you have great, healthy art production: when you change it.

IB **There's some slippage in this fine line. There's straight-out copying or, in music, sampling. Art has been borrowing and morphing and shifting for decades. Even the medium of collage brings together all these disparate parts to form a whole.**

RC My latest work is basically collage, but I'm happy to report it's all my work. I don't cut things out and use other people's work. And yes, I'm saying that with a little bit of disdain: "You're so damn lazy you can't go out and create your own imagery." That's coming from the photographer in me who thinks, No, you don't get to just cut up my work and reconstruct it into something else. Do it yourself.

You have Titian and his *Venus*, Manet and his *Olympia*. Then I do *Olympia's Boyz*. I take the flowers and the slave and the maid and all of that out, and I do a similar but completely different piece.

IB **If there's an element of critique, does that make appropriation okay? Does the individual doing the appropriating have to match the culture that is being appropriated? Where do we draw the line? I want to identify this slippery space between appropriation and appreciation.**

JA One of the articles I've written about the Kardashians is about the idea that they invented boxer braids. "Boxer braids" are not a thing. They're cornrows. Boxer braids is a name that was given to them by a magazine that I won't name but is not *Teen Vogue*, and Kendall or Kylie was credited with making them a trend. When I first learned to braid, my grandmother taught me on a doll on the floor of our kitchen. She learned down South with grass stalks and passed it down through generations. This practice has been going on in our culture for years. And then to credit a Kardashian with inventing it—it's erasure at its worst. That's the kind of thing where it's copying and then totally ignoring a sector of people and saying, "Your hairstyle is okay, but your humanity isn't." That's the message that it sends.

MDM   What we often see when things go from a local, more communal space into a popular space is a dissociation from those with whom something originated. This is true especially when it's connected to the oral or bodily traditions of a community that's marginalized or seen as *less than* because of their actual creative performances.

I'm going to read a short quote from bell hooks's essay "Eating the Other: Desire and Resistance" that speaks directly to what Jessica pointed out, that is, taking these things on without considering the actual people that they're connected to. "To make one's self vulnerable to the seduction of difference, to seek an encounter with the Other"—in this case, if we're talking about the Kardashians, we're talking about the boxer braids, known as cornrows to Black people in America—"does not require that one relinquish forever one's mainstream positionality." So often the mainstream personality is in a place of dominance or privilege—again, a Kardashian. "When race and ethnicity become commodified as resources for pleasure"—when we take on these ideas or these styles or these performances or these aesthetics to find pleasure for our own selves—"the culture of specific groups, as well as the bodies of individuals"—the actual people, the human beings who exist in those bodies—"can be seen as constituting an alternative playground"—meaning that those human beings are commodities to be played with, that their cultural productions can be playthings—"where members of dominating races, genders, sexual practices affirm their power-over in intimate relations with the Other."

This goes back to Hottentot Venus, to the founding of this nation, to the founding of the West. Sarah Baartman, an African woman whose actual genitals were on display for a long time starting in 1810, was referred to as the Hottentot Venus. She had a particular posterior that was out of place to those who were watching her—the white colonizing gaze—and it became seen as exotic, as other, as animalistic, but that also became an inspiration for a whole damn fashion trend.

JA   And for Kim Kardashian's whole career.

MDM   Yes, the whole career, even down to replicating a photo of Sarah Baartman for her *Paper* magazine cover. So the dissociation from particular cultural resonances also becomes stereotyped onto those same bodies they are taking from.

Using Black vernacular English, wearing a hoodie, or wearing certain types of pants may look and sound and be cool on a body that does not actually have to experience the resonance of being a Black person in real time in this country: those are things that are always held next to one another when thinking about what it means to replicate or engage with cultural performances that are attached to a community that is then not able to claim ownership over those things.

RC   The Hottentot Venus, that also was about forwarding colonization. It's business, it's capitalism. It's like taking one group and saying, "Look at them, they look like crap," and then putting them on display and, for Sarah Baartman, showing her like that until she dies. It took almost two hundred years, until Nelson Mandela became president, to get her remains back to South Africa.

IB   **The business element is important because at the end of the day we are talking about consumption—commodification and consumption. In music, appropriation, or how you see appropriation as most commonly functioning—sampling and improvisation—has a long and rich history. It almost feels like things become more blurred.**

    Music is not just audio, of course. It becomes about the persona and the profile of the individual—think of Elvis. That's where the commodification and consumption component comes in because you're selling that whole package that encapsulates the sounds. How does appropriation come into play here?

MDM   For me, it goes back to Renee's work around Aunt Jemima and Uncle Ben. These images have had a strong hold for such a long time on presentations of Black women and men, and they stood in for actual Black people. Within the larger arc and history of American popular entertainment and consumption, we have blackface minstrelsy. Blackface minstrelsy is at the foundation of American popular music. With the continuing genocide of Indigenous peoples on these lands, with the enslavement of Black folks at the hand of white colonizers, you have a whole class of people, a whole race of people, who were erased, who were unable to speak for themselves. Property relations in the United States developed in relation to slavery, meaning that people were considered to be property. If a person is a property owned by another person, then the person who owns the person as property also owns their cultural possessions as property.

    At the same time that these human beings, Black people in particular, were considered property under chattel slavery, the very first form of original American popular music develops. Blackface minstrelsy began with white men, Irish American men mostly in the North, darkening their faces with burnt cork and performing English and Irish folk tunes in what they imagined were Black dialect, movement, and performance. So the first form of American popular music begins with an imagined performance of Blackness by white men in blackface. As time goes on, a whole industry of blackface minstrelsy forms, which becomes the base of theatrical entertainment.

    By the end of the twentieth century, we have copyright laws to determine what property value is assigned to any particular item, including music. It wasn't until 1976 that actual recordings were considered to be copyrightable material. The record was copyrighted so that whoever owned the record, the master usually, held the property value for that particular record. But the sounds on them were not protected, and the sounds and the movements that accompanied them were often created by Black people.

Almost all forms of American music in general and Black music in particular are about borrowing and pulling and re-creating and reproducing. Sampling became a different methodology when the technology was available to take sounds from one record and re-create them for another.

IB **And those sounds were not copyrighted.**

MDM Because the sounds on the records were not yet copyrighted. In 1978, "Rapper's Delight" becomes the first popular rap song, and it's a sample of Chic's "Good Times" where Sugarhill Gang essentially loops the bridge of it and raps over it. Later on, Nile Rodgers and those folks were like, "Hey, this is our record." But the way popular music developed in the mid-century was through larger record companies taking the records of smaller R&B companies, records by Black artists, and remaking them. This is how we got Elvis Presley and "Hound Dog" and the erasure of Big Mama Thornton.

Big Mama Thornton is the originator of "Hound Dog." She was a queer Black woman—an icon within the local community. But because the record that Big Mama Thornton created was not protected as property under copyright laws, as many of the cultural productions of Black people had not been at that moment, it was able to be taken, remade, repackaged. Also, look up Little Richard's "Tutti Frutti," then look up Pat Boone's "Tutti Frutti," then Elvis Presley's "Tutti Frutti." You have to think, Oh shit, is this what was really happening here? It's also an indication of what's going on today.

IB **Does it feel more clear-cut in music? In art and in fashion, it's still a bit nebulous.**

JA It's more nebulous in fashion for sure. Unless there's a design that you have copywritten, you don't have legal standing. But designs are copywritten only if you have the access and the resources to copyright them. When we talk about Dapper Dan, what standing did he have to sue Gucci? That is a huge fashion house with a whole legal department. If it wasn't for social media, the story probably would have been buried. That's why cultural appropriation is always about access and power. When you have a dominant group that has access to spaces that marginalized groups don't, you can steal from the marginalized groups easily and then make money off them. And they don't have standing to fight against it.

IB **I'm even thinking about professional sports. How many Indigenous communities have tried to sue the Cleveland Indians or the Atlanta Braves? They've failed because it takes so many resources to fight in that way.**

JA That's why I'm slow to criticize call-out culture. Sometimes if you're coming from a marginalized group, all you have is social media. All you have is your voice and your platform. A lot of times we've seen with brands, like with H&M and their photo of a monkey hoodie on a Black child model, that outrage makes them wake up and realize they need to fix a wrong. We didn't have that in fashion before. That's why so many situations were going unchecked for so long. But with social media, we're starting to see a shift.

IB **Can appropriation be a good thing? When is it okay or "acceptable"? Who gets to decide that it's acceptable?**

MDM When we think about cultural appropriation, it's always within a system. Cultural exchange is always happening within a system, a structure, a society. That's why, at the outset, I tried to outline cultural appropriation with various stances. One that takes into account reciprocity or reciprocation in some sense, and the others involve dominance or exploitation.

IB **That's a key element, the reciprocity.**

RC And credit. You've got to credit people.

JA You've got to credit.

MDM You've got to credit.

RC History is a good thing—to know where things come from. They didn't just happen yesterday.

MDM That's something that we get away from in an easily consumable Google era. Because it is a system, we often let the consumer off the hook. It's important to bring the consumer into the fold. One of the reasons that Bruno Mars is a star is that he's really good at what he does. He also comes from a lineage of R&B singing. He's done the work and done his homework. But there is also a way that Mark Ronson, his producer, who also produced Amy Winehouse, took from the sound of Sharon Jones and the Dap-Kings. If you love Amy Winehouse, then you would really love Sharon Jones and the Dap-Kings. But it's a feedback loop. The industry is trying to create and present things that they think will be consumed; and then the consumers either consume them or reject them.

    I taught a class on music, copyright, and intellectual property. If you go through websites of court cases, you'll see many cases against Beyoncé, Jay-Z, and others by folks who don't have as much money or by companies who bought a catalog and then say, "Hey, you used this one little thing, so you need to pay us $2 million." The litigation, the power, how people move around, and the credit make a huge difference. With Beyoncé and "Run the World (Girls)," her choreography was from Tofo Tofo, the brothers from Mozambique. But Beyoncé invited them to be part of the video—she didn't just take their choreography. Cultural appropriation is about power. It could also come from people of marginalized backgrounds.

JA A lot of times I am asked, "What's the difference between cultural appropriation and appreciation, and how is it appreciation?" I look at Beyoncé's Coachella performance, which was incredible. It paid homage to historically Black colleges and universities, which she did not attend. Going back to people of color being able to appropriate, she could be called out for appropriating HBCU culture. But she hired people who worked at these HBCUs to perform, and, after the performance was over, she donated money to the schools. The culture is acknowledged and respected and then you're giving back and you're giving them a seat at the table. That's appreciation to me. When you're robbing someone's culture and you're not giving anything back and you're not hiring them and you're not acknowledging them, that's when it becomes an issue.

RC   But did the greater public know that she was doing that at Coachella? All those white kids sitting up there…did they know about historically Black colleges and universities?

JA   They should have known.

RC   I don't think they knew.

JA   Once she did "Lift Every Voice and Sing," people were looking around saying, "Oh, I've never heard this song from her albums. What album is this from?" I'm thinking, I've been singing this song since I was a kid in elementary school. A lot of them didn't know, but the media did write about the history and the inspiration. And she acknowledged it. That information is there. A lot of times, with fashion designers, that information is not there. When you ask designers what the inspiration is, they'll never say people of color or marginalized groups. With Bantu knots, for example, people will mention Björk or Gwen Stefani, not the Zulu tribe. I do credit her for giving acknowledgment.

MDM   Be an active consumer, not passive.

IB   **Being active is crucial. It can take two seconds to find out about "Lift Every Voice and Sing," James Weldon Johnson, the Black National Anthem. Being active, educated, informed consumers is so important.**

MDM   These industries rely on us not to be.

JA   Fashion is always cyclical. There's literally nothing new under the sun. There's always an inspiration.

IB   **You can say the same for music and probably for art as well.**

Audience   For me, the gray area is important. This country is the gray area, and I am patriotic about the gray area, and I'm proud of the gray area. In acknowledging the origins of what made us a complicated tapestry—it's the most beautiful thing that's been invented. There's a song by the Coasters called "Down Home Girl." The song with "Lord, I swear the perfume you wear smells like turnip greens."

    In the song, an African American in a Northern urban setting is commenting on someone from the South. The girl from the South is trying to act urban-sophisticated, but he can see and smell that everything about her is "down home girl." It's an unbelievably great song with a funky beat, written by two Jews from New York, Leiber and Stoller. It's also a document about African American culture. It's from the 1960s, and it has everything in it: the Northern diaspora from the South, commentary about the urban and the rural. It's a beautiful and complicated song.

It has been sampled many, many times. The same people also wrote "Spanish Harlem," which Aretha Franklin sang. Nowadays, they wouldn't write that song. How do I wrap my mind around these songs in this context?

MDM But they do write those songs today. It's not really complicated because it's based in history. Take "Strange Fruit," which was sung by Billie Holiday. The text itself was also written by a Jewish American. At the turn of the twentieth century, the popular music entertainment industry developed out of Tin Pan Alley, primarily by Jewish American immigrants who came toward the end of the nineteenth century. It was developed straight out of the legacy and history of blackface minstrelsy. This idea of the Southern woman coming up North is a narrative that's already seen in the figure of Zip Coon.

"Zip Coon" is one of the first blackface tunes to help set blackface as primary. Zip Coon is also a character, this urban city slicker who is in the North posing as a dandy, posing as educated. You are meant to see him and think, "You're still a Southern plantation darkie like Jim Crow." So there's an ability for Leiber and Stoller, who wrote lots of amazing songs, to enter into these flights of fancy that bell hooks talks about. One can also absorb the styles, the rhythms, the sounds. But they were making a song to be a hit, a hit that would be read as authentic by Black performers.

There are also questions about authenticity, but, in the end, we still have the folks who get the credit, meaning those who get the royalties, who are the authors and the composers. The performers receive less than the composers. So it is complicated in the sense that it's a long history, but in the history of popular music, the actual act of ventriloquizing one's own self for another by non-Black folks is part of the basis of the construction itself.

Audience If you take "Hound Dog" from Elvis, that's clearly been appropriated, but how far back do you need to go before it gets really blurry? This relates to culture, to fashion, to art, in general.

JA With cornrows, there was a lot of talk about Vikings having worn cornrows. But in this country, there are Black people who are being kicked out of classes for wearing cornrows. There's definitely a reigning perception that if you wear cornrows to a job interview, you're not going to get the job. That's something that Black people face all the time. When cornrows are on Black people, they're stigmatized; when they're on the Jenners or the Kardashians, they're praised. So I start with the originating culture or the culture that something is most associated with. Especially if a group is stigmatized for a particular fashion, you have to think twice about appropriating it.

RC Forget the Vikings, go to Africa. We were the first people.

JA Who owns this thing from culture? There are Black people who have been wearing cornrows for decades in this country. It's not starting with the Jenners or the Kardashians or 2018. That's basic information. That's a Google away. But then you can go back into history and find out where something originated and how it became popular. I did that research for myself with Ankara print, which is popular in West Africa. I had a moment where I was really into that print and making it a part of my wardrobe, so I did the research and learned that actually, it was invented by the Dutch. It wasn't invented by West Africans, but it is something that they embraced and popularized, and it became associated with that culture. Colonization obviously plays into it as well.

RC   It's cross-fertilization.

JA   When I'm wearing Ankara print, I'm very aware of all the cultural connections that are wrapped into it, but I'm also aware of the stigma that's attached to it in this country because Black people embrace it in Africa.

Audience   You talked about reciprocity. In music, a lot of people talk about how if you're just being your authentic self, you can do whatever you want basically. But for someone who grew up in a world being socialized by appropriated culture, what comes out can be problematic. How do you think a person with a lot of privilege can approach music in a way that could potentially empower people? It feels like I don't have anything to give in music that's not stolen.

RC   Look at the Beastie Boys.

IB   **A lot of us are recycling through things and putting our own imprints on them. Our guests touched on the idea of not only reciprocity but acknowledgment and being informed, so that if you're DJing or you're painting or you're creating fashion, you know that there's a rich history. Inform yourself. Know your history and be able to articulate it. That's a good starting place.**

RC   But tell your story. If you're white and privileged, tell it, find a beat for it.

MDM   Reflect on your taste. That's part of being an active consumer. There are ways that certain things are fed to us because the industry is relying on us to consume them passively.

IB   **And they don't think we're going to think on it.**

JA   And we don't.

MDM   Be thoughtful about what you listen to. If you find yourself always listening to the top 10—because that's what's streaming, that's what's on rotation, that's what's on the playlist, that's what's at the party—you're getting what's being fed to you quite often. Go beyond the top 10. Think about what you listen to and why, and in a way that it comes from your own vantage point of positionality or privilege or what have you. Then talk to people about these things. Talk actively.

RC   And also consciously, because there's a lot of negative stuff out there that is basically poison for your ears, your eyes, everything else. And people call it entertainment.

Audience — Matthew referenced bell hooks, and that made me think about a topic she often discusses: being enamored with the oppressor's gaze. What are the ways in which oppressed groups internalize the ideas of cultural appropriation?

RC — If you're talking about the gaze, I just throw the gaze back at you. I'm not going to be objectified. My work is always engaged and always looking back at the viewer. You don't get the opportunity to judge or to say whatever you want. That's been part of my practice since the very beginning—I'm not interested in being anybody's victim. If anything, I want the power and I want to own that power and I want it to work the way I want it to work, just like others before me did. I take a note from them. I'm not pandering at all. You can just give it back. You own it. You own yourself.

JA — Knowledge is so wrapped up in power, and a lot of what I try to do as a writer is to educate. If there's an instance of cultural appropriation, I'll go back to the originators and talk about its history and educate readers about it. These things aren't being taught or talked about, and I'm in the perfect position with a platform to bring that topic to a national conversation.

RC — We talk about the consumer. But really, what does the consumer know? You're asking a lot of the consumer to start digging through and trying to find information. The world is not geared for you to do that, either—in fact, it's the polar opposite. The world says not to do that. That way you can keep consuming, and you're not thinking about it. But you have a responsibility.

As an artist, I have a responsibility. Some artists say they don't have a responsibility. Some artists say, "I'm not a Black artist," whatever that means. I take issue with that. I'm Black and I'm proud to be Black. I'm not going to sit up here and tell you, "I'm just an artist." Everything that I do revolves around my Blackness. Why shouldn't I own that?

Audience — Jessica, you have educated yourself on the histories of West African textiles, but a West African woman walking down the street who sees you and identifies you as American could easily say, "She's appropriating. She doesn't appreciate my culture." Does appreciation have to be only on the inside? If not, how do you express your appreciation while still wearing those kinds of fabrics?

JA — Because I'm a writer, I express appreciation by always writing about it and educating people. Even if it's something where I'm not in my professional capacity, I'm just out and somebody remarks on the skirt, I'll say, "Oh, this is Ankara print. This is where it comes from. I bought this garment when I was in West Africa," and I'll share that information and really embrace it. Not everyone has to do that, but that's what I do, and that's what makes me feel comfortable when I'm participating in anyone else's culture. This includes food, too. I went to Thailand and learned to cook peanut-sauce dishes. When I have people over and I'm making dinner, I'll explain the history of what I'm making.

Culture is so fascinating to me. There's such a beautiful tapestry, especially in this country, and you can't get caught up in the negativity and the racism and the bigotry and the xenophobia. There are so many people who participate in other cultures in a way that is respectful, in a way that pays homage and offers acknowledgment.

RC It's totally about paying homage. My dog's name is Dogon, and people say, "What's the name of your dog?" And I say, "Dogon. They're this ethnic group in Mali. They discovered the Sirius star long before Western astronomers," and I say this whole thing about the star system and where they felt their ancestors came from. And people are blown away. I do that in the Hamptons all the time on the beach. I give people an entire freaking history lesson on the Dogon each and every time. I feel like it's my responsibility to do that. I'm not going to let them walk away and think, oh, that cute dog's name is Dogon. And I say, "Okay, now that I gave you that little background information, look it up."

JA And people do look it up. That's how information passes. It's storytelling.

Audience A discussion at large, especially on social media, has been about the separation of an artist and their art in relation to an artist's negative actions. Do you think it is an ethical decision to separate an artist and their art in our consumer-heavy society?

MDM Unless you can split a person into pieces, it's not possible. The artist exists. The person exists in society in the world that they live and create in—even if they sit inside a box for ten years. Harriet Jacobs, an enslaved woman, was isolated in a crawl space for seven years; later she would write a memoir. It was still reflective of what was happening in the world around her. So an artist declaring that their work is "apolitical" or "separate from" or should just "be seen as art" is bogus: it carries political statements and it's made by a human being who is living in this world and society in real time.

IB **It's a multilayered question. There are ethical issues that arise when you have an artist who, as an individual, is problematic. You also have their cultural output. There are ethics involved: How could this person who did X, Y, and Z, create this? At the same time, as a creative person, once you put your work out there, it doesn't exist as just work. It exists as your work coming from you as a creative cultural producer and individual. Many people would say it's difficult to separate the artist from their art because the creative output has the imprint of the creator.**

Audience This is a nuanced question. What about people who are racially ambiguous or white-passing or are of two different races or have grown up with a culture whose creations they're using but don't get the flack of the stereotype that other people do? Halsey, for instance, is white-passing and received negative feedback for wearing braids, but she's part Black.

MDM People have to exist in their own bodies in the way that they feel they belong—which also comes with dealing with one's own relationship to an awareness of both privilege and the oppression that one carries simultaneously. And those things can vary depending on where you are, who you're interacting with, and what's happening.

Because colorism is about reception, it's also about understanding how people are perceiving. So that means recognition of whether someone is white-passing is required in that public sphere because there's also a claiming of a certain Black ancestry publicly. There are concerns about capitalizing on the "one-drop rule" without actually engaging with both the privilege and the difficulty of what it means to live in that ambiguous racial space.

Audience I'm Dominican and Puerto Rican and when I see someone who's not Dominican or Puerto Rican rocking a *chacabana*, I think it's interesting that people think it's fresh and it's cool. When I talk to my parents about it—my father is an immigrant from the Dominican Republic and my mother is a child of immigrants—they are happy that people like our culture. I don't know how to respond to that—we're coming from different viewpoints. My father's a working guy. My mom is working. We're on a college campus talking about these things. How do I respond without seeming uppity?

MDM Herman Gray's essay "Subject(ed) to Recognition" hits on the difficult part of what you're saying, especially being in our neoliberal consumer commercial culture. What does it mean for people to gain visibility but that then becomes another way of consumption and erasure? The essay takes into account what it means for people to see themselves represented or appreciated in any space, which makes a difference when they have been so marginalized or jettisoned. So there's great value to that recognition that your folks have.

IB **History is important and it's incumbent on those of us who are younger to acknowledge that. My father comes out of a colonial culture in East Africa. Your parents had a different experience than you did. What may seem like a step toward positivity or a step toward assimilation for their generation could seem undesirable to you and me, but that doesn't minimize it or make it less than.**

There's a way that you can have a conversation with questions: "When you came and you wore the clothes that you wore, what did people say? What was the reception? What was the perception?" You might be amazed at some of the similarities between your parents' experiences and your current-day experience. It's a way of listening and educating yourself. We think Black Lives Matter just appeared, but it was preceded by the civil rights movement. It's educating yourself, and it's also listening to your parents' experience. Then work to establish that lineage from then until now and share your experience. It's about having that conversation with older generations where you actually have an opportunity to extend lineage. ▲

ON NAVIGATING FORGIVENESS, REDEMPTION, AND REJECTION

Alexandra Bell
A Teenager With Promise
(from *Counternarratives*)
2017
Ink on paper, wheatpasted to building

Alexandra Bell's *Counternarratives* series appropriates, annotates, and edits *New York Times* stories to reveal the underlying racism perpetuated by the news media's choices in images, headlines, and language. Bell wheatpastes her revisions in public spaces, encouraging passersby to look more closely at what they consume. She has said of the project, "Black communities, gay communities, immigrant communities feel a lot of media representations to be inaccurate, biased. There's a lot of reporting around police violence and Black men, and I realized a lot of the arguments that we were having were about depictions. I started to wonder, how different would it be if I swapped images or if I changed some of the texts… This isn't a grammar exercise. I'm really trying to see if I can disrupt subliminal messaging about who should be valued."

Is Forgiveness Enough?

Lyle Ashton Harris

Forgiveness is not really about the other person. It's really about yourself. —Jacqui Lewis, Senior Pastor, Middle Collegiate Church

More than fifty years ago, Martin Luther King Jr. embodied and espoused the philosophy that forgiveness is integral to liberation: one could not forgive another without looking at oneself. His central ethic of love required thinking about truth and reconciliation. As someone who has been in recovery for the past twenty years, I have had an opportunity to reflect on the act of forgiveness and whether this necessary healing work, repair of the psyche, is a way to deal with larger issues.

One almost has to forgive others in order to heal oneself. I find forgiveness necessary, especially for Black folks collectively, so that we don't fall into madness. It is difficult to accept major transgressions, especially around white supremacy violence (past or present), homophobia, xenophobia, and gender and trans violence. At the same time, accountability is equally necessary. My family has ties to Mother Emanuel AME Church in Charleston, and I often reflect on the 2015 attack there. The congregation forgave even though no one took accountability for racialized violence and a past climate that encouraged a neo-Nazi to shoot up a historic church. Was forgiveness enough? Henry Louis Gates Jr., in his recent book *Stony the Road*, brilliantly charts the uncanny, disturbing link between the white supremacist reaction to the nascent political agency of newly free men and women during Reconstruction and the neo-white supremacist reaction to Barack Obama's presidency.

The history of Black familial, communal, and political life in the United States has been one of acceptance, healing, forgiveness, and activism. I don't think we would be here today if we did not have that healing as part of the core of what it means to be alive. The forgiveness mustered by the churchgoers at Mother Emanuel is in itself a radical political gesture of remembrance and bearing witness. Sacrificing private grief in favor of public memorialization requires deep emotional labor. What has been the cost of that emotional labor to our collective and personal bodies? Is there a way to transform that emotional energy into a beacon for the next generation? ▲

Alexandra Bell
artist

Lyle Ashton Harris
artist

David Karp
scholar

Isolde Brielmaier **In these trying times, an open conversation about rejection, redemption, and forgiveness resonates across all communities, cultures, and perceived boundaries. We all make mistakes. But how can we learn from them? What does it mean to live in the gray and to allow ourselves to take a more fluid approach to how we see others, to how we see ourselves? To whether or how we choose forgiveness?**

Let's start with the basic concept of forgiveness. Is it a concept? Is it an action? It feels like a long and ongoing process that dates back hundreds, if not thousands, of years. Is it passive or reparative? Does it set you free? Does it require redemption? Is it simply a process of letting go?

David Karp It's a huge concept. I would start with the simple cultural formula we all know: if I accidentally spill this glass of water on you, you say, "Ouch" or, "Ah." And then I say, "Sorry." And you say, "It's okay." That's the cultural script we all know. If we deviate from it, it's almost surprising. The forgiveness doesn't come if I haven't asked for it in some way. It's pretty easy to forgive me for a mistake or unintentional accident, one that wasn't particularly painful or didn't ruin your clothes and cause a terrible mess. That formula is pretty easy.

IB **Does this formula extend across cultures, beyond the United States?**

DK The way the ritual plays out will vary, but the necessity for humans to get through difficult moments is universal. Of course, it gets harder to forgive: the worse the transgression, the more complicated forgiveness becomes.

Alexandra Bell Interpersonal forgiveness is one category, that is, if I tell a secret of yours or something like that. I can apologize, and you can accept that apology. As we start thinking about institutions, we get to a different place. I think the word *forgiveness* should not really be part of the conversation. I'm starting to think more about acknowledgment and engagement, because when I think of forgiveness, I think about absolution: "It's okay," "Let it go," "I'm moving past that," or "I'm working past that." I don't think that that's the case when you're thinking about bigger transgressions like, for instance, racism.

Lyle Ashton Harris I want to share a quote on forgiveness. I'm reading from Caroline Myss's *Defy Gravity: Healing beyond the Bounds of Reason*:

> Forgiveness is a mystical act, not a reasonable one. Forgiveness is a challenge meant to cleanse the windows of your mind, particularly those through which you can see only your need for personal justice. You can't see anyone else's pain through these windows, because, like mirrors, they reflect only you: you are the center of the universe, yours is the only pain that counts, and all that is just and fair should be based on what serves your life.

Also, a minister, Jacqui Lewis, at the progressive church I attend on the Lower East Side, has said that forgiveness is not really about the other person. It's about yourself. You might not accept a major transgression, like a deeper level of historic violence, but one almost has to forgive as a way to heal one's own self.

IB **That segues into the next question: What is this first step? David, your work has spanned a broad range of situations.**

DK It seems to me that there are parallel pathways for forgiveness. One is interactive, like I described. The other is personal and private, which is not about the other person or the system that was being unjust. It's about your own personal process and coping and transformation, whatever that may be. First steps can really vary depending on what the goal is. Some people are motivated by that personal healing journey that's independent and has nothing to do with the other side—the side that caused harm—and everything to do with either an inward journey or an affinity group, your own community that you do the work with. So that's one first step. Another first step would be interactive: I can't move forward unless I hold you accountable in some way. I can't forgive you unless you deserve the forgiveness.

IB **How much does accountability play into forgiveness, particularly when you're talking about larger issues of racism, extreme violence, genocide? Can accountability and forgiveness occur simultaneously?**

LAH I don't think we live in a world where those two are separate or one can make a distinction between them; as Martin Luther King Jr. said more than fifty years ago, it is integrated. One could not forgive the other without actually looking at oneself. That was the ethic of love in his platform. Think about truth and reconciliation in South Africa, Rwanda, Tibet. How do we do the necessary healing work as a way to reimagine, let's say, being prepared to deal with these larger issues?

AB The word *forgiveness* is a struggle for me because it feels like this final thing, like a period. And I always hear that if you forgive someone, you're freeing up yourself, and I wonder, in the absence of forgiveness, isn't there something else, another emotion that may be sustainable? It's not outright contempt or hate, it might not be fully active rage, but it doesn't mean that there's forgiveness. Accountability is a continuous, active thing. I don't know if forgiveness is required for accountability to exist.

IB **Alexandra and Lyle, how do these ideas relate to your artistic and scholarly practices?**

LAH I grew up in the 1970s, and, as a child, I had the opportunity to live in East Africa after my parents divorced. My mother took my brother and me to live in Tanzania, in Dar es Salaam, for a couple of years. There's something about being an African American in a Black African country—you cannot imagine what that meant for someone like me as a child, despite the fact that I come from a robust family. There is a particular sensibility that has resulted—having an openness around the heart.

There's an anecdote I'd like to share. On the desk in my living room is a letter from my late father's wife's lawyer. It addresses a small inheritance to my brother and me, and it relates to forgiveness in a certain sense. After my parents' divorce, my father and I didn't see each other for at least twenty years. I attempted to go see him about ten years ago, and he wasn't able or he wasn't willing to open the door. So we had a difficult relationship, and a lot of my difficulties in life have been about that primary relationship. I was resurrecting and sacrificing the "father" in my relationships with other men through aggression, etcetera, with my own self. I had to go through the act of forgiving myself as a way to open up my heart to accept my own self and to accept other people, particularly Black men. That's a life process, a life journey. When my father died, I was in Paris for a show at the Pompidou, and I called my mother in South Africa. We didn't have any expectations, but we learned there was an inheritance. What did it mean to be open to that? I wouldn't have been ready without having done the necessary healing work on the psyche.

I've created different types of work. I have explored issues of identity and sexuality, but there was something about the healing, the interior work, that allowed me to be there for others and not to annihilate others because of my own primary sense of fraction.

IB **Thinking about this in relation to some of your earlier work is eye-opening.**

LAH Isolde is referring to work that explores issues of the body, sexuality, gender. In 1994, I was in a show at the Whitney Museum of American Art called *Black Male*, curated by Thelma Golden, who is the renowned curator and director of the Studio Museum in Harlem. The work was highly controversial.

What did it mean to be young and queer as part of a show and to still be the personification of a faggot, if you will? Do I take that energy of violence and turn it on the self, or how do I transform that energy as a way to be a beacon for the next generation? I think about Thomas Lax, the young Black curator at the Museum of Modern Art. What did it mean for him to go to the Whitney and see *Black Male* and see a queer Black man in full glory on the wall? So although I might have experienced trauma, what does it mean to pay forward through the act of making work, through the act of the sacrificial?

AB My work actually deals a lot with rejection. I'm interested in looking at language and imagery and media and deconstructing dominant narratives around marginal communities.

I have two series right now. *Counternarratives* involves me marking up and reworking headlines and articles from the *New York Times*. The second series looks at the Central Park Five. In April 1989, a twenty-eight-year-old investment banker was jogging in Central Park in the evening, and she was raped and attacked. Five young boys were sentenced to jail. They served between seven and thirteen years before the real perpetrator, Matias Reyes, a serial rapist, came forward. We now know that the confessions of these five boys were coerced. And many of us knew then that their confessions were coerced. But later, the convictions were vacated.

I'm looking at a lot of the reporting around that. The boys are referred to as a "wolf pack." So my work isn't at all about forgiveness: it is really about rejecting these narratives. I'm not interested in forgiveness or absolution in that sense. My work is oftentimes either a pushback at something or a protective gesture toward members of a particular community.

I'm interested in creating, through art, ways of equipping people to be able to critique media in a responsible way. There's this idea that something happens and it's over and done with. But looking back and digging through certain events and drawing connections between then and now is interesting. You see a lot of repetition in the way things are reported.

What's been difficult for me is to think critically about whether forgiveness has a place in my practice. The healing is very much in feeling that I have agency to say that this does not apply or there's something wrong with this or this is incorrect. I can do that at institutions. The first work of *Counternarratives* features Michael Brown. I'm trying to deconstruct the original *New York Times* article on Michael Brown and Ferguson, Missouri. Michael Brown and the officer who shot and killed him, Darren Wilson, had parallel articles on the front page of the *New York Times*. This was a problem for me because it suggested that they were peers. The work that I'm doing is trying to turn that on its head. When I strip that piece down, I leave people with: there's a white cop who killed this Black kid, there's a Black kid who was killed by a cop. It's the bare bones.

When I hung up a large print featuring this story, I did it anonymously. When people found out it was my work, they said to me, "I needed that." They didn't forgive the *Times*; they needed to feel like somebody hijacked the page and rejected what had been such a dominant, aggressive, and repetitious narrative about Black youth and police violence. The work that we can do doesn't involve forgiveness; it is about sifting through things and finding a way to see them differently.

IB **The materials of Alexandra's work, news stories, are persisting and continuing to unfold. The Central Park Five, now the Central Park Exonerated, settled with the City of New York in 2014 for more than $40 million. I'm not sure of the impact of spending ten years in jail. But the narratives are ongoing, and if one case closes, there's another case or incident or story that we can expect to unfold.**

AB Although I've never really thought about my work in the context of forgiveness, or at least not with that word, it has been important because the work is about race and race relations. People want a moment of apology. The *Times* has the Overlooked series, where they're publishing obituaries of people who have been overlooked. I commend this active excavating. You have to continue to do these things.

Newspapers used to have festive articles about lynching. They're referred to as "Negro barbecues" or "lynching went off as planned." They're very passive; they didn't take an active stance against lynching. So you now have papers writing these editorials, saying, "We did these bad things." The *Montgomery Advertiser* published an apology about how they reported on lynching. That's great, but I don't necessarily think it requires that I forgive those past actions. In fact, the onus is on the paper to continue to do better. What good are the best apologies unless they change the behavior?

DK I want to throw out one concept that a colleague writes about: earned redemption. It speaks to the notion of a newspaper losing the trust of the community through the way that they control a narrative and earning their way back into that trust. Restorative justice is about people getting to tell their stories and not have their stories told about them or for them. It's about creating the conditions where it's possible for someone to take responsibility for harm they've caused. Almost everything in our culture is designed to ensure that someone denies responsibility. In every context, we're told, "Say nothing, because if you do admit it, you're just going to get hammered for it." There's no real incentive to take responsibility. We see this every day in the #MeToo movement—denials because no one can accept the label that comes with being a sex offender or around racism. People go into this denial mode because they can't entertain rejection, another word in tonight's panel title.

IB **People skirt around or deny because they're afraid of being rejected. That's maybe at more of a one-on-one level or a group and community level. But then I think back to history, to racism or genocide. One of the first times I heard about restorative justice was with Rwanda. Is it denial because they're fearful of rejection?**

DK Rwanda is a perfect example where, postgenocide, thousands and thousands of people were incarcerated for horrible, horrible crimes. At some point, the government had to let people go; they just couldn't afford to incarcerate in the way that they did. They were terrified about what would happen if they released people back to their villages or if the conflict resurfaced because of retaliation. They needed a mechanism to reintegrate people into the community. Gacaca courts were the mechanisms to create conditions where it was possible for someone to say, "This is what I did." To ask, "Is there a place for me in this community?" The courts offered people a way to navigate coexisting. They don't have to be friends and they don't have to forgive and forget. There's still accountability that's needed. But it's a huge undertaking.

LAH There's illness, so there's pathology. Racism has consequences, such as what happened in Charleston, at the Mother Emanuel AME Church, in 2015. We have to look at the models where there has been healing. If you think about the history of Black familial life in this country, it has been one about acceptance, healing, and forgiveness. We wouldn't be here today if we didn't have that as part of the core of what it means to be alive today.

Looking at the horror of all the people who were killed in Charleston, I see there is a direct link to my family as my grandmother attended Mother Emanuel until 1923 before moving to New York. I'm interested in an analysis of what it took to summon the forgiveness to be able to go on, to be able to resurrect a healing modality as opposed to total chaos. It's important to acknowledge that force.

DK The church was acting out of faith through a personal journey of forgiveness. That's independent of the shooter, Dylann Roof. They weren't asking anything of Dylann Roof in their forgiveness journey.

LAH They were asking the country and the world to witness in a similar manner to Emmett Till's mother, who sacrificed her son to ask the world to witness. That's not personal; it's political, a radical political gesture.

DK We're pretty good at holding resentments and letting them build. And right now, we mostly don't have ways for people to work through these issues. I teach about restorative justice and do research, but I'm also part of a team that works with different communities, campus communities, K-12 schools, to use restorative practices. We got a request from a Texas university where a fraternity member was in a chat with his friends, which was meant to be a private chat, but it got out because of social media. He's a white guy, and the things he was saying were awful: how it would be great if Trump would allow people to hunt illegal immigrants and they could buy hunting licenses and that would generate revenue for the government. It feels pretty unforgivable.

Step one was the behavior. Step two was the outrage. There were demands that the university take action and expel this student to demonstrate that the university does not tolerate this kind of hateful speech. The university consulted their lawyers, who said that the chat was First Amendment speech. It's offensive speech but not a direct threat toward anyone in particular. Under the university policies, they couldn't do anything—they were stuck. And they were looking for some other mechanism to address the community outrage and search for accountability.

This guy was quickly ostracized. We're talking about rejection after rejection. It was a social death. He was a big man on campus—fraternity guy, Interfraternity Council president—and he had all kinds of access to senior administration. Then he lost all of his friends, his position. He had something like three thousand death threats. He went from everything to nothing. He was pretty shattered, so when the restorative justice opportunity was offered to him, he saw one possible pathway toward redemption. He was willing to do whatever he could to make amends for what he had done. My colleagues organized a restorative process that would bring him together with people who were harmed by his speech. Groups of students and representatives of communities went around the circle and talked about the impact that his behavior had on them.

His mother was sitting next to him through this process. One young woman said the night that she read the chat, she had a nightmare that her parents were murdered. These students talked about how they were simply frightened not just by that incident but by everything else that's happening—frightened of white people, frightened to cross paths, frightened of being accused of being an illegal immigrant. They were able to share some significant stories of harm, and he was able to respond and take responsibility for his actions. It's not direct as in, "Okay, you did that but we forgive you." It was along the lines of, "We want to know who you are, and we want you to demonstrate that you understand." We crafted an agreement.

One of the more powerful moments, as this was told to me, was that members of the Latinx community said, "We want you to come to our clubs. We want you to experience our community the way we experience it." And he said, "I'm game, but I'm scared. If I go, people are going to beat the crap out of me. I'm not going to survive if I go." They said, "No, because you're going to come with us. We will be in solidarity because it's a learning journey that you're on, and we're going to make sure that you understand." He was up for that.

One other thing that I thought was meaningful was that the students were saying that they did not feel like they had access to the administration in the same way his white fraternity did. They wanted him to help facilitate the kind of access that he had. So their engagement was about changing the nature of the relationship between the administration and students as well as about more personal changes.

IB **I think that many of us who hear these stories are not surprised. This has been our lived experience, that a chat gone wrong hits social media. How does it work when you're an individual or a community that time and time again experiences oppressive situations like this? When we talk about racism, sexism, homophobia—these things aren't going away. In this situation, there's a part of me that questions who's doing the work, the emotional labor.**

DK The model is not to put the offender in the center of the circle, where we all point and say, "This is what we're going to do to you for the thing that you did." It's to put the issue or the incident in the center of the circle, where we all speak to it from our individual perspectives: "This is how this affected me," "This is what's hard about this for me," and "This is what I want to see happen."

The question for the circle is: What does each individual want? What might we get out of this situation? We always ask about what's not working and what could help, and then people give voice to their own answers. When we have a chance to put out what we each want, we're not just signing on or being tasked with something that was imposed on us; rather, we have the agency to decide for ourselves whether this is what we want.

Usually in these kinds of situations, the question involves affinity circles first. So the Latinx community would have a circle about what it wants for its own healing and for its own steps forward, and then they would bring that to some kind of intergroup dialogue and decision-making process. It's important to consider the narrative problem: who controls the narrative? If we can decide that this is the story we want told, which might include the fact that we're tired of having to tell this story, then we put it to the group. Usually, it's a downhill slide. It's painful and hard. But when we get to collaborative decision making, it can get creative, which builds energy from something that felt hopeless before.

IB **This model may be relevant in the context of a university or a smaller group. But what about when we're dealing with big, systemic issues, issues that have been around for hundreds of years?**

LAH It's important to not have these great divides. I'm thinking of Eve Ensler, the author of *The Vagina Monologues*, who wrote an editorial addressed to white women in *Time* magazine on the eve of the Kavanaugh confirmation vote. She wrote, "I couldn't help focusing on the women behind [Donald Trump] who cheered and laughed" when he mocked Dr. Christine Blasey Ford. She said she was laughed at in the past, and, as a child, her mother sided with her father over her. The mother would not acknowledge that she was raped and would rather be in alignment with the patriarchy than protect the sanctity of her own daughter. Eve was telling white women to start having a level of accountability.

AB Part of what stands out about the situation in Texas is that it's about an individual. It's much easier when you're dealing with a smaller space to force someone's hand through ostracism or the like. I am from Chicago, and I went to an all-Black magnet school where we celebrated Kwanzaa and we were very pro-Black. The school I went to was about reclaiming our roots. We weren't interested in redemptive narratives; instead, we were finding our own little segregated space. As a gay Black woman, there are other hierarchies and things within my community that I want to overcome, and I don't have time to pull someone along.

In an institutional sense, it's difficult to have such a positive outcome. People don't understand that my work is not just about this Central Park Five reporting. In a book that I read, one woman said she was afraid to hire any kids from Harlem. These narratives reverberate, and they collectively impact my position in the world. Some of what's restorative in this story is that this student, having lost all his power, was willing to say, "Okay, you can have some, too." But what does restorative justice look like in other situations, with major institutions, like newspapers or the government? I just don't see that happening in the real world. What I see is me showing up and a bunch of people pulling me to the side and saying, "Oh, your work is magnificent." Then they're still where they are.

I went to a *National Geographic* storyteller summit. They were proud that the roster was diverse. Three of us were Black—and none was a *NatGeo* photographer. We were these external people that had been brought in. We were all artists, and we were all critiquing imagery. Every single person I engaged with who was in some position of stature was a white person. People want to be able to have their cake and eat it, too. You want to tell me something positive, but you don't want to acknowledge the fact that the portrayals that you've pushed forward have probably kept me out of a position at your organization. Some of it is giving up and letting go. It's easier to imagine that in a small, interpersonal space.

But when we start to think about sacrifice, that's what's wrong with a lot of white women—they don't want to sacrifice their position and proximity to white male power. So they don't vote the way they should. What I find really difficult and why forgiveness hasn't even entered the conversation for me is that there's that inability to say, "You know what? I'm going to have to give up something." I feel like it's in my best interest to find a way to shield myself as opposed to trying to elicit an apology, which is probably thin anyway.

Why were the people in Charleston so forgiving? How were they able to move forward? That's interesting to me. But I'm also interested in why the narrative around the young white guy who shot people wasn't naming him as a terrorist.

LAH Yes, it's an act of terrorism.

I want to be clear: I'm not suggesting or supporting the fact that they forgive. For me, that forgiveness is so that Black folks, collectively, don't go into the element of insanity. There's a necessary healing process.

One more quick excerpt, this one by Reverend angel Kyodo williams from *Radical Dharma*:

> Movements for Black liberation cast their bodies into resisting the systems and instruments of oppression. Our bodies take the shape of, and thus illuminate, the contours of the most insidious force of systematic dehumanization and destruction ever imagined, one which has led the global community into a downward spiral of self-annihilation... We are propelled by the essential human compulsion for freedom, but we can also be driven by centuries of pain and carry a burden greater than people should have ever known. Our healing cannot wait until the structures acquiesce, are dismantled, or come undone. We must take a seat.

The seat is in reference to healing oneself. This is critical.

IB **What if you are an individual who has historically been and currently is disenfranchised, and discriminated against violently? I'm talking about Black and brown people, LGBTQIA+, immigrants, Indigenous communities, victims of sexism... I think that Alexandra is saying that we can push and move and effect change and maybe a system will give or shift.**

DK I'd love to have the answer to this problem. From a restorative perspective, it starts with the premise of storytelling. That's what you're trying to do at the very beginning. We can't get engaged unless we share something about ourselves. And we can't trust one another unless we know one another at some level. So the first step to preventing the kind of dehumanizing policies that exist or structures that exist is to know one another. That's why I think stories are important, even if we're tired of telling them.

Even if it may have been triggering for the Latinx community, they dragged this guy in Texas to their events to say: "If you knew us, you couldn't say these things." If we're able to humanize what's been dehumanized, that's the first step. And that's interpersonal. This is a leap, but if there are people in positions of power, people who feel that human connection, it will be harder for them to maintain the policies that they try to deny. Or they may be more open to creating more seats at the table and have those policies challenged—if not by them personally, then by the people they've brought in. That's a hope.

LAH Could you give us an example in your life with a high position—how that has happened for you and what was the leap, what sacrifice? It's authorship that I'm asking you about: How has that experience ricocheted in your own life? What type of transformation has that work effected in your life and in relation to your family and your kids? How has that reverberated?

DK Personally, I like to live pretty emotionally safe. I'm a social scientist. I can be behind my computer, and I've sat in enough restorative circles to recognize the limitations of that and the value of vulnerability.

One example that is coming to mind is a circle where a young guy had just vandalized somebody's car wash. It was a dialogue with the car wash owner and this kid regarding a couple of thousand dollars of damage to the car wash. The kid didn't have the money. Instead of there immediately being a sentence to pay restitution and being put on probation, the owner wanted to hear the kid's story. Then they entered a collaborative decision-making process. The owner said, "I want you to pay me back. But I want you to put the money into a bank account. If you go to college, I want that money to go toward your tuition. And if you don't go to college, I want the money to pay me back for the damage that was done."

That kind of solution says that there's accountability. It's not saying, "Don't worry about it"; you have to do something, but now there's reinvestment in the kid with this creative solution that could never happen in a criminal courtroom. What's moving for me is the power of the circle process to generate solutions that no one would come up with otherwise. It was a form of forgiveness, but it wasn't just forgive and forget. It was forgive, but you have to earn it. That's the earned redemption piece.

Audience   A question that has come up quite a bit with my family and friends is: Can ignorance be forgiven? In terms of earned redemption, can someone earn their redemption by learning? I'm thinking of situations that have horrible consequences where there are violent acts of racism or sexism. People sometimes say, "It's the community they grew up with. They didn't know any better. There was no way they could have known any better." What would you say to situations like that?

AB   Ralph Northam is the governor of Virginia who appeared in blackface in 1984. As opposed to him stepping down, his advisers and his staff are having him read *Roots* by Alex Haley and a book by Ta-Nehisi Coates. I was watching a clip of an interview he did with Gayle King, and he's having this very proud exchange, and he refers to 1619, when slaves arrived in Virginia, and he calls them "the first indentured servants from Africa." And she sits for a second, and then she says, "Also known as slavery." He answers, "Yes."

I think there's a point where—*forgiveness* is not the word—you earn back a particular kind of redemption. But it's on you. If there's something you didn't know, it's on you to gain that knowledge. It's not on me to teach you about blackface. If we're talking about forgiveness in the sense of forgiving someone who is in office, I think that you can stay in office and also do that work—though that isn't necessarily the case for Northam, given the constituents who voted him into office. You have a duty as a public official to understand, learn about, and represent the interests of the people. You can't do that when you don't know and you don't have that knowledge.

DK   For me, there are two issues. One is, if you caused harm, what can you do to repair that harm? There are steps to try to address that harm directly even if you can't fix it fully. The other issue is trust: it might be a different set of steps that you need to do for me to regain trust in you. Part of it might be around learning and knowledge: I don't trust you as long as I think you're ignorant on this issue, but it might be reassuring once you demonstrate to me a full understanding of this issue. Or maybe, unless you address these issues in treatment in some way, I won't trust you.

Or maybe it's about being isolated or disconnected from the community: if you are engaged and contributing in a positive way, I might trust you again. So there may be many separate pathways.

Northam has done damage to the governor's office. Stepping down might be an appropriate way to acknowledge that this harm is irreparable—having someone else step into the office might be an appropriate thing to do. That's more about the harm; that's not necessarily about my trust. So I think there are many things to do, and something that might work for me is not going to work for you. Maybe there's something else that is meaningful for both of us.

IB **Also, some things may just be unforgivable. Is it okay to just say that that was reprehensible and it's unforgivable to me? Must the end goal always be about forgiveness and redemption?**

DK Then what? If I'm not forgiving you, what does that mean? Does that mean you have to be excommunicated or punished?

Audience I'm interested in the origin of the social script David talked about, where you do something wrong, you say you're sorry, and you're forgiven. For me, forgiveness and redemption have a strong association with Christianity. Does the social script come from Christianity and it being so widespread as a result of colonialism and imperialism?

DK There are some anthropologists who will say that this predates any current organized religions. I think it is a universal necessity: for humans to have social cooperation, they need methods of conflict resolution. Whatever it may be, there's got to be some mechanism to resolve a transgression other than all-out violence. ▲

FOOD FUTURES
Food Justice, Sustainability, and Well-Being

Kate Daughdrill
Community dinner, 2014
Burnside Farm, Detroit

"Burnside Farm is an urban farm and artistic hub on the east side of Detroit. It's a place where art, plants, neighbors, and healing come together. During the growing season, the neighbors and artists of Burnside host regular dinners in the garden—most of the food coming right from the garden and grilled on a homemade cinder block grill. The spirit of the farm is to cultivate a life-giving, healing space and an overall sense of well-being in the people, plants, neighbors, and animals who are a part of it." —Kate Daughdrill

Fighting Metabolic Dominance

Anthony Ryan Hatch

1 David Axe, "This Scientist Wants Tomorrow's Troops to Be Mutant Powered," *Wired*, Dec. 26, 2012.

2 Anthony Ryan Hatch, *Blood Sugar: Racial Pharmacology and Food Justice in Black America* (Minneapolis: University of Minnesota Press, 2016).

3 Cedric Robinson, *Black Marxism: The Making of the Black Radical Tradition* (Durham: University of North Carolina Press, 2000).

In 2002, the Defense Advanced Research Projects Agency launched a new military biomodification program called *metabolic dominance*.[1] Its purpose was to create a supersoldier whose biochemistry could be manipulated to overcome the biological limits imposed by their environment, such as the need to eat, sleep, breathe. Like Captain America, they would no longer be subject to the normal metabolic constraints of the human body. Imagine the military implanting microcomputers into soldiers' endocrine glands that can turn on the hormonal signals that say "eat" or "stop eating." A soldier could fight for days without having to sleep or perhaps swim underwater for much longer than expected. It makes sense to me why the US military would be interested in metabolism as a medium for the production of supersoldiers. From a biomedical perspective, metabolism encompasses all of the chemical reactions that unfold within the body, processes that allow us to derive energy from food, take oxygen from air, and interact with a host of biochemicals that flow between us and our environment.[2] Manipulating the basic metabolic functioning of organisms is an extreme form of Foucauldian biopolitics where bodies become the very battlegrounds on and through which biological warfare is waged.

Metabolic dominance also offers us new language to talk about food futures, racial power, and bodies. Metabolic dominance is all about using a wide range of technologies to control and transform the biochemistry that creates interdependence between bodies and ecologies. While the military has been trying to tinker with the metabolism of its troops, transnational food companies and governments have long successfully altered and profited from the transformations of our collective metabolisms.

In this broader social sense, metabolic dominance begins with the system of racial capitalism established by European and American colonial powers: monocropping through slavery-based agricultural production systems. The term *racial capitalism* comes from Cedric Robinson, who sought to theorize and historicize the worldwide system of capitalism in its full racial context.[3] He argued that European societies were already racially and ethnically organized when the transition from feudalism to capitalism took place. Racial distinction and subordination were metaphorically baked into the cake of capitalism.

4 John Bellamy Foster, *Marx's Ecology: Materialism and Nature* (New York: Monthly Review Press, 2000), 158.

5 John Bellamy Foster, Brett Clark, and Richard York, *The Ecological Rift: Capitalism's War on the Earth* (New York: Monthly Review Press, 2011).

Under racial capitalism, the mass production and consumption of the major colonial agricultural commodities—sugar, rice, tobacco, coffee, and cotton—exploded. These forms of agriculture and economy, imposed by colonizing settlers on Indigenous lands and populations all over the world, have been a principal driver of climate change, ecological toxicity, and human death and disability. In other words, they constitute the systems that enforce metabolic domination in our time.

Karl Marx also used the concept of metabolism in his social theories "to describe the complex, dynamic, interdependent set of needs and relations brought into being and constantly reproduced in alienated form under capitalism, and the question of human freedom it raised."[4] For Marx, metabolism is the process by which human labor generates and redistributes the productive energies trapped within nature, a process that was on full display in the rise of industrial agriculture. By laboring in agriculture (either for subsistence or under enslavement), humans cultivate and transform the energy in food into a form of social exchange that doubles a means of biological subsistence, much like the way in which the microbes that live within our gut digest (or metabolize) the food we eat. But the transformation of energy from one form into another has breathtaking consequences.

The system of racial capitalism is at war with the Earth and its inhabitants.[5] Over an astonishingly short period of time, racial capitalism has transformed ecological and multispecies life to the point where no material things exist outside of the system of private property. Literally everything is thoroughly commodified, including life itself.

Through the hyperproduction and -consumption of agricultural commodities under racial capitalism, humans have created what Marx called a *metabolic rift* that disturbs the complex ecological relationships between species and ecosystems. By using more land, more machines, more chemicals, and more monocrops to grow food for profit, we are destroying the metabolic processes that sustain life on Earth. This rapacious system ravages the land, us, and everything with it. The disruption of complex nutrient and waste cycles, the transformation of interspecies relationships, and the mass extraction and burning of fossil fuels are forging the metabolic rift at the precipice of the Anthropocene. The greater the rift, the more jagged its

[6] Anna Brones, "Karen Washington: It's Not a Food Desert, It's Food Apartheid," *Guernica*, May 7, 2018, https://www.guernicamag.com/karen-washington-its-not-a-food-desert-its-food-apartheid.

edge, and the deeper the alienation that separates humans from the rest of nature. This metabolic rift has both ecological and social costs, the most important of which may be climate change and catastrophe.

How can the global peasantry take for itself the inalienable right to food sovereignty, good health, and environmental justice from racial capitalism? The current unequal distribution of resources is not an accident. Eight people hoard as much wealth as half of the people living on Earth—these folks are not going to give up the loot without a fight. Private corporate interests have completed the regulatory capture of our governments—corporations, especially food corporations, are today able to fund political campaigns, write new laws, and police their own bad behavior. Moreover, the thin veneer that perhaps once protected science and medicine from the corrupting influence of private money has long been pierced. Our major institutions of economy, government, and science have all matured and ripened in the context of racial capitalism and work to support the subordination of billions through metabolic pathways.

As we yearn for a future in which food is produced sustainably (by means of vibrant, local, organic polycultures) and for the benefit and well-being of all creatures, human and nonhuman alike, we have to confront the systems of metabolic dominance that keep that future at arm's length. A socially just and equitable world is inconceivable in a racially unequal silent spring. It is hard to envision a futuristic Garden of Eden with solar panels and organic gardens built from the bones of the dead within segregated "green zones" (think Iraq) for the poor and "blue zones" (exceptionally healthy places) for the privileged and lucky. Without a direct challenge to racial capitalism, our food future will continue to look and feel more like what activist Karen Washington rightly calls "food apartheid."[6] We can't stop climate change and ecological destruction until we dismantle racial capitalism.

A People's Food Police

Former North Charleston, South Carolina, police officer Michael Slager is currently an inmate in the Federal Correctional Institution, Englewood, serving a twenty-year sentence for violating the civil rights of fifty-year-old

7 American Heart Association Statistics Committee and Stroke Statistics Subcommittee, "Heart Disease and Stroke Statistics—2017 Update: A Report from the American Heart Association," *Circulation* 135, no. 10 (March 7, 2017).

8 Miriam Van Dyke et al., "Heart Disease Death Rates among Blacks and Whites Aged ≥35—United States, 1968–2015," *CDC Mortality and Morbidity Weekly Report* 67, no. 5 (March 30, 2018).

father and Coast Guard veteran Walter Scott. We all watched in horror as Slager shot Scott in the back following a botched traffic stop on April 4, 2015. Slager discharged his weapon eight times, hitting Scott three times in the back, once in the leg, and once in the ear. Not only did Slager lie in official reports about Scott stealing his Taser and lunging at him with it, he also planted evidence of the lie at the crime scene. Scott was unarmed when he was killed.

When the police shoot to kill a Black person, they often do so based on the erroneous and racist claim that Blackness in general and this particular Black body represents an imminent threat to the racial police state, and to the concept of whiteness, and to white bodies themselves. In reality, quite the opposite is true: the racial state is a danger to Black bodies.

The function of the actual police is to protect the property and constitutional rights of America's original gangsters—settlers and plantation owners. What if we could have the *people's food police*? The traditional food police governs people's food choices with scientific facts about what's healthy for people and the planet. They issue tickets: moral condemnation from a position of ethical superiority (often tied to systems of gender, class, and racial advantage) that perpetually blames individuals and groups who have no sovereignty to produce the foods they are forced to buy. To punch back, the people's food police would work on behalf of all people, especially the least among us, to turn control over the entire food system back to the people. This force would be made up of freedom fighters working on the side of those of us who need to eat to live and don't want to die from eating.

In 2015, US police killed 104 unarmed Black people, which results in a rate five times that of the killing of unarmed white people. In stark contrast, chronic metabolic illnesses (heart disease, diabetes, stroke, obesity) have killed scores more Black people. In 2014, diabetes, stroke, and heart attacks killed 68,990 Black adults.[7] Back in 1968, there were no racial disparities in heart disease death rates; rates for all groups have decreased substantially since the late 1960s. Yet the Black-white disparity in heart disease death rates increased 16.3 percent from 1968 to 2015.[8] These Black deaths and racial disparities are not caused by inherent biological, genetic, or heritable traits

[9] Walter Scheidel, *The Great Leveler: Violence and the History of Inequality from the Stone Age to the Twenty-First Century* (Princeton, NJ: Princeton University Press, 2017), 437–44.

that are specific to Black people; these Black deaths are caused by white supremacy as envisioned and institutionalized through metabolic domination.

If one goal of antiracism is to end the killing and devaluing of Black bodies, shouldn't Black people have their own food police who are empowered to stand their ground against an anti-Black food system that kills thousands each year? Corporations are people, too, says the Supreme Court, but is it murder to kill one? Can Black people mobilize "stand your ground" defenses against social institutions that seem to be out for our blood (sugar)?

I wish we could shift the awesome power of the police state to initiate a technologically advanced and well-funded militarized campaign against the industrial food system. We could call it "food regime change." Instead of brutalizing the Black and brown masses with guns, tanks, and prisons, this food police force would act with immunity and impunity and dark hearts, taking out all the pumpkin spice cakes and Sysco truck-refueling stations and soda-manufacturing plants—just like the US military did in their "shock and awe" operation in the sovereign nation of Iraq. Decapitating corporate regimes would be facilitated with a "most wanted" deck of cards identifying the executives of murderous companies and their coconspirators in government and science.

Break in Case of Emergency

I have a vision of those glass boxes with "Break in Case of Emergency" etched on the front. What emergency protocols for the global peasantry sit behind the glass? What are the prospects for the scale of social, technological, and ecological transformations required to turn back unprecedented inequality, climate change, ecological degradation, and the food crisis? In this context, it's really challenging, *for me*, to consider the soft reform approach sufficient for the building of a world order that puts the last first and the first last. The global peasantry needs a new world order. A provocative book called *The Great Leveler* by Stanford historian Walter Scheidel argues that peaceful social reforms "may well prove unequal to the growing challenges ahead"; only total thermonuclear war can provide the seismic jolt needed to fundamentally reset the current distribution of resources.[9] No doubt this is a radical proposition. But we have to be sober about the kinds of systems we are facing and the kinds of force relations that are strong enough to dislodge and dismantle them.

The global one-percenters are already in emergency mode, building luxury militarized yachts to prepare for rising oceans and the inevitable collapse. I think of them as modern-day arks, like those represented in the Roland Emmerich film *2012*. These yachts are equipped with anti-aircraft missiles and advanced communication and life-support systems. They are getting ready for another great flood.

Maybe this is what President Trump's Space Force is all about. Too bad about all that space garbage that will make the Space Force difficult to deploy. Maybe Elon Musk or Jeff Bezos has a solution, but watch out. They might not have space for anybody from the 99 percent. While white-controlled private corporations develop robust rocketry systems in an attempt to establish a for-profit market for the wealthy, the rest of us are stuck in the terminal crisis without an emergency plan. On this very point, listen to Jarobi in the 2016 song "The Space Program" from A Tribe Called Quest:

> Molotov the spaceship though before that bitch is taking off
> It always seems the poorest persons are people forsaken, dog
> No Washingtons, Jeffersons, Jacksons on the captain's log
> They'd rather lead us to the grave, water poisoned, deadly smog
> Mass un-blackening, it's happening, you feel it y'all?
> They'd rather see we have a three-by-three structure with many bars
> Leave us where we are so they can play among the stars
> We're taking off to Mars, got the space vessels overflowing
> What, you think they want us there? All us niggas not going!

Unlike Elon Musk and Jeff Bezos, we can't leave planet Earth. And I'm not necessarily advocating direct violent action against corporate targets. Rather, I'm suggesting that we need to resist the dynamics of metabolic dominance in this world. A converging set of terminal metabolic crises—unprecedented wealth inequality enabled by crippling political corruption, catastrophic climate change, metabolic health pandemics, and total environmental toxicity—is upending our planet. If our metabolic crises come to pass, the Earth will remain, changed by us yet sooner or later without us. ▲

Kate Daughdrill

artist

Anthony Ryan Hatch

scholar

Leah Penniman

farmer

Isolde Brielmaier — **Good, healthy food nourishes the mind, body, and spirit. Food now and in the future must be considered in relation to equity, social justice, sustainability, and the well-being of all people as well as of our planet. Where and how do we conceive of the basic concepts of food justice and food security? How are they connected to us as individuals, in your work, and in communities locally and globally?**

Leah Penniman — It's so important to define words in the context of who created them. The idea of food justice and food sovereignty is rooted in Indigenous communities around the world, as seen in La Via Campesina network. Previously, folks were talking about food from the access point of view. Who has it, who doesn't, how many greens are on the plate, how many chips are on the plate? That certainly matters. But when we talk about food justice, we're getting into power and control, into democracy, and into the economy.

We need to start asking not just who's eating food, but who controls the land? Who gets to farm? Who controls the seed? Who controls the markets? Who decides what's grown? What profit share is going to farm workers as compared to multinational corporations? As my daughter, Neshima, says, the food system is everything it takes to get sunshine onto your plate. It's about justice all the way through.

At Soul Fire Farm, it is about paying attention to the whole food system. We run a farm on eighty acres; we grow vegetables, eggs, and all that is necessary; and we box that up every week and bring it to the doorsteps of people who need it most. That includes refugees, new Americans, folks impacted by mass incarceration, and they pay whatever they can afford. And we're training and supporting the next generation of Black and Indigenous farmers—this is a generation that has been excluded from leadership in the food system in the United States. We're working on reparations and policy change. So it goes beyond access.

Anthony Ryan Hatch — The term *food security* was established by the US government to give the government a way to describe patterns of access to food. You're either food secure—you have access to food locally, within a mile or so—or food insecure. That was the central metric by which the government was looking at questions of food, health, and nutrition. It was all about access and proximity.

The term *food security* places food in the context of a discourse of war and of the state and its power. Some of my thinking looks at food as a technology of war and how we wrestle that out of the hands of people who seek to make war on us through food and take it in another direction. This is more about *food sovereignty*, where we actually have a place to grow and a place to have some control over our food. We want to shift the conversation away from thinking about securitization and who is secure and insecure. We already know who that is.

Kate Daughdrill — I found my way into farming organically. When I finished graduate school at Cranbrook Academy of Art, outside of Detroit, I volunteered at Earthworks, a farm in the city. It was the most diverse group of people that I had worked with: people with homes, without homes, all ages, all backgrounds and races, all ethnicities. There were thirty of us. We gardened, and then we'd sit in a circle and talk about race and food justice and how all people deserve access to good food. We would discuss what's getting in the way of this. I had never before experienced people of different backgrounds coming together to work and then to talk about these issues. I hadn't been a "plant person," but I just naturally started to become one after that first encounter.

I bought a house in Detroit, and there were vacant lots next to it. So I said, well, it makes sense to garden. I invited my neighbors to garden with me, and we started gardening. Growing food completely changed my life. My art practice and my gardening practice fused, and I began to see how food could bring people together as a creative medium around dinners, around edible creative activities. My neighborhood is really diverse—Bengali, Yemeni, Black, white. It used to be made up of Polish and Ukrainian auto-worker homes. That mix of different people coming together and seeing how each person has something to contribute to the garden, and also to their own gardens, has been magical. I came to food justice from a sense of seeing this elemental life-giving thing that we all need—how are people taking control of that for themselves? And with people from all these different backgrounds, how are we working together to do that? Where do we have strengths to help one another?

IB **All three of you have raised notions of power and access. Who are the different actors in food politics? Who influences decisions and policies around the control, distribution, and access of food production?**

ARH Scholars use the idea of a food regime to describe the constellation of actors, laws, policies, and regulations that govern the food system. While we have to see it as a global system that has local roots, we're really talking about two central institutions of power. On the one hand, nation-states have for 150 years used food, both its production and consumption, as a tool of international relations. More recently, multinational corporations have privatized the food system in ways that wrestle power away from everyday citizens all over the world, including farmers. So we're talking about big institutions, and we're talking about trade policy.

We're also talking about World Trade Organization rules, which govern how much of a given commodity a country can make, how much they can export, and the prices for those commodities, which limit the resources that everyday farmers can garner for the commodities they grow. These are big macro-institutional forces that are largely hidden from us. When we go to the grocery store, whether it's the local farmers market or the Whole Foods or the traditional supermarket, we don't really know the institutions that touch the food we eat. That part is something we have to demystify.

When you demystify it, you see people getting together to put things in the earth and then magically, actually chemically, things grow. But corporations would have you think that they are the only ones who can do it. Think about rendering visible these big institutional forces that remain largely hidden from us. How was it that they got to do this? Who decided that it was okay for them to have power over us like this? To have power over us in this way, for people to be able to govern us like this, requires that we acquiesce to it, that we voluntarily submit to it in some way. We have to decide that we're not going to be governed in this way anymore. To wrestle back power means to reject the mystification that corporations and states wield over us in terms of food.

IB **We're also talking about lack of information. Leah, what you're doing with your community is focused on this.**

LP In terms of the amount of money, the Farm Bill is the largest piece of legislation we have in this country. It governs our entire food system. Because I have direct contact with thousands of Black and brown farmers, my job has increasingly become to have my ear to the ground to see how these massive policies and corporate contracts impact real people and then translate that for the folks who are lobbying. I was on a call with the National Black Food and Justice Alliance earlier today and the HEAL Food Alliance last week to develop these campaigns.

Farming is a highly subsidized industry. Until the 1980s, there were price supports that guaranteed a minimum price for your milk or your grain. That was dismantled and replaced with crop insurance. Almost every farmer gets some kind of government money; otherwise, they would close down. It's why we have cheap food. It's why the market is flooded with commodities like wheat and corn and soy. But over generations, Black farmers have been excluded from these subsidies.

Martin Luther King Jr. gave a famous speech shortly before he was assassinated in which he talked about how the federal government had provided the white peasant farmer with land through the Homestead Act: land grant universities, loans with low interest rates to facilitate mechanization, and payments to not farm as part of the Conservation Reserve Program, which protects soil fertility. But Black farmers didn't get this assistance. As a result, there was a decline from Black farmers making up 14 percent of farmers in 1910 to 1 percent today. Then, in 1999, Black farmers won the Pigford Case, the largest class action civil rights suit in the history of this country. But by then most of the farmers were in their eighties and nineties. They'd lost their land and moved out of their communities. I did a study with *YES!* magazine a couple of years ago, and we found that even though the USDA has been called to account, there are still huge racial disparities if you look at how their money is actually being distributed. So we're pushing for distributing loans and technical assistance fairly among all farmers. And there needs to be redress for past harms.

Another story of how big institutional forces affect real people is around the earthquake in Haiti in 2010. My maternal lineage is Haitian. One part of the Farm Bill is called tied aid. It says that if we're going to give food aid, it has to be from US farmers, shipped on US ships, and processed by US corporations. All fine and good, right? But think about rice harvest season. All the peasant farmers in Haiti are getting ready to bring their rice to market. At the same time, Monsanto conveniently brings barge-loads of free hybridized and genetically modified seeds to dump on the Haitian market.

Monsanto would be very happy to give out this seed to decimate the Haitian economy and to create dependency. But the president of Haiti tells the ship to turn around. Monsanto refuses, and the peasant movement, which we're a part of and with which we organize, burned the shipment when it came in. They won a global food sovereignty prize. They said, "No thank you, we have our own creole rice, and we're going to share it among ourselves the way we always have. If you want to help us, you can support our local food economy, but you can't supplant it with this corporate hegemony." US policy impacts not just farmers here, but also peasant farmers in Haiti and around the world.

IB **Kate, do you think about some of these larger structures? How do you bring that down to a more local, community level?**

KD A lot of my journey with food and the land really did come from this inside-out experience. My journey started from the level of my own body and my own eating and my own healing and my own relating to one plant and learning how to do that in a community and with other people and through getting engaged with my local farmers market.

Detroit has the biggest historic farmers market in North America, in terms of land size. It's a thriving area where people of all different backgrounds come together. It honestly feels like church to me. Everyone has food that they feel a connection to. It's a beautiful thing. Keep Growing Detroit is an amazing program that equips people with starts and with seeds and with education for growing. People grow food in more than four thousand farms or gardens in Detroit. Three times throughout the growing season there is a big day where people all come and get their starts. There's this element of people and organizations equipping one another with the tools for growing their own food.

The goal is to be 51 percent food sovereign, meaning 51 percent of the food consumed in Detroit is being grown by Detroiters. Detroiters could actually do that with just 4 percent of the vacant land that we have available—it's a unique situation. I learned about that and met other people and heard about the deep, long work that has been done, specifically by Black Detroiters over the last thirty or forty years. Starting in the 1950s and 1960s, capitalism and certain consumer systems left Detroit, business trickled out, and people were learning to take care of themselves and growing their own food and making windmills in the city and starting to harvest their own energy. It became essential to ask, If there aren't as many 9 to 5 jobs, how do we take care of our own basic needs? What's work in a more expansive, creative sense? What does it really mean to be a human? You need food, water, some energy, and you need to trade with people to figure out how to build things.

The Osborn neighborhood in northeast Detroit received a public art grant, and they invited me and Mira Burack to create an Edible Hut. The community wanted a place to come together, to rebuild trust, and that was centered around food as a healing tool for their relationships in a neighborhood where there's a lot of vacancy and crime. So we built a gathering place out of an old garage. The whole roof is covered with living, edible plants—a living sculpture. But the real work of it was creating a group for neighbors of the Edible Hut. We had potlucks on the site of this place every month for four years before it was finished and when it was completed. We built an amazing association of schools and neighborhood groups. We cooked, we shared healthy food, we ate from the roof. The space really became this way to hold space for people wanting to take care of themselves and one another.

I had the direct physical experience of seeing how people provide food for themselves—how I, a lot of my neighbors, and the growers in Detroit became more empowered.

IB **How do we make the connection between hands-on training, education, and individuals and communities? What happens on a day-to-day level with people?**

LP Fannie Lou Hamer is well-known for her work with the Mississippi Freedom Democratic Party. She is less well-known for her work with the Freedom Farm Cooperative, which was a family housing co-op and farm she founded in the late 1960s. It provided food and education and scholarships for Sunflower County, Mississippi. I think of her as an ancestor when it comes to practicality, because she would gather a bunch of activists in a room to organize for political power. And she would say, "Y'all, if you have four hundred quarts of greens and gumbo soup canned for the winter, nobody can push you around or tell you what to do. If you don't have those four hundred quarts, you might go and rabble rouse and scream and yell, but as soon as they shut down that grocery store, you're going to be begging and pleading for them to get that machine going again because you don't have the means of your own survival." That is really where our day-to-day is rooted. We believe that to get free as a people, and in this case, we're talking about Black, Indigenous, and people of color, we need to be able to feed ourselves.

One of the programs that came out of that desire for community self-determination at Soul Fire Farm is called "BIPOC FIRE! Black-Indigenous-People-of-Color Farming in Relationship with Earth." It is a fifty-hour, week-long beginner training in farming. It covers everything from bed prep to seed to harvest to marketing and business planning, infused with a trauma lens that is about rewriting the story of our relationship to land as something wider and deeper than just the oppression that took place there. We're up at 6:00 a.m., and we do a little stretch and say, "Thank you for the day." It's a hands-on class—we cook and eat together, we have classroom activities, we have ritual, we have storytelling, we have history. We really become a family through it.

There is a lot of power in creating food and community on land. Once folks have gone through the program, they're forever Soul Fire family. We follow up with mentorships and help getting land, a job, a scholarship, a fellowship. We do everything we can to make sure that our alumni can enact the food sovereignty plans that they create while they're in the program, whether that's urban farming, rural farming, or some type of advocacy project.

Gaining access to the land is not to excuse the need for wholesale reparations. But there has been a shift in consciousness, and people have put together the fact that 80 percent of wealth in this country is inherited. Most of that is property, and about half is traceable back to slavery. If you include the genocide of Native people, that's almost all the wealth. According to Pew Research, today the average white baby is born with sixteen times the wealth of the average Black baby.

You add up all those facts, and if you're a conscious person with a heart and you've got some wealth, you probably realize it's not really yours. It was built on stolen land and stolen labor and a whole series of policies that are clumped together as white affirmative action. So we've catalyzed what we're calling a voluntary reparations project. We have a map where BIPOC put up their farm projects, and they might need a tractor, they might need forty acres—the forty acres and a mule that were never given, by the way. We have about seventy or so people on this map, and thirteen folks have gotten land through this project. Many of the donors have also gone through Uprooting Racism trainings that have been offered by alumni and folks in our network. It's been inspiring to know that people to people, heart to heart, mind to mind, we can actually catalyze this change and just get going.

ARH One astounding fact to share is that Monsanto and Bayer Pharmaceuticals have merged. Monsanto controls most of the genetic information about the seeds that are grown all around the world, and Bayer Pharmaceuticals is one of the largest drug companies in the world. Why? Why would it be a good idea to have food and pharmaceutical companies under the same umbrella of capital? My suspicion, which I articulate in my book *Blood Sugar*—it's a little conspiratorial—is that the foods we are fed make us sick. The book is about metabolic syndrome, which is a way of measuring who's at risk for a heart attack or a stroke. Overweight, hypertensive, high blood pressure, high blood sugar, high cholesterol, inflammation—if you have multiple of these risk factors simultaneously, you're said to have metabolic syndrome. My book analyzes the science of this construct that when you're made sick, you're forced to go to the pharmacy to buy medicines that are supposed to heal you. I think that we should, as a citizenry, as a people, be greatly concerned about the coming together of the food and pharmaceutical industries in the United States and around the world. Why would they do that unless it's a good idea for them?

I was thinking about this in relation to my own family. I have type 1 diabetes. I have been on injected insulin for twenty-six years. We just did the food budget for my family of four. If we're honest about how much money we spend, the food budget for the grocery store alone is around $1,800 a month. Most folks can't afford $1,800 a month—I'm not sure we should afford $1,800 a month. But it's really hard to go from having two parents working full time to participating in a food sovereignty program.

KD I can share a little on that because I grew up eating cheese, hot dogs, cookie dough…I even remember eating Gatorade powder. I would eat it with a spoon because it was so good. So that's where I came from—not having an intimate relationship with the earth or with gardening or with plants or with food. Then I started to be near the earth—physically gardening and planting one plant and watching it grow. Then I ate the food of that plant and I realized how amazing it tasted. It wasn't like food from a grocery store. It tasted different, and my body started to feel different. It wasn't because someone told me, "You should eat healthy and here's how to eat healthy"; it was the direct experience of doing it.

I was lucky to get a house off an auction very cheaply. I lived with one extension cord from the basement and no fridge for nine months; I put in a wood stove for my heat. It's a dramatic example of how you make it work. But I decided I wanted to feed myself from this land, work with my neighbors, go to the farmers market and get the things I needed there to supplement what I grew myself. I've lived off $12,000 a year for the last eight years because I own my house, I can eat much of what I grow, and I freeze food. I've found ways to do it simply, but it does take my whole life to provide for myself.

As an artist, there are times when I see my art and my farming come together. But to live simply and eat well and make that shift takes so much of my time. As I travel to connect with people and to learn and share, I ask myself, Where do I buy food that's affordable to me in living simply, and how do I provide for some of my own needs? There have to be some ways that the pie can be sliced where we're between paradigms or we have different tools of trying to live in a more nourishing way with food. But it's a mystery to me as I travel.

IB **So many people in the world have food sovereignty integrated into daily living and have had it so for generations. But for many other people in the world, we're making a shift—it's a different experience. How do we begin, especially when it is not for lack of wanting but maybe lack of access to information?**

LP It's challenging when we put the onus on the individual, because we're in a societal context. I knew how to farm when I was living in the south end of Albany, which is a food apartheid neighborhood. There was no supermarket, no grocery stores, no room in the community garden. We didn't have a car. The only way we could get fresh vegetables for our children was to walk 2.2 miles up the hill to a CSA dropoff at the Quaker meetinghouse, pile the vegetables on top of the two-year-old in the stroller with the baby in the backpack, and walk the 2.2 miles back down the hill. The cost of the vegetables was more than our rent. And that's unreasonable. A lot of times we have this myth that if folks get educated, they will know they need to eat healthy. We've had thousands of young people, teenagers—hoods up, earbuds in, cute sneakers—and every single one of them loves the food from the farm. Why? Because they grew it. It's not a desire thing. There are a lot of solutions that need to be made.

Let's look at Costa Rica as a long-term example. They pay farmers subsidies for environmental services. If you are increasing the number of pollinators in your area because of your farming practices, if you are increasing the amount of carbon in your soil, if you are engaging in watershed protection, you will get a government subsidy. Right now, subsidies in the United States are flipped. We give you money to trash the planet and drive the climate to chaos. So we need to look at the systemic things that drive the price of good food down and make it accessible to people.

One great thing that I've had to learn and remember is that our ancestors had all the answers. There are literally hundreds of Black- and brown-led organizations working on food justice that have thoughtful campaigns, policy platforms, information on what you can do. So it really is a question of opening up our awareness and saying, "How do I engage with these solutions that are already in motion on the ground?" We don't have to make up something new.

IB **It's an incredibly complex ecosystem that consists of individuals, communities, and governments.**

ARH Because I'm a sociologist by training, I'd be remiss if I didn't pick up on Leah's brilliant comment that this is not a problem for the wills or choices of individual people. These are systemic institutional crises. The food crisis is linked to the ecological crisis, and the ecological crisis is linked to a crisis in governing. Our rulers have decided that this is the way they want things to be.

Food is at the center of the climate crisis. If you look around the world, the forces driving climate change are grounded in the soil: what's put in it, what's taken out of it, the whole system. For example, we know about cows and cow gas, about pesticides, about biocides being put into the soil to grow commodity crops. At an institutional level, we're at a crisis point. Unless we envision a different way of governing these systems, our time is limited. These times call for dramatic institutional transformations and the kinds of reversals that Leah suggested in terms of incentivizing the good and de-incentivizing the harmful, in terms of putting power back in people's hands.

IB **It's important to frame the crisis historically, because it's not as if these issues have just popped up. Those systems need to be examined and not only disrupted but dismantled, because they're clearly not working or they're working for a select few.**

ARH The point is very simple: the systems were designed to do just this. They're not random; they're not broken. They were designed to do exactly what they're doing. They need to be reengineered and redesigned so that they serve different interests.

KD Monsanto has literally engineered their seed so that you cannot save it to then plant it. They are saying: "You have to rely on us and give us your money to get the seed again." The most essential human thing in the world is that life begets life. But the system is literally designed for a company to have power and money. A way we can engage is to grow food or to get it directly from someone we know who grows it, even if it's a small slice of how we get our food, and to know that we have this power as individual creators—even if it's just herbs in our windows. That fuels this conversation and care to also keep working at the big policy level.

Audience — What do you think of the current political approaches to climate change, specifically the Green New Deal?

LP — I met this morning with leading Black farmers and advocates from across the country about the Green New Deal. We have some suggestions, but overall, we're for it. The policy summary mentions that the people most impacted by climate chaos are front-line communities—BIPOC and farm workers—but it does not translate how those communities are going to have a central role and voice in how the policy is laid out. We think it's important to center the voices of those communities. Farm workers are not mentioned, even though heat stress from climate chaos is impacting farm workers disproportionately. Also not mentioned are climate refugees, Black farmers, and land loss. So it's missing an analysis piece, and it's also missing a piece about community self-determination. But it's on the right track.

ARH — That makes me think of the danger posed by the Green New Deal. That is, in order for it to be politically palatable in the United States, it's going to have to be seen to benefit white people. This is a well-known principle called interest convergence: we're not going to do anything to help Black people or poor people unless it also benefits those of us who have power. This is a framing issue. For the Green New Deal to win, it has to be strategically framed so that those who hold the reins of power have an interest in changing the conversation about power—the power that they themselves hold. That's hard. We've seen this again and again and again in this country: policy suggestions that ostensibly are going to improve conditions for the great majority of us end up not improving those conditions, and then we just think that it didn't work. It was designed not to work. It was designed to do exactly what it did.

LP — The original New Deal was an amazing package. We had substantial workers' rights legislation for the first time, social security. But the southern Democrats would not vote for it if Black people were included in the legislation. I'm not being sensationalist: you can read the transcripts of the committee reports. So they created exclusionary clauses in the Fair Labor Standards Act and the National Labor Relations Act, which said all this good stuff about overtime pay, the right to unionize, child labor protections, limits to the workday, on and on. White folks can have it. But farm workers and domestic workers, who at the time were almost entirely folks of color, cannot have it. To this day, most of those laws have not been changed. Right now, there's Fairness for Farm Workers legislation being proposed that would rectify the FLSA and, for the first time, give farm workers the same legal protection that all other workers have.

ARH — In other words, it's not a scientific question vis-à-vis Republicans and their belief in climate change. It's about political questions that support or challenge white supremacy.

LP   We're going to write an open letter from hundreds of organizations, and other people can sign onto it. I'm not putting all my faith in politics to solve our problems, but we do need to engage with the opportunities that we have.

ARH   For the Green New Deal to be successful as a policy, we as a nation have to address the health-care crisis. Those things are tied together. There's a ton of research that shows the links between the environment's health and our health. That's the piece that's missing from the Democrats' current plan.

KD   I have seen a real shift in consciousness around food from many people, and a more mainstream consciousness around food. It's a first step: more people are reconnecting with the planet, and the planet is screaming for us to do something and shift the way that we're living. We're starting to see that; people are ready and they're open. We just need those avenues of learning.

Audience   Farming is really hard. Even if you're able to swing the pendulum back toward smaller-scale farming and fairer political and economic frameworks for farmers, is there a next generation of young people who will want to accept that lifestyle? Will they put themselves at risk of flood, drought, all of that, as the climate gets worse and the conditions for farming are even harder? Do you see enthusiasm for people to step into farming to an extent that would allow us to feed ourselves?

LP   That's a really important question, and I think it's a yes and a no. We really are in a crisis. The farming population is aging. Among Black farmers, the median age is around sixty-seven; it's a little bit younger for white farmers. Suicide rates are through the roof, particularly among dairy farmers here in New York.
     Farming gets romanticized, but it's tough. Certainly the demand for our training programs is high—we have a multiyear waiting list. But less than half of those folks want to farm at the scale it takes to feed the community. There are a lot of people who want to do admirable urban gardening and community gardening. But in terms of really feeding folks, we need to have that national conversation about how we make the conditions possible for farmers to survive. Right now, 95 percent of small farmers in this country rely on outside income. What are we going to do as a society to make sure farming offers a viable living? Because we can't survive without farmers. This is the problem of our generation.

Audience   Veganism is often framed as the saving grace of a sustainable diet. But that's not the case, because often you have to cut down rainforests to plant soy to have protein to be a vegan. And it's unaffordable for a lot of people. It feels impossible for an individual to have a large impact with a personal diet. Do you think that perpetuating the myth of one way to eat, one way to be, is at all helpful or does it do more harm than good?

ARH   Look around the world. There are seven billion folks on the planet. There are many varied cultures of eating around the world. Veganism is not going to save anybody from anything. And while you might be harming animals less, you're harming humans: by purchasing more fruits and vegetables and grains, you're keeping an exploitative system in place.

It's usually a good idea to eat things that don't come in boxes.

LP I definitely concur that, as a world, we need to cut down on our meat consumption. There's no question that there's just not enough water and land and green space. We need to adjust not the scale but the absolutism of veganism. This is coming from a thirteen-year vegan, and I had my heart handed back to me while living among Indigenous communities. I came to understand that this one-size-fits-all diet can be super imperialist. There are whole communities that are excluded from their traditional hunting grounds by organizations like the Nature Conservancy. They proclaim an ethos of saying, we've trashed all of our resources, so we're going to preserve yours; you can't have your traditional ways of eating, which are actually super sustainable. If you are eating small animals that browse on native vegetation, that's sustainable because the small animals can take a high-fiber plant that's not edible to humans and convert it into an edible protein. It's important to live in that nuance and not be absolutist or imperialist with our diets. There are myriad ways to eat well for the sustainability of the planet.

Audience What is your perspective on the role that philanthropy plays in community farming or farming in general?

KD In Detroit, so many people are farming at a small scale and supplementing how they live. I have mentors at Oakland Avenue Urban Farm, which just received a $500,000 ArtPlace grant to bring together art and farming. It helps the farm, but even so, Jerry Hebron and Billy Hebron, who run the farm, are getting a minimal salary. My friends who are full-time farmers and have an acre of land in the city are making a maximum of $16,000 a year from farming.

I've seen challenges of big grants. I received one big grant to produce art events and other events for Burnside Farm that would bring our diverse neighbors together around food. It was so stressful that I actually just wanted to give the $12,000 a year back. I wasn't ungrateful for it, and it was a beautiful program to facilitate, but the grant world comes with its own set of bureaucratic expectations, posturing, and the sudden need to document everything. I wanted separation from grant funding to have something more simple and pure. I'm trying to be at the scale of a one-block family farm, so I have a lot of respect for the needs of bigger operations.

LP We have a guide for philanthropic organizations to help them be less oppressive and less white supremacist. We actually had one organization offer money but then said they'd need someone on our board of directors to direct the future of the organization. No, no, no. Philanthropy needs to be accountable to front-line communities, not the other way around. It's an honor for them to share their wealth with the people who are doing the work on the ground. And there are coalitions like Grantmakers for Effective Organizations and EDGE Funders Alliance that are trying to shift the philanthropy world.

Audience   I have become much more aware of the public health crisis around the consumption of added sugars in the American diet and in diets globally. It doesn't seem that we're going to interrupt that trend anytime soon. It's not just a governance issue—it's systemic and it has infiltrated everywhere. I'm curious about smaller interventions. A tax on drinks with sugar added has been instituted in Berkeley, California, and it has resulted in a reduction of the consumption of sweetened beverages. But there have been lots of people who've said that type of tax is regressive and makes poor people who live in neighborhoods where soda might be the easiest source of calories pay a tax while the system itself remains untouched. Are there smaller-scale interventions that some of us might want to lobby for or be alert to and supportive of?

ARH   I've been studying sugar biologically and socially for a while now. At the end of the 1800s, we were producing around eight million metric tons of sugar globally. This year, we're probably going to produce around two hundred million metric tons of sugar globally. It's been a linear increase, and someone's got to eat all of that. We see the direct effects of sugar flooding our food ecosystems and our bodies and the land. I'm beginning to take the approach of the Anti-Saccharrites, eighteenth-century abolitionists who stopped eating sugar because of its role in the exploitation of people in the colonies.

At the super-local level, think about all the added sugar you ate today and try to cut that in half tomorrow. It's remarkable how easily and insidiously sugar finds its way into everything we eat. For example, in a traditional grocery store, it's very difficult to find bread that doesn't have added sugar in it. So that's an invitation for all of us to rethink how we consume. The boycott still works as a political tool to push back against people who run things. If you don't buy it, what are they going to do?

KD   One interesting thing we've done at Burnside Farm is a community cleanse. It's small scale, but for a week we agree to do this cleanse together. It's easy to look at food packaging, and then you start to become aware of what's in your food—it's cleanse as educational experience. People will make a small shift based on what they learn. That's a local, grassroots technique that's worked for me.

Audience   When I was in agricultural school, everybody was talking about sustainable agriculture. Right now, we're looking at regenerative agriculture as a way to heal the planet. Something like three hundred local farms working at a small scale can feed large communities of people. Do regenerative agriculture, farmers markets, and CSAs offer enough support directly to farmers that they can actually make a living and continue to feed people into the future?

LP   Regenerative is not new—it's super old. A whole generation before the Rodale Institute, considered the start of organic agriculture, there were Black farmers at Tuskegee University in Alabama getting together to learn to farm from George Washington Carver. Carver is probably most famous for his support of the peanut. It's a legume, a magical category of plants. Turning atmospheric nitrogen into organic nitrogen is what makes agriculture possible. So in the late 1800s, Carver had farmers doing leguminous cover cropping, sheet composting, rotational grazing, and diversified horticulture. These are Indigenous technologies, but he taught them in a university—he was the first to do so—and he called it regenerative farming. This Black farmer in Tuskegee was the father of organic agriculture.

In the next generation, Booker T. Whatley, also a Black farmer at Tuskegee, realized that Black farmers weren't making any money. He said, "Why don't you get out of the mono-crop business? Forget about tobacco and sugar. What you need to do is plant a bunch of fruits and vegetables. Then invite these city folks who are pining for the country out to your farm. They will harvest the food and pay you, and you will call it 'pick your own.'" He had a newsletter so that people felt connected. He had a CSA. A lot of today's co-ops and food hubs come from the Black farming community in the Deep South. These solutions are old, old, old. We need to give credit where it's due, and we need to continue to innovate on the technologies that those who have been closest to the earth have known all along are the right things to do.

ARH You have to consider that the food in our elementary schools, middle schools, and high schools, in our prisons, in our hospitals, and in our nursing homes is all connected institutional food. In fact, food that's grown in prisons is sold to schools. Every single prison system in the country has a program where they sell various commodities to the state, and food is one of the central ones. Another thing is Michelle Obama's "Let's Move" campaign. Because of pressure from food companies, it became more about movement and exercise and less about food and actually transforming the food system. That was a real missed opportunity.

LP To add to that, the USDA Food Pyramid—the diagram that recommends what we should eat every day—is driven by the food lobby. The reason it's a cup of milk a day is because of the dairy lobby. The Food Pyramid is not designed for us to do well—it's designed to make sure that we get rid of commodity crops in the appropriate quantities. I appreciate the work of Oldways. This organization has created heritage food pyramids based on traditional Indigenous diets around the world. So there's a Mediterranean food pyramid, an African food pyramid, an Asian food pyramid. In a Black food pyramid, the fundamental thing at the bottom—what you're supposed to eat the most of—is green vegetables. Right above that are tubers and fish. These are our traditional foods, and, for many of us, our bodies are designed to thrive on those cultural foods. ▲

CONTRIBUTORS

Jessica Andrews is Deputy Fashion Director at Refinery29 and formerly the Fashion Features Editor at *Teen Vogue*. Her essay on cultural appropriation at Coachella was one of the magazine's most-read articles of 2017. She has contributed to *ELLE*, *Vanity Fair*, the *New York Times*, the *Daily Beast*, *Essence* and the award-winning *Glamazons* blog.

Amir Baradaran is the Creative Research Associate at Columbia University's Computer Science Department (CG and User Interfaces Lab) and a New York–based Iranian Canadian performance and new media artist. His pioneering Augmented Reality {AR}t works question the role of machines and the promise of artificial intelligence in our everyday life.

Alexandra Bell is a multidisciplinary artist who investigates the complexities of narrative, information consumption, and perception and explores the tension between marginal experiences and dominant histories, particularly around race, politics, and culture. She received the 2018 International Center of Photography Infinity Award in the applied category and was a 2018 Soros Equality Fellow and a 2018–2019 Bard at Brooklyn Public Library Fellow.

Ian Berry is Dayton Director of The Frances Young Tang Teaching Museum and Art Gallery and Professor of Liberal Arts at Skidmore College. His research and teaching interests include underrepresented modern and contemporary artists and the intersections of race, gender, and identity in art and museums.

Dan Borelli is an artist and Director of Exhibitions at the Harvard Graduate School of Design. In 2010, he started an art-based research inquiry, funded by Harvard Innovation Learning Technology, ArtPlace America, and NEA Our Town grants, into the Nyanza Superfund Site in his hometown of Ashland, Massachusetts. His project makes public hidden narratives of cancer clusters, human loss, activism, and ultimately regeneration.

Isolde Brielmaier was the Tang Teaching Museum's Curator-at-Large from 2016 to 2019, during which time she developed and moderated the Accelerator Series, a conversation series on big ideas and big issues. Currently, she is Curator-at-Large at the International Center of Photography and Assistant Professor of Critical Studies in the Department of Photography, Imaging and Emerging Media at New York University's Tisch School of the Arts. Her practice areas include contemporary art, global visual culture, and examining media and immersive technology as platforms within which to rethink storytelling and the politics of representation. Brielmaier is the former Executive Director and Curator of Arts and Culture at the Oculus at Westfield World Trade Center and continues to advise on cultural strategy for a range of organizations. She has written extensively on contemporary art and culture and has received fellowships from the Mellon and Ford Foundations as well as the Social Science Research Council. She serves on the Board of Trustees of the New Museum and on the board of the Women's Prison Association.

Farai Chideya is a multimedia journalist, radio host, political and cultural analyst, and novelist. Now the journalism program officer at the Ford Foundation, she covered the past six presidential elections for outlets including FiveThirtyEight, NPR, and CNN.

Matthew Cooke is a filmmaker, actor, director, producer, and editor who worked on the 2006 Oscar-nominated documentary *Deliver Us from Evil*. His social justice and prison reform advocacy commentaries have garnered over a hundred million views on Facebook and are shared and promoted widely.

Renee Cox is a photographer and mixed-media artist. Her self-portraits of her nude and clothed body at once celebrate Black womanhood and critique societal attitudes about race, desire, religion, feminism, and visual and cultural aesthetics. She started her career as a fashion photographer for high-profile magazines before turning to more conceptual photography. Her work has been featured at numerous art institutions throughout the country, in the 2006 Jamaica Biennial, and elsewhere.

Kate Daughdrill is an artist, urban farmer, writer, and speaker who lives and works on Burnside Farm in Detroit. She currently cultivates gatherings, sculptural environments, and dinners that explore the connections between plants, ceremony, and artistic energy. She has shared her sculptures, performative dinners, cooking, yoga practices, ceremonies, writing, and creative immersions all over the world. Her work has been exhibited at the Museum of Contemporary Art Detroit, Cranbrook Art Museum, the School of the Art Institute of Chicago, Kunstverein Wolfsburg, and elsewhere.

Kimberly Drew is a writer, curator, and activist with a passion for innovation in art, fashion, and cultural studies. Former social media manager of the Metropolitan Museum of Art, she received AIR Gallery's inaugural Feminist Curator Award and was selected as one of *Brooklyn Magazine*'s "Brooklyn 100."

Sam Durant is a multimedia artist whose work engages a variety of social, political, and cultural issues. His work has been exhibited in group and one-person shows at museums throughout the United States and abroad as well as in the 2017 Yokohama Triennale, Japan; dOCUMENTA (13), Kassel; the 2004 Whitney Museum Biennial, New York; and the 2002 Venice Biennale.

Natalie Frank is an artist whose paintings and drawings revolve around women's bodies, desire, and narratives based on literature—fairy tales and everyday fantasy. Recent exhibitions include drawings of the erotic novel *Story of O* at Half Gallery; *Dread and Delight: Fairy Tales in an Anxious World* at the Weatherspoon Museum; and a collaboration with Ballet Austin in 2019 on sets, costume design, and animations for a world premier full-length production based on her book of the unsanitized Grimm's tales.

Eric Gottesman, a cofounder of For Freedoms and Assistant Professor of Art at Purchase College, State University of New York, is an artist who makes images and social interventions that address themes of nationalism, migration, conflict, structural violence, colonialism, and intimate relations. Gottesman is a recipient of the Creative Capital artist grant, the ICP Infinity Award, an Artadia Award and a Fulbright Fellowship in Art.

Hassan Hajjaj is a self-taught artist whose work includes portraiture, installation, performance, fashion, and interior design, including furniture design. Heavily influenced by his North African heritage, African studio photography, and the hip-hop, reggae, and club scenes of London, Hajjaj's work combines the personal with the political. He was the winner of the 2011 Sovereign Middle East and North Africa Art Prize and was shortlisted for the Victoria & Albert Museum's Jameel Prize for Islamic Art in 2009.

Lyle Ashton Harris, Professor of Art and Art Education at New York University, is an artist with a diverse practice that includes photography, collage, installation, and performance art. His work explores intersections between the personal and the political, examining the social and cultural impact of ethnicity, gender, and desire. His work is in the collection of the Museum of Modern Art, New York, and has been exhibited internationally and throughout the United States.

Anthony Ryan Hatch is Associate Professor of Science in Society at Wesleyan University. Hatch's areas of interest are science and technology studies, medical humanities, critical race theory, radical ecology, and sociology of knowledge. He is the author of *Blood Sugar: Racial Pharmacology and Food Justice in Black America* (2016) and *Silent Cells: The Secret Drugging of Captive America* (2019), an investigation into the use of psychotropic drugs to pacify and control inmates and other captives in the US prison, military, and welfare systems.

Elizabeth Hinton, Assistant Professor of History and of African and African American Studies at Harvard University, focuses her research on the persistence of poverty and racial inequality in the twentieth-century United States. She is the author of *From the War on Poverty to the War on Crime: The Making of Mass Incarceration in America* (2016).

Duron Jackson is a multidisciplinary artist whose work explores the social inter-relationships of "Blackness" within the broader context of contemporary culture and focuses on social and political histories in relation to mass incarceration, constructions of criminality, and state surveillance. His work has been shown in group and solo exhibitions nationally and internationally.

Michael Joo is a multimedia artist known for making art with a scientific lens. He has had numerous solo and group exhibitions in the United States and abroad. Joo represented South Korea at the 49th Venice Biennale in 2001 and was awarded the grand prize at the sixth Gwangju Biennale in 2006. In 2012, Joo was a Smithsonian Artist Research Fellow, studying 3-D scanning and the relationship between art and technology.

Titus Kaphar uses painting and sculpture to interact with the history of art by appropriating its styles and mediums and then altering the work in a nod to hidden narratives and unspoken truths about the nature of history. His work has been exhibited at the Savannah College of Art and Design, The Studio Museum in Harlem, the Seattle Art Museum, the Smithsonian National Portrait Gallery, and elsewhere. Recipient of a MacArthur Foundation "genius" grant, Kaphar is cofounder of NXTHVN, an art space in Connecticut offering artist fellowships and apprenticeships.

David Karp is Professor and Director of the Center for Restorative Justice in the School of Leadership and Education Sciences at the University of San Diego and formerly Professor of Sociology and Director of the Project on Restorative Justice at Skidmore College. He has published numerous academic papers and six books, including *The Little Book of Restorative Justice for Colleges and Universities* (2013). He is on the board of directors for the National Association of Community and Restorative Justice.

Treva B. Lindsey is an Associate Professor of Women's, Gender, and Sexuality Studies at The Ohio State University. She is the author of the award-winning book *Colored No More: Reinventing Black Womanhood in Washington, D.C.* (2017) and was the inaugural Equity for Women and Girls of Color Fellow at Harvard University. Her work on race, gender, culture, history, and sexual politics has been published in *The Washington Post*, *Cosmopolitan*, *Grazia UK*, *Al Jazeera*, and *Huffington Post*.

Matthew D. Morrison is Assistant Professor in the Clive Davis Institute of Recorded Music at New York University's Tisch School of the Arts. He has held numerous fellowships throughout the United States and in London and has written extensively on music and musicology. His forthcoming book, *American Popular Sound: From Blackface to Blacksound*, considers the implications of positing sound and music as major components of identity formations, particularly the construction of race.

Richard Mosse, born in Ireland, is a documentary photographer and filmmaker whose recent project *Incoming* (2014–2017) is concerned with the refugee crisis unfolding across Europe, the Middle East, and North Africa, and prior to that he worked extensively in eastern Democratic Republic of Congo to create *The Enclave* (2010–2015). Mosse received the Prix Pictet, the Deutsche Börse Photography Foundation Prize, a Guggenheim Fellowship, and the Leonore Annenberg Fellowship.

Karyn Olivier, Associate Professor of Sculpture at the Tyler School of Art and Architecture, is a sculptor and installation artist whose work engages the "blind spots" of public spaces and history, including in Philadelphia's historic Vernon Park for Philadelphia's Monument

Lab program and New York's Central Park for Creative Time and the city's Percent for Art program. Her work has been exhibited at the Gwangju and Busan Biennales, the Whitney Museum of American Art, MoMA PS1, and elsewhere.

Leah Penniman is an educator, farmer, writer, and food justice activist and cofounded Soul Fire Farm in Grafton, New York, in 2011, with the mission to end racism in the food system and reclaim ancestral connection to land. Penniman's work and the work of Soul Fire Farm have been recognized by the Soros Racial Justice Fellowship, Fulbright Program, Presidential Award for Science Teaching, New York State Health Emerging Innovator Awards, and Andrew Goodman Foundation, among others.

Johnny Perez, drawing on the wisdom of thirteen years of direct involvement with the criminal justice system, is Director of the US Prison Program for the National Religious Campaign Against Torture, an interfaith membership organization comprised of 325 religious organizations working to end US-sponsored torture and cruel, inhuman, and degrading treatment. Through his leadership, Perez coordinates NRCAT's existing campaign efforts to end the torture of solitary confinement, adding value and strategic insight to building the capacity of faith leaders and directly impacted communities to engage in education and legislative advocacy across the United States.

Amy Richards is a writer, producer, and organizer. Richards produced the VICELAND series *WOMAN* and curated a series of talks to accompany Annie Leibovitz's traveling exhibition *WOMEN*. She is the president of the lecture agency Soapbox Inc., the creator of Feminist Camp and an executive producer of *The Glorias*. Her books include *Manifesta: Young Women, Feminism and the Future* (2000), *We Are MAKERS* (2019), and *Opting In: Having a Child Without Losing Yourself* (2008).

Minita Sanghvi is Assistant Professor of Management and Business at Skidmore College. Her research centers around gender and intersectionality in marketing and consumptionscapes. Her book *Gender and Political Marketing in the United States and the 2016 Presidential Election: An Analysis of Why She Lost* (2018) has been deemed a "must read" by gender scholars in the field of marketing and history as well as practitioners who work with female politicians. Sanghvi is cocurator of the exhibition *Never Done: 100 Years of Women in Politics and Beyond* (2020) at the Tang Teaching Museum.

Tanya Selvaratnam is a writer and producer who has collaborated with Planned Parenthood, Aubin Pictures, the Vision & Justice Project, Glamour Women of the Year, Mickalene Thomas, and Carrie Mae Weems. She is an advisor of For Freedoms and a cofounder of The Federation. She is the author of *The Big Lie: Motherhood, Feminism, and the Reality of the Biological Clock* (2014) and *Assume Nothing: A Memoir of Intimate Violence* (2020); and her essays have been published in the *New York Times*, *Vogue*, *CNN*, *Glamour*, and *McSweeney's*.

Dara Silverman is a consultant, somatic coach, and trainer with twenty years in organizations and movements for social, racial, economic and gender justice based in Beacon, New York. She partners with trainers of color to lead organizational change and leadership development initiatives centering racial justice, equity, and liberation. Previously, she was the founding Director of Showing Up for Racial Justice and the Executive Director of Jews for Racial and Economic Justice in New York City.

ACKNOWLEDGMENTS

This volume celebrates the tremendous commitment of many toward the goal of affecting change in our world. Deep gratitude goes to all of the contributors to this book and to those who contributed to the Accelerator Series at the Tang Teaching Museum from 2016 to 2019. Thank you for sharing your experiences, insights, and wisdom and above all, for keeping it real at all times. Thank you to our writers and panelists: Jessica Andrews, Amir Baradaran, Alexandra Bell, Dan Borelli, Farai Chideya, Matthew Cooke, Renee Cox, Kate Daughdrill, Kimberly Drew, Sam Durant, Natalie Frank, Eric Gottesman, Hassan Hajjaj, Lyle Ashton Harris, Anthony Ryan Hatch, Elizabeth Hinton, Duron Jackson, Michael Joo, Titus Kaphar, David Karp, Treva B. Lindsey, Matthew Morrison, Richard Mosse, Karyn Olivier, Leah Penniman, Johnny Perez, Amy Richards, Minita Sanghvi, Tanya Selvaratnam, and Dara Silverman.

    Conceptualizing, organizing, and executing these conversations was a major collaborative effort. At the Tang, a special thank you to Dayton Director Ian Berry for his support of this program, as well as to Rebecca McNamara for her ongoing partnership, along with Rachel Seligman and Tom Yoshikami—all of whom pushed the program forward and participated in seemingly never-ending brainstorming sessions. To Annelise Kelly and Michael Janairo for getting the word out about each panel. To Jean Tschanz-Egger for her constant creativity and design work. To sound engineer Frank Moscowitz and videographers and photographers Zach Durocher, Jacob Hopper, Shawn LaChapelle, Logan Pinchbeck, Nick Spadaro, and Raymond Stockwell at Modern Mix for documenting these important events. To Patti Sopp and kelly ward for their organizational prowess. Thank you to my team: Jill Smith and Cheyanne Epps, for ideating, discussing, and keeping things both up-to-date and on track. And to The Andrew W. Mellon Foundation, whose generous funding supported many of our visiting artists and speakers.

    For helping to create this book so that these conversations endure and continue to spark dialogue and change: thanks to designer Beverly Joel, editor Andrea Monfried, and at the Tang, Ian and Rebecca for their astute edits and project management. Thank you also to Sophie Heath for proofreading, and to the artists whose images are reproduced here.

    And I would be remiss to overlook how important the Skidmore and Saratoga Springs audiences—students, staff, faculty, and regional community—have been in propelling ideas and exchange forward, often through some challenging terrain: a heartfelt note of gratitude to you all. Onward!

Isolde Brielmaier

This publication accompanies the 2017–2019 Accelerator Series of public conversations held at The Frances Young Tang Teaching Museum and Art Gallery at Skidmore College, Saratoga Springs, New York.

Culture as Catalyst

The Frances Young Tang Teaching Museum
and Art Gallery at Skidmore College
815 North Broadway
Saratoga Springs, NY 12866
T 518 580 8080
F 518 580 5069
tang.skidmore.edu

The Accelerator Series was catalyzed by a grant from The Andrew W. Mellon Foundation, *Accelerate: Access and Inclusion at The Tang Teaching Museum.*

All rights reserved. No part of this publication may be reproduced or transmitted in any form or by any means, electronic or mechanical, including photocopy, recording, or any other information storage and retrieval system, or otherwise without written permission from the publisher.

© 2020 The Frances Young Tang Teaching Museum and Art Gallery at Skidmore College

ISBN: 978-0-9982422-4-8

Library of Congress Control Number: 2020941761

Photography
9–22: Shawn LaChapelle, Raymond Stockwell
27: Jeremy Lawson
57: Arthur Evans
83: Courtesy of Jack Tilton Gallery
111: Courtesy of the Rockefeller Collection, Asia Society Museum, New York | Photograph by John Nye
135: Courtesy of Half Gallery and Sean Fader
159: Steve Weinik
183: Courtesy of the artist and Blum & Poe, Los Angeles/New York/Tokyo | Photograph by Joshua White
203: Jim Gipe and Stephen Petegorsky
227: Courtesy the artist
245: Kate Daughdrill

All images in this publication, unless otherwise noted, are copyright of the artists.

All transcribed panel conversations have been condensed and edited with participants' approval. Original transcripts are available to researchers at the Tang Teaching Museum.

Designed by Beverly Joel, pulp, ink.

Printed in Italy by Conti Tipocolor